PRACTICAL PATTERN MAKING

Owing to the antiquity and rarity of this book, certain pages are regrettably absent, and readability is compromised due to the blurring of the original text. If you possess any insights regarding the availability of these missing sections, kindly inform us. Your assistance is crucial in ensuring the completion of this significant work for the benefit of future generations.

PRACTICAL PATTERN MAKING

WITH NUMEROUS ENGRAVINGS AND DIAGRAMS

EDITED BY

PAUL N. HASLUCK

GYAN

Published by

Gyan Publishing House
5, Ansari Road
Daryaganj, New Delhi-110002
Phone: 011-47034999, 9811692060
E-mail: books@gyanbooks.com

Distribution Network
gyanbooks.com
India, USA, Canada, UK, Australia

ISBN: 978-93-6208-380-7 (PB)
First Published, 1905

2nd Impression 2024

Printed at: Gyan Press, Delhi.

PRACTICAL PATTERN MAKING
Editor: PAUL N. HASLUCK

PRACTICAL PATTERN MAKING

WITH NUMEROUS ENGRAVINGS AND DIAGRAMS

EDITED BY

PAUL N. HASLUCK

HONOURS MEDALLIST IN TECHNOLOGY
EDITOR OF "WORK" AND "BUILDING WORLD"
AUTHOR OF "HANDYBOOKS FOR HANDICRAFTS," ETC. ETC.

PHILADELPHIA

DAVID McKAY, PUBLISHER

610, *SOUTH WASHINGTON SQUARE*

1905

PREFACE.

PRACTICAL PATTERN MAKING contains, in a form convenient for everyday use, a comprehensive digest of information, contributed by experienced craftsmen, scattered over the columns of WORK, one of the weekly journals it is my fortune to edit, and supplies concise information on the general principles and practice of the art on which it treats.

Readers who may desire additional information respecting special details of the matters dealt with in this book, or instructions on any kindred subject, should address a question to WORK, so that it may be answered in the columns of that journal.

P. N. HASLUCK.

La Belle Sauvage, London,
September, 1905.

CONTENTS.

LIST OF ILLUSTRATIONS.

PRACTICAL PATTERN MAKING.

CHAPTER I.

FOUNDRY PATTERNS AND FOUNDRY PRACTICE.

A FOUNDRY pattern is a counterpart of a casting, and is used to form the mould into which the molten metal is poured. Pattern-making is thus a very important part of foundry work, and the pattern-maker must be a craftsman of experience and of more than ordinary intelligence. Pattern-making is done usually in a shop having only two or three workmen, each one of whom must be able to make any description of pattern that may be wanted. Thus one man soon comes to command a wide range of the art, and is obliged to be conversant with a great number of processes widely different in character the one from the other. The competent pattern maker has a knowledge of practical plane and solid geometry and of mechanical drawing; he is constantly required to lay upon an uneven angular surface lines which the ordinary draughtsman can get much more easily on the smooth surface of paper. He must know the nature of the woods or other material used, and be able to construct and form with accuracy any conceivable shape of body, so that it will best stand the strains of the work required, and keep its size. He must understand how the pattern can best be moulded, since he is required to decide how much of a pattern is necessary, and where and how to make the parting, taper, prints, core-boxes, etc.

The object of a pattern being to facilitate the making of a mould, the pattern-maker must know the capacity of the moulder and his appliances. Some moulds can be made more cheaply without a pattern by the use of strikes, others with a combination of strikes and parts of pattern, others with cores, while others require a full pattern of the size and shape of casting required, plus the allowance for shrinkage. Thus a pattern may be made to cost more in the pattern-making, and less in the moulding, or more in the moulding, and less in the pattern-making, according to which workman can do the work the cheapest. The number of castings expected to be made will also affect the construction and finish of a pattern. For instance, if twenty castings are required from one pattern, and one hour's work more on the pattern would save the moulder five minutes on each mould, there would be an economy of forty minutes saved by the extra hour spent in pattern work; while if there was but one casting to be made, and the one hour's pattern work was still put upon it, there would be a loss of fifty-five minutes, seeing that the moulder was saved but five minutes' work. After the pattern-maker has considered all the requirements of the moulder, he must follow the casting in his mind into the machine shop, and consider the shrinkage, finish, and the ultimate strength and soundness of the parts.

A mould is an impression in sand shaped to correspond with the required casting, and it is best produced by ramming up in the sand a pattern or model of the article required. This pattern must, of course, be withdrawn from the sand before the mould can receive the molten metal, and the pattern must therefore be so constructed that it may be withdrawn from the sand without disturbing the mould. The non-appreciation of this essential is the cause of frequent indifferent and useless patterns being made. The first important point in pattern-making is that a pattern must be tapered to allow for withdrawing it from the mould (exceptions will be dealt with in their place). A well-tapered pattern readily "draws"; the act of withdrawing a pattern is known as the "draft."

Most works on pattern-making give detailed information on the many varieties of woods used, describe the tools employed, and attempt a course of instruction in the use of both materials and tools. But that is quite outside the present scope, and, indeed, is quite unnecessary here. Pattern-making is such an intricate craft that the whole of the space here available is necessary for an adequate consideration of the methods of forming the patterns themselves. Detailed information on tools and materials must be looked for elsewhere. The whole subject of woodworking is dealt with comprehensively in "The Handyman's Book of Woodworking," a book of 760 pp. produced under the direction of the editor of this work.

Wood for pattern-making should be well seasoned, and practically all kinds are in use for the purpose. Large, long and flat patterns are made of white or yellow pine, on account of its lightness, cheapness, and freedom from warping and splitting, but it has, of course, the other disadvantage of being soft and more liable to receive injury when made up. Choice Canadian red pine is harder, but should be selected as free from knots and turpentine as possible. Still harder is white fir (spruce fir), which is admirable for large wheel patterns; the harder the wood, the finer does it look when sawn, but the working of this material is troublesome when catfaced, that is, when some parts are smooth and some rough. Teak is light, strong and durable, and easily worked, but punishes the tools a little, and is somewhat liable to split. Any part of a pattern which has to be turned may be made of beech, which has a uniform grain. Much elm, oak, maple and sycamore is used also.

For small patterns the Germans use cherry-tree wood, well seasoned, because it is hard and close grained; but in England, mahogany (chiefly baywood) comes into use for small work, and will be found to suit nearly all patterns; it warps less than other woods, shrinks but little in drying, and can be worked at the ends easily, its corners keeping sharp; but the tools used must be in good condition. Boxwood also is an excellent wood for small patterns.

A very important point in pattern-making is the due allowance for shrinkage. Castings in iron vary in shrinkage, according to their mass; for metal 1 in. in thickness, allow $\frac{1}{10}$ in. to the foot in making the pattern, while thinner castings require more, and thicker a shade less allowance in proportion.

Brass shrinks rather more, and $\frac{1}{8}$ in. may be substituted for the $\frac{1}{10}$ in. afore-mentioned. For castings under 1 ft. long, shrinkage need scarcely be taken into consideration;

the rapping of the pattern by the moulder usually suffices. This rapping, which is done to loosen the pattern before drawing, is usually done by boring a hole in the pattern, and inserting a spike in the same, and then rapping the spike on all sides with a hammer. This necessarily tries the strength of the pattern, and if many castings are required off one pattern, it is well to cut a small mortise when the rapping hole is wanted, and insert therein a small iron plate with a hole in it, thereby saving the wood from the actual contact with the spike.

In making patterns of articles which have to be worked up before use, it is well to allow sufficient metal for the process. A file or lathe will easily remove a superfluous

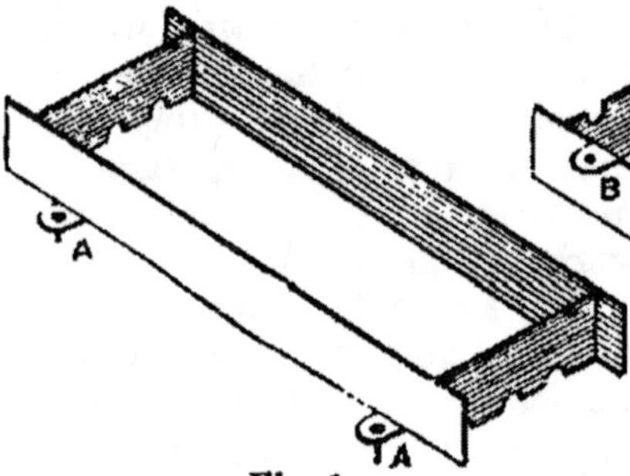

Fig. 1.

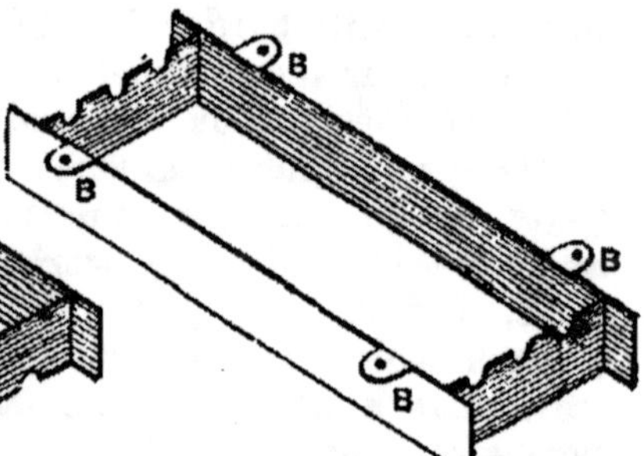

Fig. 2.

Figs. 1 and 2.—Peg-side and Eye-side of Flask.

$\frac{1}{16}$ in., but no mechanical method can satisfactorily add that amount if it be lacking at the first.

Metal patterns are used when a large supply of castings is required. Iron, brass, or white metal is commonly used for patterns. Core-boxes are made of the same material as patterns. Iron has to be protected from rusting by varnishing or beeswaxing; brass and white metal do not need protection. As the thickness of metal is often shaved down as slight as possible, plaster of Paris is frequently used to obtain exact thickness before casting the final pattern or core-box. An alloy of lead and tin is also used for patterns. The patterns should be chased up and finished to the very finest degree, and if made in two or more parts the necessary fitments for fixing them should be soldered on, so that the portions when cast may fit together easily. Exact making and finishing of the patterns will be advantageous, as better castings will result, and the fitter's work is rendered very much easier.

An outline of foundry operations will now be given to enable the worker to construct patterns intelligently, and with their ultimate use well in mind.

The sand moulds into which the molten metal is poured are made in flasks or moulding frames. These consist of a pair of shallow frames, without top or bottom, and usually made of cast-iron, having lugs on the one side as at A (Fig. 1), and lugs with holes in on the other side as B (Fig. 2). Wooden flasks are used in brass foundries,

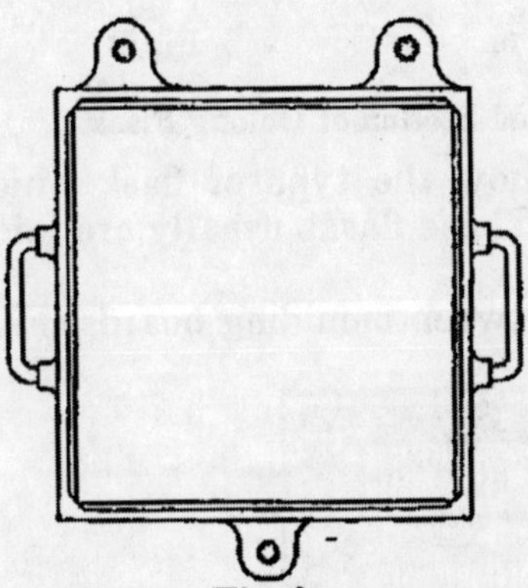

Fig. 3.

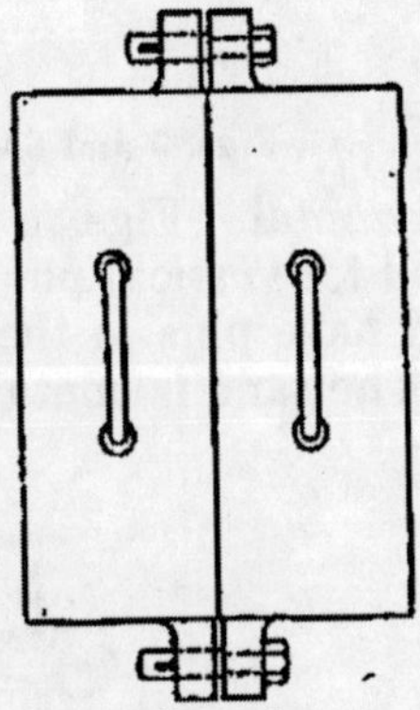

Fig. 4.

Figs. 3 and 4.—Plan and End of Square Flask.

though they are seldom seen in English iron foundries. The fitting of the pegs and the eyes of each pair of frames forming a moulding box must be very exact, so that there may be no shifting. In the pair of frames forming the brass founder's flask, one is called the peg-side, while the other is the eye-side. In iron foundries the two parts are called the cope and drag, and these are fitted with lugs having matching pins and holes, the two being either cottered together, or weighted and poured while laid horizontal on the sand floor. There is one type of brass founder's flask, however, which is not employed by the iron founder, that in which the mould is poured while the flask stands vertical, or in a slightly sloping position. Figs. 3 and 4 show a flask used by brass founders and iron founders, and made in sizes from about 9 in. to 18 in. square, usually without bars or stays. Such flasks are poured while laid

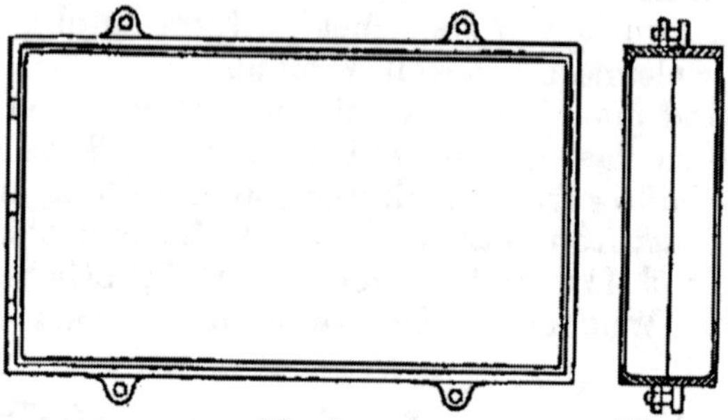

Fig. 5. Fig. 6.

Figs. 5 and 6.—Plan and Section of Oblong Flask.

horizontal. Figs. 5 to 7 show the type of flask which is used for vertical pouring. These flasks usually are jointed, and have pins in the lugs.

The sand is contained between moulding boards (Fig. 8),

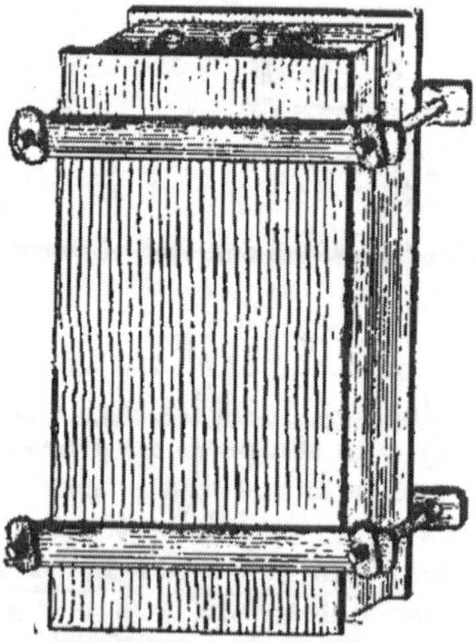

Fig. 7.—Flask ready for Vertical Pouring.

upon which the flasks are rammed, and by which the mould is confined during pouring by means of clamps (Figs. 9 and 10). The boards are of deal or oak, and the ends are tongued to prevent warping. They are from $1\frac{1}{4}$ in. to $1\frac{1}{2}$ in thick. Flasks that are made of wood are strongly dovetailed or tenoned, and clamped at the corners, and

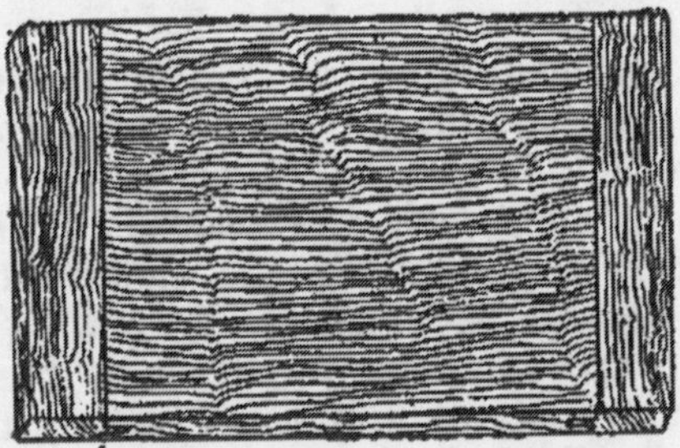

Fig. 8.—Moulding Board.

the top end, which is pierced with holes, is made of iron, or protected with iron.

A flask made wholly of iron costs rather more in the first place than a wood flask, but it is practically everlasting, besides being more rigid. In Figs. 5 and 6 a rib is shown cast round the edges of the flasks next the faces, against which the boards are clamped. In some American flasks the section is grooved in order to confine

Fig. 9

Fig. 10.

Figs. 9 and 10.—Side and Edge Views of Clamp.

the sand more efficiently. The clamps are of wood, and so are the screw nuts shown in Figs. 9 and 10.

In brass foundries the moulding tub to contain the sand

usually consists of an iron casting about 6 ft. long, 2 ft. wide at the bottom, and about 2 ft. 3 in. at the top by 15 in. deep. This is placed on brick supports, one at each end, so that its top edge is about 2 ft. 3 in. from the floor (see Fig. 11). In smaller foundries very frequently the work bench is made a part of the moulding tub, the advantage being that the sand is handy in the tub beneath the bench, which forms the cover of the tub. When a plain bench is employed, the sand is brought in small quantities from the sand bins or tubs, and placed in a small heap at the back of the bench. The moulding trough of the brass founder is shown by Figs. 12, 13, and 14, which illustrate a plan, side elevation, and end elevation; this tub affords at once a receptacle for sand and

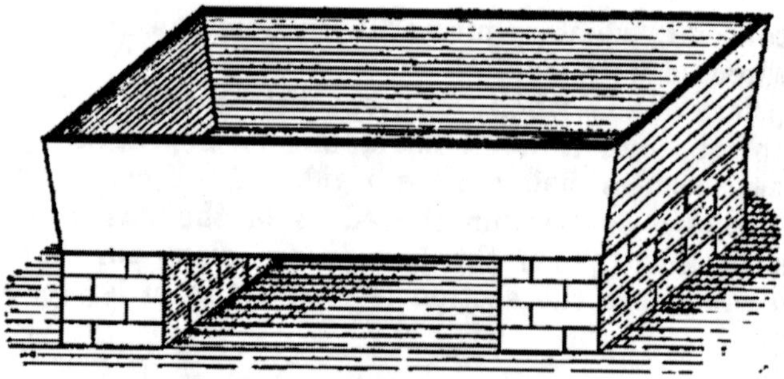

Fig. 11.—Moulding Tub.

a work bench. It stands against the wall, and is about 2 ft. 6 in. high and wide, and of any length. The tub shown is for one man, the work being done upon the sliding board A, beneath which is the trough, which contains the sand. The trough is made of deal of about 1¼ in. thick, dovetailed or nailed at the corners, and tapered at front and sides for convenience of shovelling out the sand.

When preparing a mould the sand is first tempered by the addition of water, and passed through a sieve of about five or six meshes to the linear inch. Raw sand must be employed, as used or burnt sand does not possess the adhesiveness necessary for the purpose, since it contains proportions of charcoal and other substances, such as peaflour, brickdust, etc. The sharp edges of the sand grains too have been rounded by use; they cannot, therefore, wedge together so firmly.

The moulding of the odd-side is begun by taking an eye-side frame, and placing it on a board. The inside of this frame is dusted over with parting sand, and then the side is filled with black sand, to which some raw sand has been added. This is rammed down tight, first with the

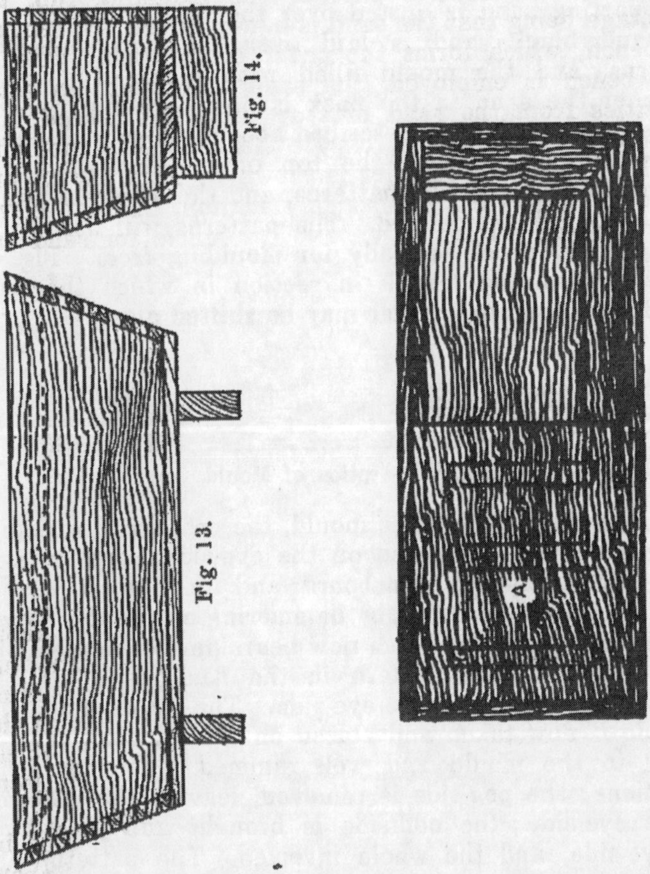

Figs. 12 to 14.—Top, Side, and End Views of Moulding Frame.

palms of the hands, then with the knuckles, and, lastly, with a wooden mallet; occasionally the workman will tread it down firmly as the final operation. The sand is then scraped level with a bar of iron, a moulding board is laid on the top, and the frame with its entire contents is inverted.

The patterns to be moulded are now laid very carefully

on the face of the mould, and the dust bag shaken over them; this leaves on the sand a clear outline of the patterns. These are now lifted off, and the sand is carefully cut away, leaving the patterns embedded half-way.

A peg-side frame, to fit on the odd-side, is placed on the eye-side, as illustrated by the sectional view (Fig. 15), and then parting sand is dusted over the sand, a mixture of raw and black sand is laid over the half embedded patterns, and the mould filled with black sand. The whole of the sand in the flask is now carefully rammed as tight as possible, as described above. A second moulding board is placed on the top of the flask and well hammered to loosen the patterns, and the whole is turned over and again hammered. The patterns will now be in the eye-side, which is ready for moulding from. Fig. 16 shows a moulding trough in section in which the flask is supported on boards that may be shifted along.

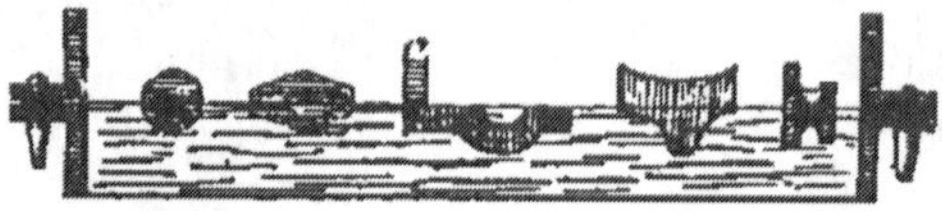

Fig. 15.—Section of Mould.

For making the peg-side mould, the process is repeated, a peg-side frame is placed on the eye-side, sand pressed in as before, covered by a board, and the whole inverted. The patterns are loosened by hammering on the top board, and the odd peg-side, which now bears perfect impressions of one-half of each pattern in the flask, is taken off, leaving the patterns in the eye-side. The frame called the peg-side is now taken and placed on the eye-side, sand is placed in the mould and well rammed, as in previous operations; the peg-side is removed, leaving the patterns in the eye-side; the odd-side is brought and placed on the eye-side, and the whole inverted. The patterns are loosened by hammering, the eye-side is taken away, and, the patterns being left in the odd peg-side, all is ready for use again, and thus the odd-side can be repeatedly used for moulding purposes.

In many cases where large quantities of castings of similar work are required, there are two other methods adopted in moulding, namely, platework and gatework.

These methods are excellent, and might be adopted with advantage to a much greater extent. They are suitable for use either in hand moulding or in conjunction with a moulding machine. The chief advantage of machine-over hand-moulding is that a perpendicular lift is ensured, thus diminishing the risk of the breaking down of sand in a deep face.

In platework the patterns are attached to a match plate or board, while in gatework a number of patterns sufficient to fill the standard flask are riveted or soldered to the gate-piece, practically forming one pattern. Platework and gatework have each their own merits, but generally it is better to put the patterns on plates than

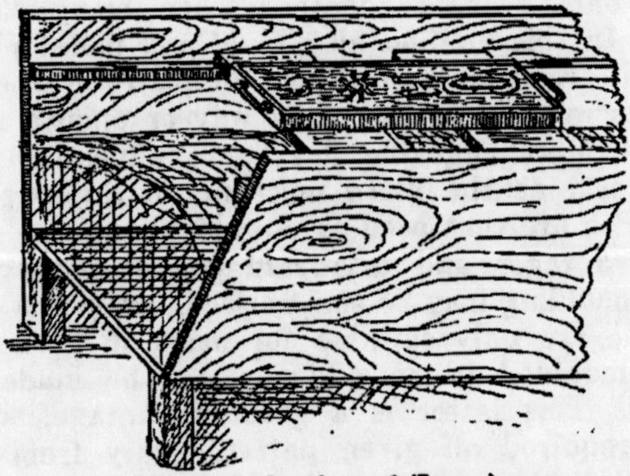

Fig. 16.—Section of Trough.

to gates, whenever it is possible to do so. Bib-cocks, plugs, handles, stems, globe and other valves, the parting lines of which are straight, can all be made on the plate principle, thereby saving the time that would be expended in making odd-sides, trimming the joints of the mould, etc., necessary with gated patterns.

There are several kinds of plated patterns, the methods of moulding being different in certain cases. The simplest plated work is that in which two portions of a pattern are put on opposite sides of a plate, wood being employed. The two portions of the pattern are precisely like those which would be used if there were no plate interposed, these portions being those which go into the opposite halves of the flask, the thickness of the plate being immaterial. In moulding, the two sides of a flask are rammed on opposite sides of the plate, being cottered together through it, and the flasks being turned over for the ramming of opposite sides.

A superior and more permanent pattern plate is made of iron or brass. In this the opposite portions of the pattern are prepared as though for moulding in the ordinary way, and then they are screwed to the opposite sides of a metal plate about ⅜ in. or ½ in. in thickness, and the flasks are rammed from the opposite sides of the pattern. In another method the two halves of a pattern are moulded on a separate plate instead of on opposite sides of the same one, and the flasks are rammed apart, and are only brought together when being closed for pouring. In this method also wood and metal plates are both used. Each of these types of plates is used either with flasks rammed in the usual way or upon a moulding machine. Interchangeable flasks are almost a necessity in platework, as the plate must fit on the peg-sides of flasks, which are thus used as dowels.

The advantages and disadvantages of platework and odd-side moulding may be summarised. Patterns once put on a plate are only suitable for using in groups, while patterns moulded in an odd-side can be made in any groupings. This latter is a great advantage, when the numbers required off given patterns vary from time to time; work put on plates should be arranged so that sets shall be completed without any parts being in excess on the one hand, or insufficient in numbers on the other. To mount metal patterns on plates is costly, and is only economical when large quantities of castings are wanted. The fitting must be done most accurately, otherwise there will be lapping joints and cores out of truth. Small brass work can only be done cheaply and well by the adoption of odd-side or plate moulding, and the choice must be controlled by circumstances. When the platework or gatework method is adopted, the advantages are that the time of bedding a pattern temporarily into its cope, and of making the joint face and sloping joints on which to ram the drag, is wholly saved. The time in cutting runners is also saved. These occupy a good deal of time when a number of patterns are moulded in one flask, and especially when they are of shapes involving the making of numerous sloping and curved down-joints. These methods of moulding are generally practicable when doing a large run of standard work, but they are seldom available in small foundries, and therefore the odd-side method is generally preferred in these.

The sand floor usual in a foundry is useful for bedding the heavier work, which is covered with copes. It is also used to lay the flasks upon when moulded and prepared ready for casting. As the sand is receiving constant additions from the new sand used in facings, a depth of from 3 in. to 6 in. will be sufficient to lay down at starting. It is employed over and over again for box filling, re-

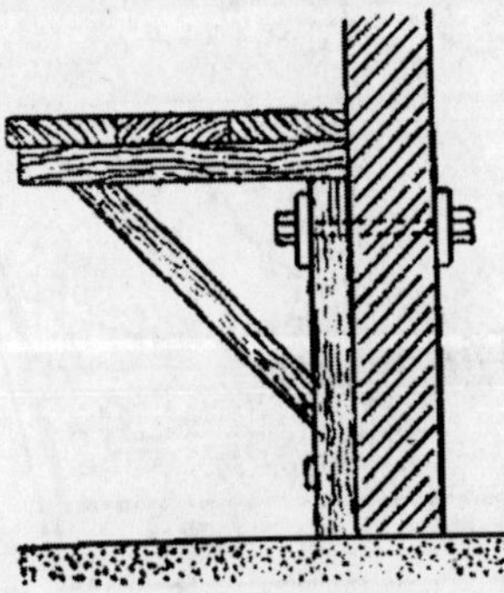

Fig. 17.—Ramming Bench Bolted to Wall.

Fig. 18.—Ramming Bench Supported by Legs.

serving the new special sand for facings—that is to say, for the stratum of sand which is immediately next the pattern to a thickness ranging from ½ in. to 1 in., hence called pattern facings. In the smallest moulds facing sand alone would be employed. Partings for brass moulds are made of burnt red sand or of red brickdust. Peameal dusted over is used for facing green sand work, both light and heavy. So are flour, powdered chalk, whiting, and sometimes charcoal. Lime mixed with water is used for facing dry sand moulds and cores for brasswork.

In a small foundry it is necessary to have a bench, on which moulds except those occasionally made in the sand floor will be rammed. The bench will be of dimensions most suitable to the work required. It may be of iron, but wood is suitable, 3-in. deals being supported on wood brackets, the latter being, if practicable, bolted to the wall with through bolts and wall plates, as shown in Fig. 17. If this cannot be done, the support may be afforded in the manner illustrated in Fig. 18. Three 11-in. or 9-in. deals will afford sufficient width of bench for the average run of brass founders' work.

When moulding a large number of small patterns in a single flask, they, with their runners, must be so arranged that the metal shall not cool before the moulds farthest from the ingate are reached. To this end it is desirable to maintain something like uniformity in size and mass of the several patterns included in any one flask; to have

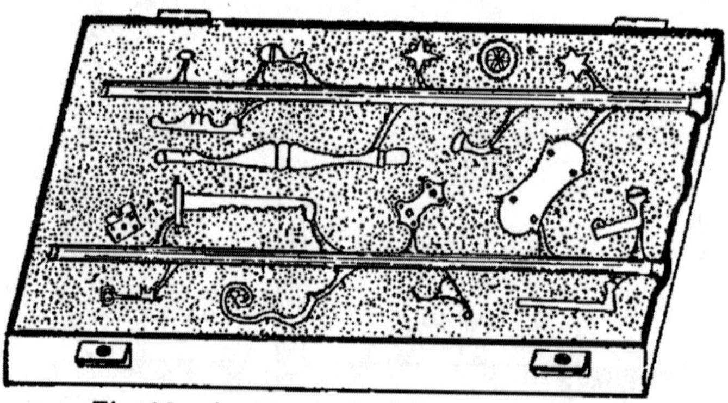

Fig. 19.—Arrangement of Runners in Mould.

the runners of sufficient area; and to pour the metal sufficiently hot to ensure its running to the farther end of the mould. There are two general arrangements of runners. In the one they pass from mould to mould in a flask, the metal running through the successive moulds to the last one. The other is that in which the metal runs down a ridge runner, and passes thence through sprays to the moulds arranged on one side, or on both sides, to right and left.

A ridge of large area and small sprays is the ideal arrangement. This is shown in Fig. 19. The patterns are so arranged in a flask that during the pouring some amount of pressure is imparted by a head of metal. Generally, this takes the form of a continuation of the head of the ingate a few inches above the front or top mould. The more dense the metal is required the deeper must this head be. Castings for hydraulic work, which have to stand test pressures of 1,000 lb. or more to the inch, have to be very dense. If sufficient head is given above the mould, it is not necessary to cast supplementary heads upon the castings themselves. Such heads are sometimes cast on the ends of pump liners and other cylindrical work; but that is more with a view to take the sullage which gathers in a deep mould.

Before the moulds are finally closed, channels must be cut in them connecting the various small impressions with the runners and gates, in order to convey the molten metal to the necessary parts of the moulds. A very good way of making the main ingate or git-hole is to procure a thin piece of tinplate tubing, and with it cut a hole through the sand in the top box to the parting, afterwards withdrawing the tube and tapering off the mouth or top part of the hole to a trumpet or bell shape, and forming also a small air-hole from the top box, at the other end, through to the parting. This allows the escape of the gases which generate within the mould whilst the metal is being poured, and prevents the casting turning out blown, or damaged by small holes. The channels must be sufficiently large to allow the metal completely to fill the impression made in the mould, but must not be larger, or waste of metal will result. It is usual to put the runners or channels in the eye-side, while if any cores are used they are placed in the peg-side.

The moulds, even in common work, are usually dried a little by placing before a stove fire, although this is not absolutely necessary if the impressions have been carefully prepared and dusted with charcoal, it must not be omitted if fine castings are required. If both sides of the casting be required fine, both sides of the mould must be dried. When sufficient moulds have been made to constitute a heat—say five or six—they are placed against the spilling trough, and are then ready to receive the molten metal.

Other details of foundry work necessary to the proper understanding of the craft of the pattern maker will be given as occasion demands.

CHAPTER II.

JOINTING-UP PATTERNS.

THE halving joint is largely used in pattern-making, and the method of joining two pieces of wood together by this means is apparent from Fig. 20. In making this joint, mark one side of each of the pieces to be joined to indicate the face side. Set a gauge to half the thickness of the stuff, and gauge lines on the edges where the pieces are to be placed. Always gauge from the face side, so that even if the gauge was not set exactly to half the thickness the joint will still come even. Screw the pieces together, and then, if the fit is good, take them apart, put on glue, and screw them together again while the glue is hot.

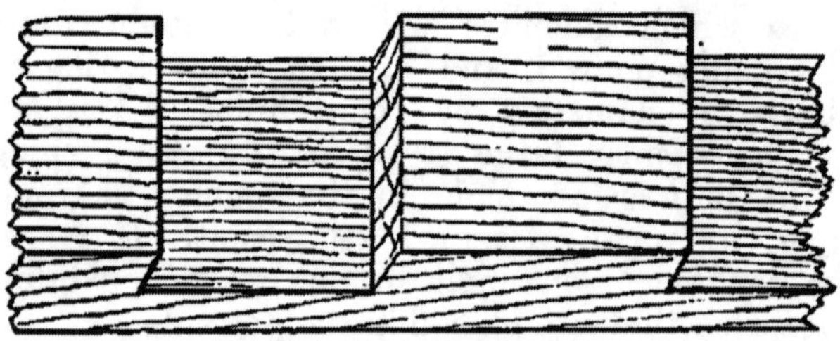

Fig. 20.—Halving.

Corner half-checks are generally cut the whole width of the stuff, as in Fig. 20, but for middle pieces the check is sometimes made short, so as to leave a portion of the timber the full thickness, adding thereby to the strength of the frame, as in Fig. 21.

The dovetail half-check is shown in Figs. 22 and 23; its use is not to hold the pieces together (the glue and screws do that) but to enable a portion of the frame to be hollowed out, and yet not reduce the cross-grained parts (where the pieces butt together) so much as to make them weak and brittle.

The ordinary half-check answers this purpose also, provided the tongue and the space which it fits be narrower than the stuff is wide.

Other joints used in pattern-making are the simple butt joint and mitre. Wheel patterns necessitate some joints that are out of the common.

Fig. 21.—Middle Half-check.

The three-part check (Figs. 24 to 26) is used for wheels with six arms, it allows three pieces to be joined together in the thickness of one. To make it, find the centre in each of the three pieces; with a radius equal to half the width of a piece, describe a circle on one side of the top and bottom pieces, and on bot` iides of the middle piece. Set a bevel to 60°, and with it draw lines touching the circles, as shown in the figures. Divide, by gauge lines, the thickness of the pieces into three equal parts. Let all the portions of the pieces be cut away as shown. The middle piece is to be cut in on both sides as illustrated,

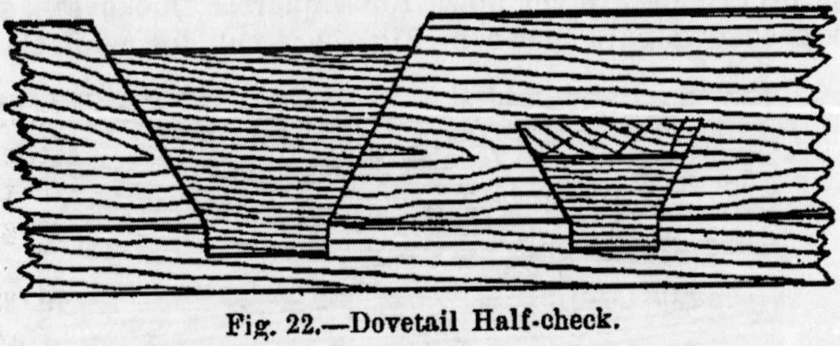

Fig. 22.—Dovetail Half-check.

leaving one-third part in the centre. Cut away the top piece at the part represented by the cross shading for a depth of two-thirds of the thickness.

The four-part check (Figs. 27 and 28) is the joint used for making an eight-arm wheel. As before, circles are described on one side of the pieces shown by Figs. 27 and 29, and on both sides of that shown by Fig. 28. With a bevel set to 45°, draw lines touching the circles. Three-

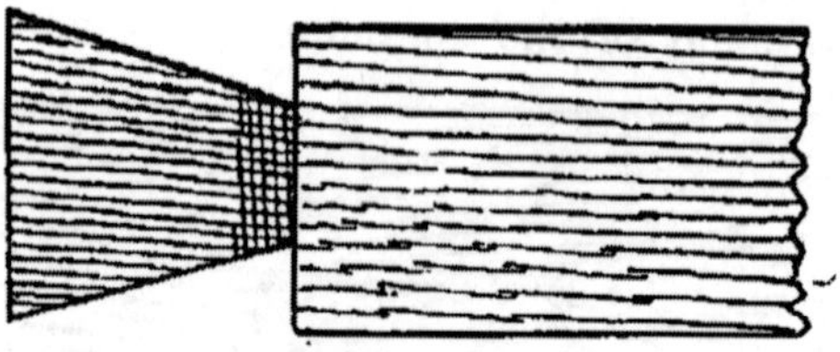

Fig. 23.—Dovetail.

quarters of the thickness of the piece shown by Fig. 27 must be cut away as illustrated. The two middle pieces are exactly alike on one side. The part cross-shaded must

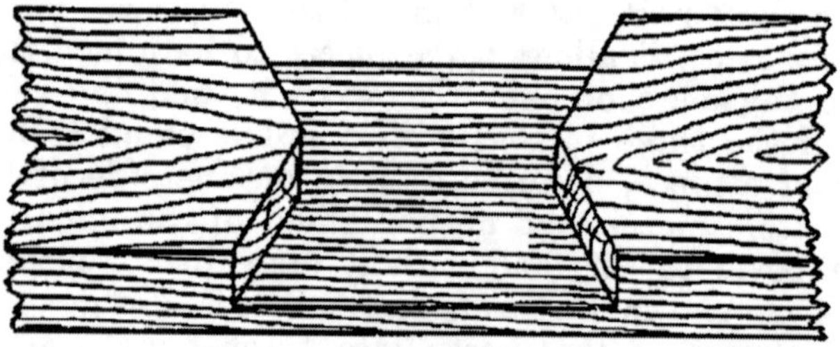

Fig. 24.—Three-part Check.

be cut down to half the thickness; the little corners and the other side are cut down for a quarter thickness. The cross-shaded part shown in Fig. 29 is cut down for three-

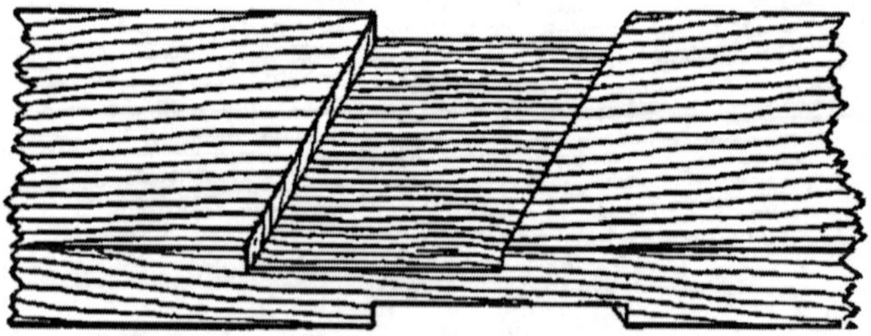

Fig. 25.—Three-part Check.

quarters of the thickness; the corners shown lightly shaded are cut down one-quarter only.

In the construction of patterns, glue should be used

as little as possible. It frequently swells out when the damp sand comes into contact with it, and a glued-up

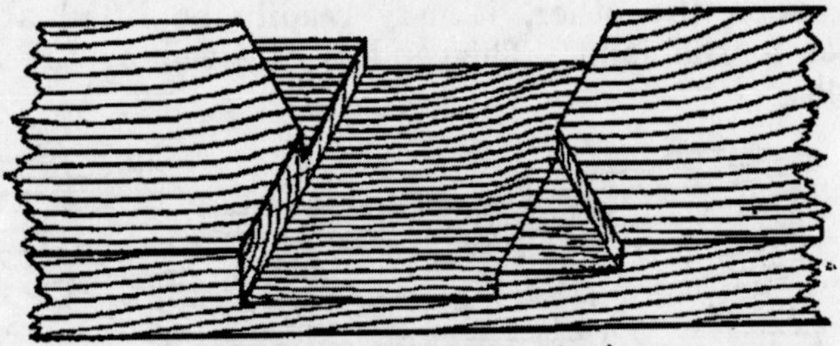

Fig. 26.—Three-part Check.

pattern which possibly has taken hours to prepare often comes to pieces almost the first time of using. As far as possible use joiners' brads, or, better still, slender steel

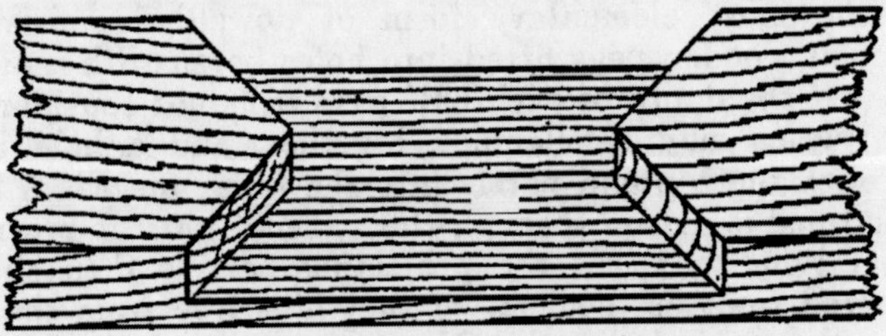

Fig. 27.—Four-part Check.

"wood" screws. When, however, glue is necessary, only the very best should be used; have it thin and fresh. A little quick-drying linseed oil, well stirred in while the glue is

Fig. 28.—Four-part Check.

quite hot, increases its resistance to moisture; but even then a coat or two of a good oil paint is necessary to protect the joint from the moisture arising from the sand.

It is frequently desirable to make a foundry pattern or a core-box in two parts, so that, while one part cannot slide upon the other, it may readily be lifted at right angles to the joint. This end is attained by the use of dowels.

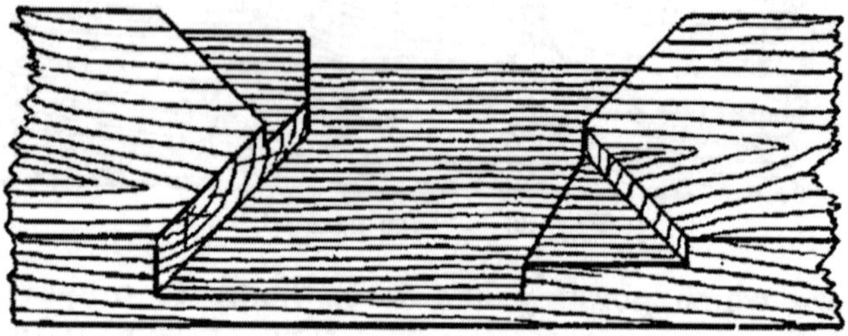

Fig. 29.—Four-part Check.

The most elementary form of dowelling consists of circular wooden pegs fitted into holes bored with a centre-bit. If the depth of each half pattern is not considerable, the pieces may be clamped together, and a hole bored through the top and partly into the lower piece. A hard-wood peg is driven through the [illegible] half until it protrudes from ½ in. to ¾ in.; the projecting part is then slightly tapered towards the end, so that it is free from the hole immediately it is lifted. Of course, a dowel should fit so that no perceptible lateral motion shall be possible.

For permanent patterns, malleable cast-iron dowels, such as are shown in section by Figs. 30 and 31, and in plan by Fig. 32, are generally used. These consist of pairs of plates, one (in Fig. 30) carrying a turned peg, the other

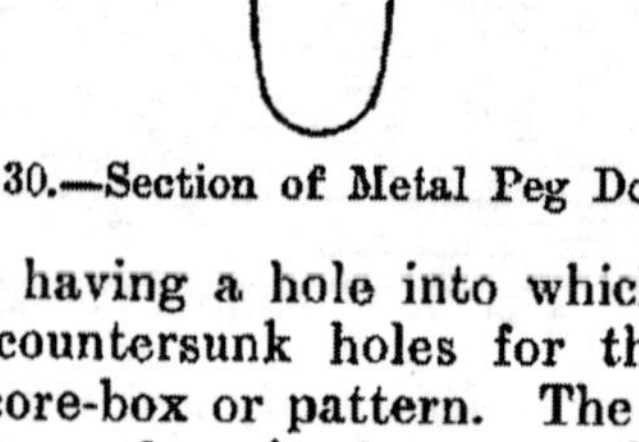

Fig. 30.—Section of Metal Peg Dowel.

(Figs. 31 and 32) having a hole into which the peg easily fits. Each has countersunk holes for the screws which fasten it to the core-box or pattern. The upper plate has two or more sharpened projections, usually at the corners of the plate (see Fig. 30).

The plate dowel (Figs. 31 and 32) being laid in position, its outline is scribed upon the wood. The plate is then removed, a hole bored in the centre of the space marked, and a recess cut so that the top surface of the plate when fastened down sinks slightly below that of the wood. The

Fig. 31.

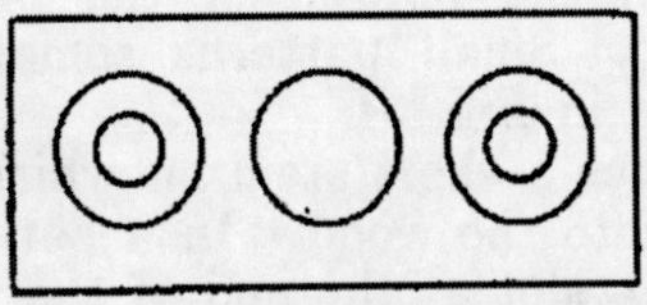

Fig. 32.

Figs. 31 and 32.—Sections of Metal Plate Dowel.

peg dowel is then placed in position, the other half of the pattern is laid upon it, and a sharp blow struck upon the wood. The projecting spikes therefore fix the position of the peg dowel, which may then be inserted and fastened as before.

Usually, at least two pairs of dowels are required, and in many cases more; in such circumstances, if misplaced in the least degree, the dowels may bind, or even refuse to enter the holes when the two parts of the pattern are brought together. This may sometimes be remedied by a sharp lateral blow upon one of the dowelled pieces of wood when they have been forced together.

Fig. 33.—Round Plate Dowel.

To find out where the binding takes place, smear the sides of the hole with red-lead and oil; the peg is then forced into it by a blow, and, on examination, shows where the red-lead has adhered. The dowel is then moved to relieve that part.

Some workmen insert all the plate dowels, then lay in place all the peg dowels, and mark them at one blow; but it is better to mark and insert the peg dowels one by one, as then any inaccuracy may be detected and corrected as it arises. Dowels of this type are sometimes made of stamped brass, but are of little service if the pattern is roughly or frequently used. Dowels of the shape shown in Fig. 33 may be let into the wood by making centre-bit holes of the same diameter as the circular parts of the plate, spikes on the bottom of the plate marking the centres required. Small patterns sometimes have brass dowels as shown in Fig. 34.

The peg carries a short stem on which depressions are turned to lock into the wood. In a better kind the stem is screwed, and a slot at the end of the peg enables it to be inserted with a screwdriver. Rings are also turned on the outside of the ferrule or socket. To insert these dowels a hole is bored, into which the cup dowel may be driven tight, but just before it is driven home the other piece is laid over it, and receives a blow which imprints upon it the shape of the projecti _ part of the cup dowel. The latter may now be completely driven home, and the peg inserted in the centre of the circle thus marked.

An alternative method is to place between the surfaces household pins whose heads occupy the places selected for the centres of the dowels. A sharp blow presses the head of each pin into both pieces of wood, and marks the centres for the boring tools.

The joint face of each half of a pattern should have screwed upon it a stout rapping plate of wrought- or malleable cast-iron, having two holes, one tapped for a lifting screw, the other clear for a rod by which the moulder loosens the pattern in the sand preparatory to withdrawing it. The top of these plates should be, say, $\frac{1}{16}$ in. lower than the surface of the wood, as the rapping burrs the edges of the hole. If the pattern is small enough to be lifted by one hand, the lifting hole should be vertically above the centre of gravity of the pattern. This point may be found experimentally by driving in a bradawl and suspending the pattern in the hand.

When screws are used to connect parts of a pattern, their heads must be made flush, particularly where they would slide upon the sand during the lift. If the thickness of the wood through which the shank of the screw passes is not less than ⅜ in., the neatest method is to make a centre-bit hole and sink the head of the screw below the surface. Wooden plugs are then glued in and cut off flush. With thin stuff the holes are countersunk, the screw head being very slightly below the surface; this depression, with the slot in screw head, is filled with ordinary putty. A paste made of whiting and shellac varnish hardens quickly, but when mixed it must be used at once.

When angles in a casting are left square, the strength of the casting is much less than when filled in with a

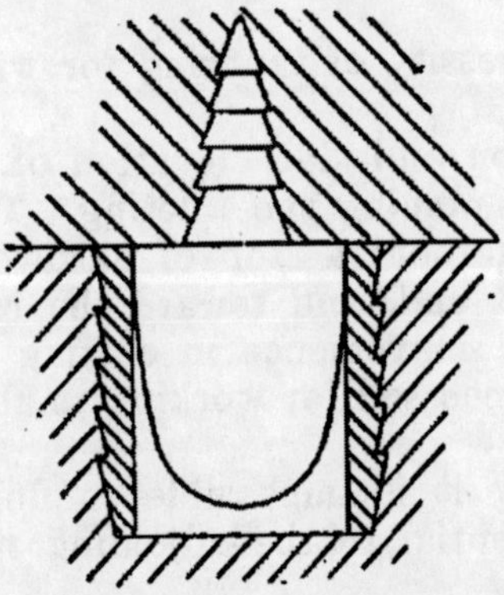

Fig. 34.—Cup and Peg Dowel.

Fig. 35.—Feather-edged Fillet.

curved fillet. This is due to the crystallisation of cast-iron when cooling. The tendency of the crystals to form with their axes at right angles to the cooling surface of the mould causes a weak junction between the two sets of crystals when two parts of a casting are inclined to each other. The introduction of the fillet gets rid of this weakness. Moreover, the additional metal is an advantage at the angle where the regular formation of crystals is interfered with. Practically it is an advantage to the moulder by relieving him of a fragile salient angle of sand.

For straight lengths of filleting, the usual practice of the pattern maker is to plane strips of wood to a triangular section, which are then hollowed out with a round-soled plane, as in Fig. 35. This is termed "feather-edged" filleting, or "angling." If the angle A is slightly more obtuse than a right angle, the fillet will fit close to the corner and reduce the tendency of the edges to curl up. Moreover, the angle in the pattern is seldom or never

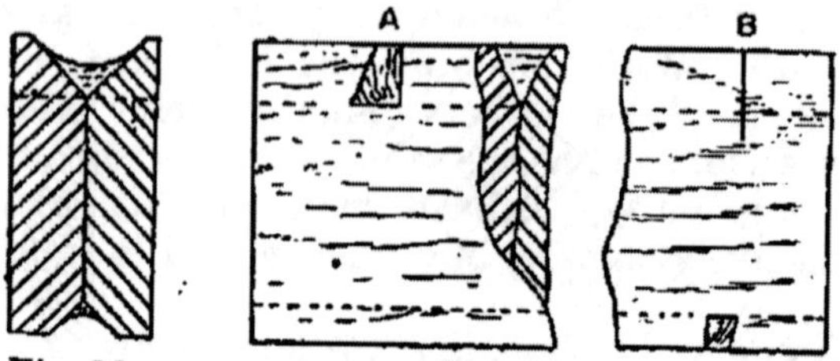

Fig. 36. Fig. 37.

Figs. 36 and 37.—Angle-board for Planing Filleting.

square itself owing to the necessity of tapering for withdrawal from the sand.

Figs. 36 and 37 show section and side elevation of an angle-board which is used for planing the filleting. Two chamfered strips are fixed together; a stop of hardwood A is dovetailed in at the front end, and toward the rear a cross saw-cut B is made for convenience in cutting off lengths. The bottom edge is recessed for working smaller sizes.

With feather-edged filleting it is impossible to finish off the edges to a curve tangential to the adjoining sur-

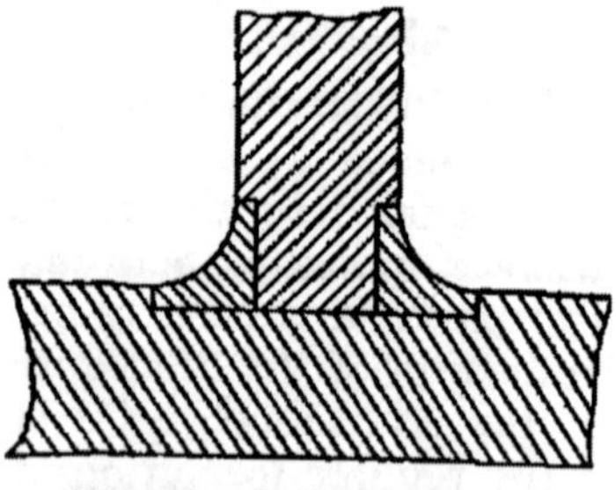

Fig. 38.—Inlaid Fillets.

faces, for this would mean working sharp, fragile edges. In patterns of the most perfect finish and durability, fillets may be inlaid as in Fig. 38. This form would be desirable in such a case as is shown at A (Fig. 39), for a feather-edged fillet here would be at once fragile and clumsy. In this case the fillets are of different curvature, the most shapely finish being obtained by taking tangents at the same height above the horizontal part.

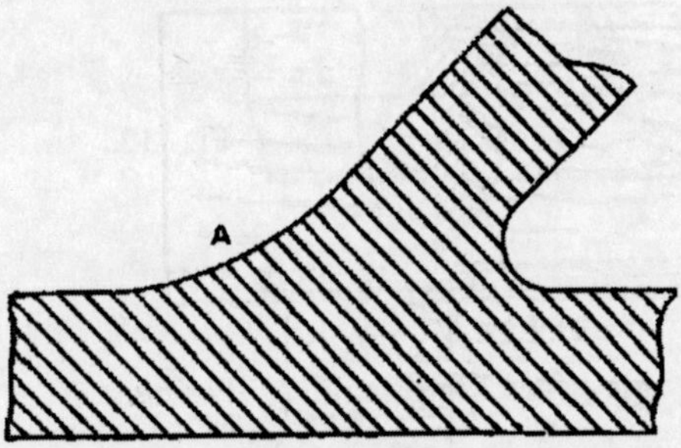

Fig. 39.—Inclined Rib.

Fig. 40.—Leather Strip for Curved Fillet.

When one or both of the adjoining surfaces to be filled in are of a curvature to which a straight fillet cannot readily be bent, a strip of leather of section shown by Fig. 40 is soaked in water to make it pliable, glued, and then pressed in with a short stick of wood turned with a rounded end; or a strip of soft metal rolled to the required section is pressed in, and cemented with a solution of shellac. Such sections are supplied by dealers in pattern-makers' requisites.

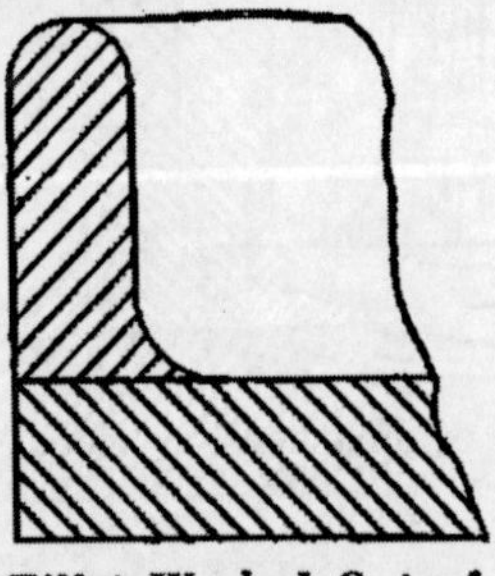

Fig. 41.—Fillet Worked Out of Flange.

In some cases it is desirable to work fillets out of the solid, and one such instance is shown in Fig. 41. Here, the additional base given to the shallow flange is of great advantage in fastening the parts together, without adding greatly to the work—assuming, of course, that the flange is curved in plan. If the work is built in segments, the bottom segment may be made wider, to allow for working the fillet.

A cheaper expedient for curved work is to fill in the

Fig. 42.

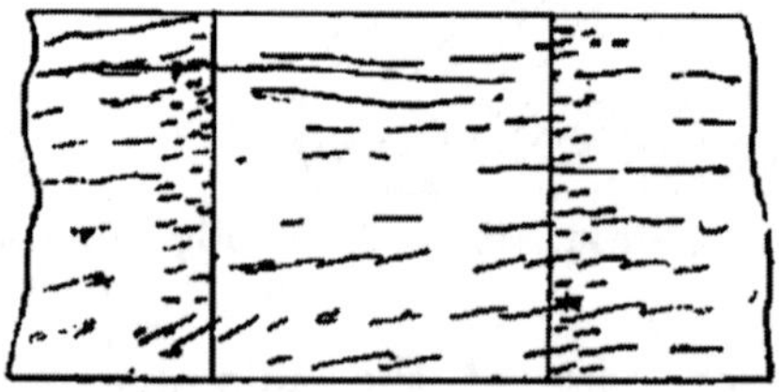

Fig. 43.

Figs. 42 and 43.—Strong Form of Feather-edged Fillet.

space with a mixture of beeswax and resin. This cement is melted and brought to shape with a heated iron, having one end shaped a half-round. Occasionally beeswax alone is used, but generally it is too soft.

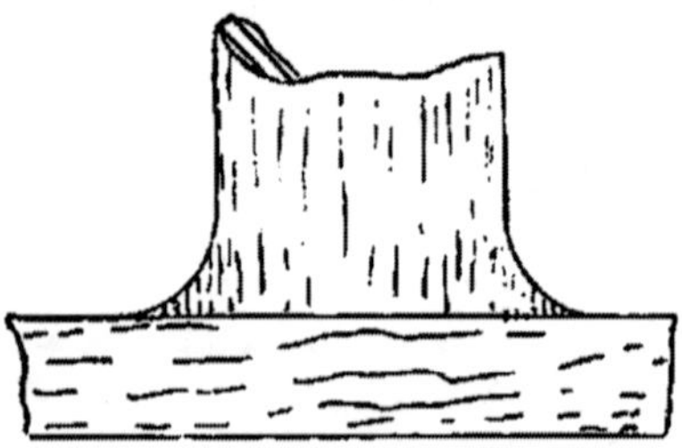

Fig. 44.—Weak Form of Feather-edged Fillet.

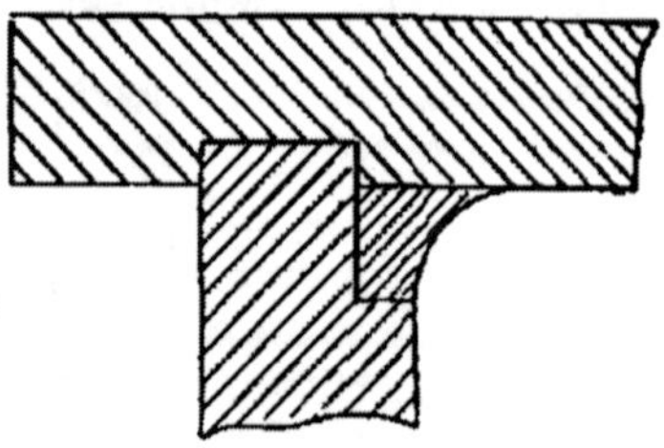

Fig. 45.—Fillet for Core-box with Loose Ends.

The strength of feather-edged filleting depends greatly upon the disposition of the grain of the wood. In Figs. 42 and 43, for instance, it is arranged in the most advantageous manner, whilst in Fig. 44 the shortness of the grain would render it so weak as to be useless in a pattern, even if it could be worked successfully. In such cases it should invariably be let into the lower piece.

In Fig. 45 is shown a combination of feather-edged and inserted filleting, used when one part of the core-box or pattern is not permanently attached to the other.

Sometimes, as in small brass fittings, the angles may best be worked out of the solid, as, for instance, in the

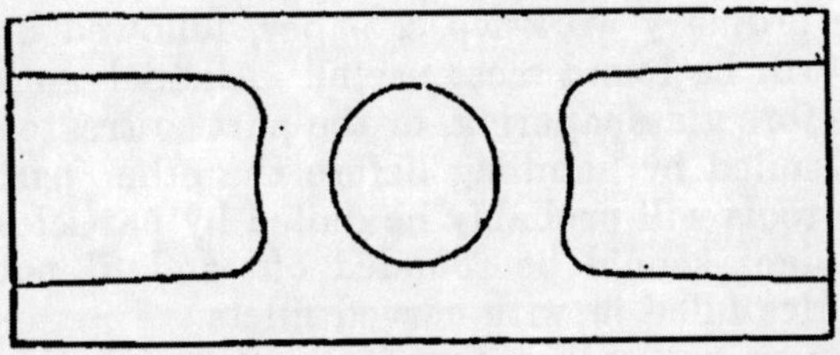

Fig. 46.

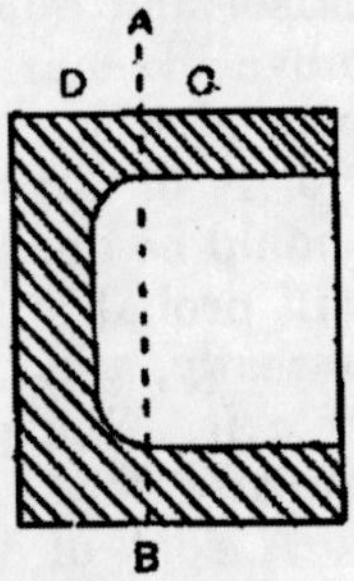

Fig. 47.

Figs. 46 and 47.—Fillets Worked out of Solid.

guide blocks in Figs. 46 and 47. If the pattern is formed of two pieces jointed in the plane A B (Fig. 47), the two may be taken apart, and C, being worked straight through, its shape is scribed upon D, and the small pockets in that piece are cut out with carving gouge and chisels.

About half the thickness of the metal is usually sufficient for the radius of a fillet; if it is too great, metal will be concentrated so much as to draw or become spongy.

CHAPTER III.

FINISHING PATTERNS.

A PATTERN that has been brought to a curved shape by chisel and gouge must be glasspapered afterwards to remove the marks of the tool; in planed work it is best dispensed with. In ordinary work No. 2 paper, followed by No. 1½ or No. 1, will be found most useful. All tool work should be done before glasspapering, or the part so treated will probably be soiled by handling before the other part is ready, and the tools will probably be dulled by particles of grit. Sharp edges should be rounded off, and, if not already done, angles filled in with curved fillets.

A coat of varnish prevents a foundry pattern absorbing moisture from the damp moulding sand. The varnish is made by dissolving shellac in methylated spirit, and is applied with a camel-hair brush. When the first coat has dried, the surface will be found to be roughened by the raising of the grain of the wood. It must be rubbed down with a piece of used glasspaper, and another coat of varnish applied. After this, lightly rub down again and apply a third coat.

Red-lead is sometimes put in the varnish to give more body to it, and to fill the pores of the wood more thoroughly. Whilst the pattern body is thus coloured yellow or red by the varnish used, core prints and parts on which loose pieces are to be wired are rendered conspicuous by varnish to which lampblack has been added. Further, to inform the moulder of the shape, the section should be hatched on the joint face on one half of the pattern with another coloured varnish.

Patterns should be stamped with a number, and all loose parts should also have a similar number to show the pattern to which they belong, and in addition a distinguishing mark, to be repeated on the pattern near the position of the piece. A number of loose pieces belonging to one pattern may be kept together by threading on wire passed through small holes bored in the pieces.

Searing signifies the smoothing and hardening of the surfaces, or portions of the surfaces, of wooden patterns in order to render them more easy to draw, and better able to resist the action of moisture in moulding sand. It may be used with or without an after protective application of shellac varnish. Searing is used for rough work as being more rapid of accomplishment than the action of cutting tools and of glasspaper, and it is adopted also in certain sections of good work to produce uniformity and precision of results which could not well be obtained in any other way.

There is one application of searing which consists in going over large flat surfaces with a hot flat iron. Many years ago, the flat surfaces of large patterns were quite com-

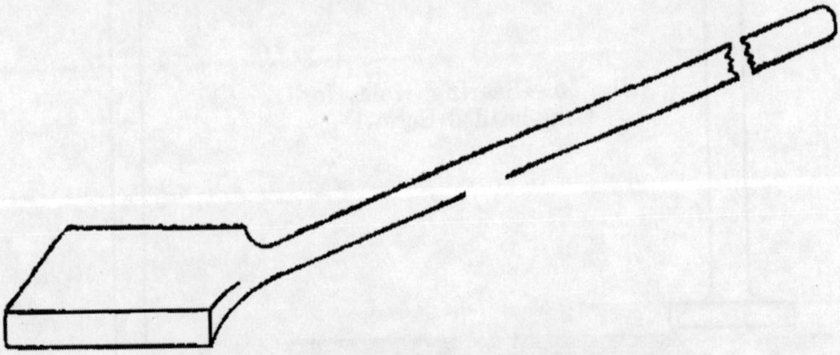

Fig. 48.—Iron for Searing Plain Surfaces.

monly seared or scorched in order to smooth and harden their surfaces, and so assist their delivery from the sand.

The old millwrights and the early pattern makers did not use shellac varnish to anything like the extent to which it is employed in the modern shops. It was reserved chiefly for the smaller patterns, and so much pains was not taken with patterns then as now. Standard patterns now in shops doing repetitive work are got up almost regardless of cost. And it pays to do so. In a few of the very best shops the wood patterns are almost like cabinet work, and the iron ones as good as high-class fitters' work. The millwrights made their patterns more in the style of country carpentry, accurate enough for the purposes for which they were wanted, and mouldable, but with no attempt at finish, often not even glasspapered, and often without any provision for rapping and lifting. Those were the days when searing irons were employed.

The irons used were of the shape shown in Fig. 48, differing only in dimensions. An average size for the flat portion was about 5 in. by 3 in. by 1 in. Some were shorter and narrower, some wider. They were brought to a low red heat in a clear fire, the face just rubbed over with a

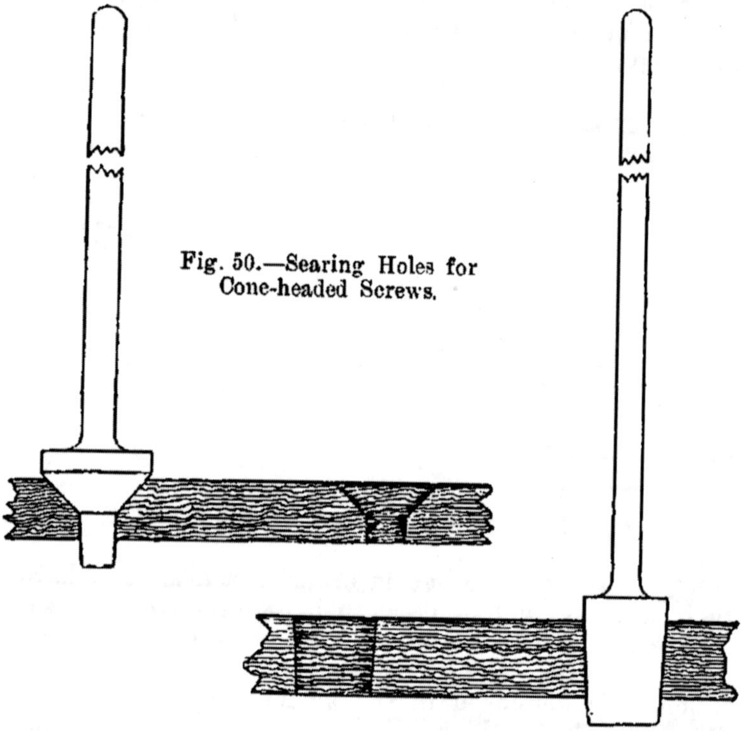

Fig. 50.—Searing Holes for Cone-headed Screws.

Fig. 49.—Searing Plain Bolt Holes.

file, and then the surface of the pattern was seared with the broad face. A quick man could go over a reasonably large pattern at one or two heatings of the iron. It was just a light skinning, not a charring of the wood. It closed and smoothed the grain, obliterated plane marks, and gave a variegated brown and white appearance to the surface. Glasspapering was not necessary either before or after, and the pattern so treated came from the sand freely.

The method was only applicable to plain surfaces. The iron could not be worked round into corners or concave parts, but such parts would be glasspapered or left rough from the tools. Searing was very well adapted to large

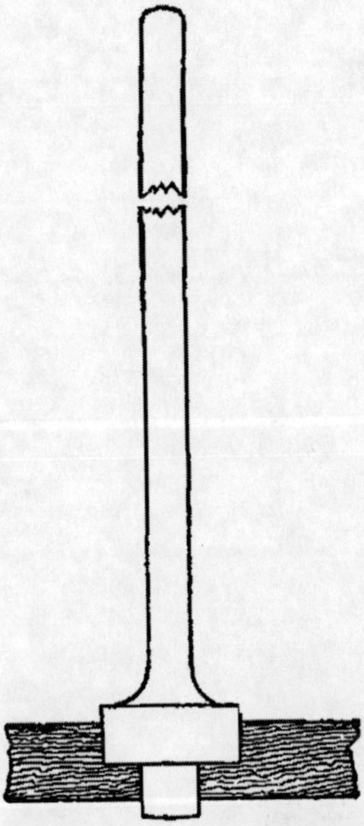

Fig. 51.—Searing Hole for Cheese-headed Screw.

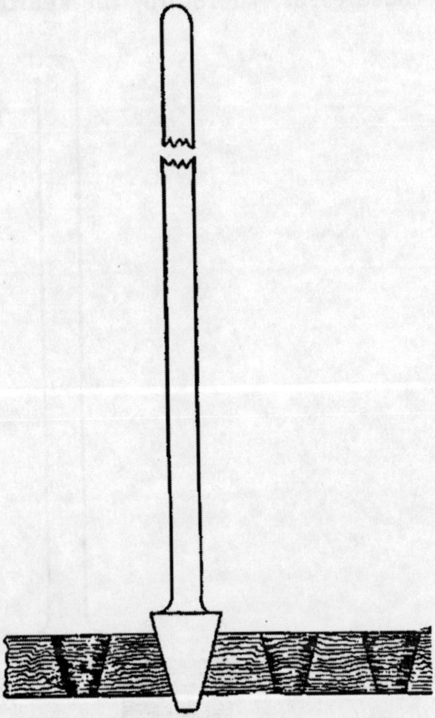

Fig. 52.—Searing Holes in Strainer Core-box.

plain patterns, saving the cost of varnishing or painting, and leaving for all practical purposes as good a surface. It did not protect the grain from the warping effects of moisture so well as paint or varnish, but that is seldom considered of much account in large plain patterns, which are, in fact, often broken up after use.

The method, however, survives in another way. Holes for self-delivery are seared in this manner more rapidly and quite as efficiently as by glasspapering. In thin castings for which holes are cast for black bolts, or for cheese-head or cone-head screws, the holes are often made to deliver themselves in the sand instead of being cored out with prints. The holes which are cast in pipe strainers, though cored, are not inserted in print impressions. In these cases, therefore, the searing iron is used. Figs. 49

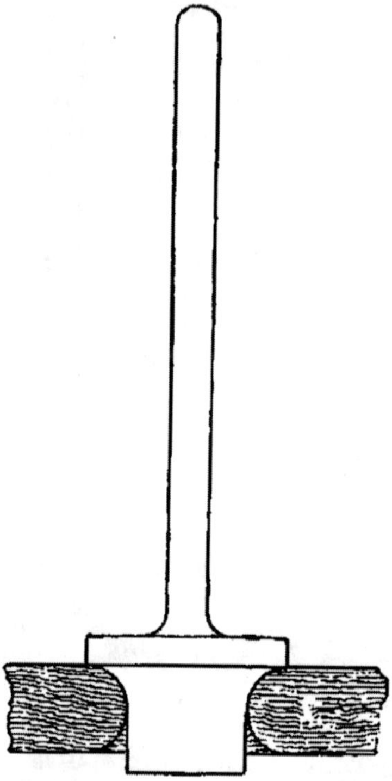

Fig. 53.—Searing Hole of Convex Section from Opposite Sides.

to 52 illustrate the shapes of iron of this class. Fig. 49 shows one used for plain bolt holes. The amount of taper given to it is just sufficient to permit of free delivery in the moulded holes. The effect of a slight amount of taper in much black fitting work is of no consequence. In the holes for cone-headed screws (Fig. 50) the correct form is obtained much more truly and cleanly than by the use of cores, and with a far less expenditure of time and trouble. Holes for cheese-headed screws (Fig. 51) would be very troublesome to form accurately without the burning iron. When many holes have to be seared in a strainer core-box (Fig. 52) they can be done uniformly and quickly. Fig. 53 shows some work in which the hole has to be seared from opposite sides.

These searing irons are made of wrought-iron or steel, and the burning ends are turned to correct form. If not overheated they will last for years. The handles are from 18 in. to 2 ft. long.

When cutting holes which afterwards have to be seared, it is not necessary to observe such exactness of form as when they are finished by glasspapering and varnishing. The holes are bored small enough with a centre-bit; that is sufficient when the form of the hole is, as in Fig. 49, just plain tapered. When it is of any of the forms shown by Figs. 50 to 53, it must be cut nearly to shape and dimensions with a gouge. The burning out of a parallel hole to form a considerable taper would char the timber too deeply; the art of searing consists in just burning the mere surface to a brown or brownish-black tint. The iron must not be too hot, and a contact of a second or two is sufficient. It is not necessary to do anything further previous to moulding, but the application of a coat or two of varnish to patterns or core-boxes for repetition use prevents the roughening up which results from frequent moulding.

CHAPTER IV.

CIRCULAR PATTERNS.

In describing a pattern to be used for making a mould, it will be well to begin with one of the simplest kind. Fig. 54 shows a knob to be turned up in the lathe; it is not given as a model design, because a pattern made to the exact shape shown is almost sure to give trouble. The hollow part A has parallel sides, and lumps of sand will remain in the hollow, with the result that corresponding lumps will be found on the castings. Sometimes patterns are made of the shape indicated in Fig. 55—that is, with the hollow undercut—and such a pattern will not leave the sand. The proper shape is given in Fig. 56; there it will

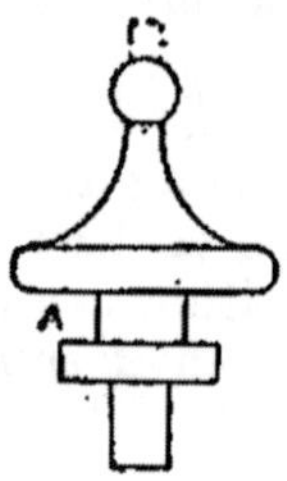

Fig. 54.—Knob Pattern with Chucking Piece.

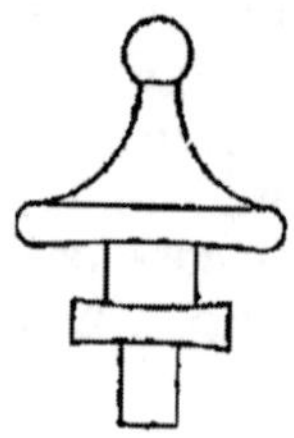

Fig. 55.—Undercut Knob Pattern.

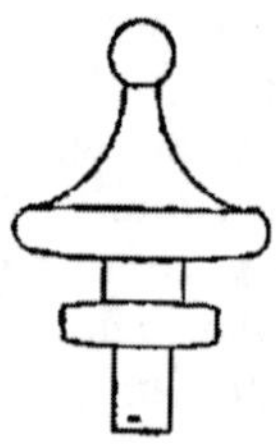

Fig. 56.—Correct Shape for Knob Pattern.

be seen that all surfaces are sufficiently inclined to allow the pattern to be taken out of the mould without clogging the sand.

When about to make such a pattern, first decide as to size, and then as to the quantity of castings likely to be required. If a great number, make the pattern in brass; if only a few the usual method is to make it in boxwood. Beech is much used for large turned patterns, but for the present requirements is useless.

The pattern may be turned in the lathe with ordinary turning tools, and smoothed with fine glasspaper, a good finish being got by taking a handful of clean box turnings and holding these against the pattern whilst the lathe is run at a good speed A boxwood turned pattern finished in this way has a surface that is practically perfect, and will not need varnishing, etc. When making patterns of castings to be finished in the lathe, it must be decided beforehand how they are to be held for turning. The knob here shown will need something by which to hold it, and the plain projecting piece shown at the top of Fig. 54 should be left on for the purpose of chucking it. A screw can then be cut on the foot, or it can be drilled and tapped without removal from the lathe.

From such a pattern as the one just described, it will be but a step to the making of spindles and more ornamental work, but if these are of considerable length, as Fig. 57, they must be supported at both ends in turning. This is accomplished by leaving on the dotted portions,

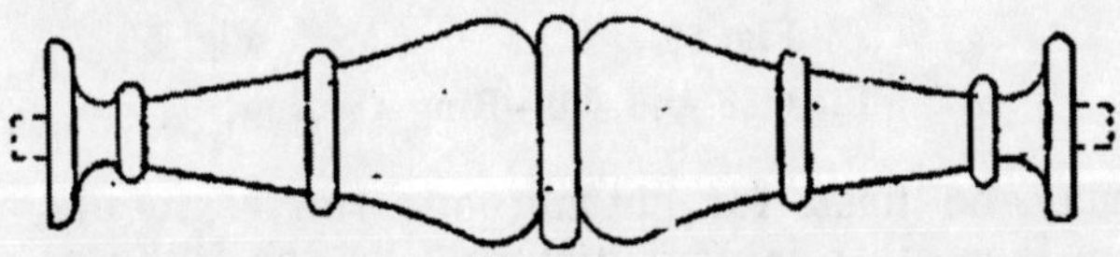

Fig. 57.—Pillar with Chucking Pieces at Each End.

and one end is held in a chuck on the lathe, while the other end is supported by the back-centre.

Segments are chiefly used by the pattern-maker in the construction of circular patterns that are to be turned to shape on a face-plate, such as the rim of a wheel, a piston, ring, etc. Assuming that a casting has to be made, such as Figs. 58 and 59, first prepare a template of the required segment from thin stuff (Fig. 60). The space between the dotted lines and the outline is an allowance of $\frac{1}{8}$ in. to $\frac{1}{4}$ in. for turning the pattern and jointing the ends. The pattern for a turned casting has an extra $\frac{1}{8}$ in. on each turned surface. The smallest patterns usually have four segments to the circle, whilst larger ones have six or eight; only very large patterns have more. The number of segments that can be cut out of the width of a board is next ascertained, and the length of material required is computed. The thickness of wood for ordinary work is from $\frac{5}{8}$ in. to $\frac{7}{8}$ in. For very slight and fragile work, the thickness is from $\frac{1}{4}$ in. to $\frac{3}{8}$ in.

If the segments are small, say less than 12 in. long, the wood may be cut into convenient lengths for planing, and each piece faced perfectly flat. The template may then be used as a guide in marking out the segments on the face of the board. A band-saw, bow-saw, or compass-

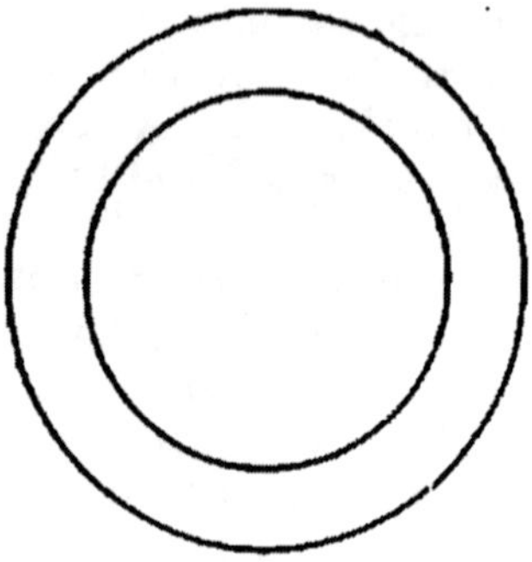

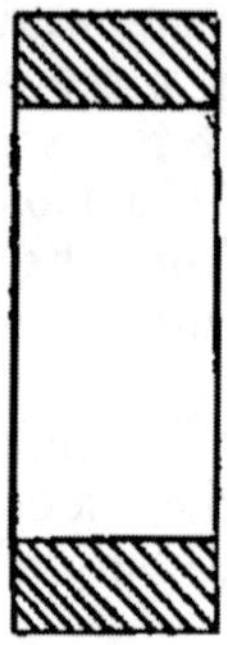

Fig. 58. Fig. 59.

Figs. 58 and 59.—Ring Casting.

saw may be used for cutting out the segments, and a wooden face-plate is next mounted on the lathe as a foundation for building upon. To trim the ends radially, if a small allowance only has been left, hold the segment on a shooting-board and shoot the ends with a trying-plane.

For making similar segments, the sawing-board (Fig. 61) will be an aid. On a rectangular piece of board D, about 1 in. thick, are screwed two blocks E and F, each having

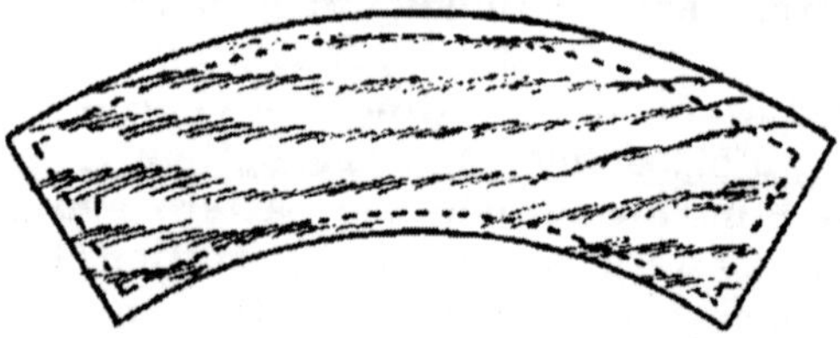

Fig. 6 .—Template for Segments.

a thickness slightly less than the depth of a tenon-saw blade. H is a template about $\frac{3}{8}$ in. thick, one edge, butting against E, being planed parallel to a tangent of the circle of the segment where it is cut by the line B C, and recessed so that the segment A, when brought against it, has bearing points at the ends only. In the line B C, and perpendicular to the base board, a tenon-saw cut is made through E and F to form a guide for the saw. Beneath the base at the front edge a strip is screwed, which, being gripped in the vice, keeps the appliance steady when in use. After one

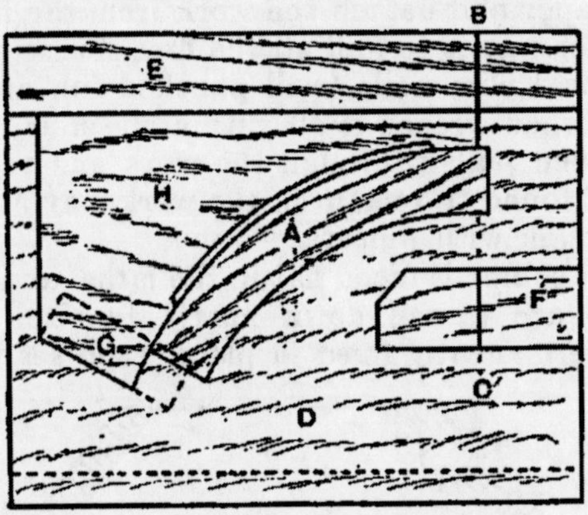

Fig. 61.—Sawing-board.

end of each segment has been sawn off true, another piece of wood, shown dotted at G, is fixed above the template to form a stop when the segments are reversed to have their other ends sawn off; the radial line to which this is set should be marked on when the template is set out. In setting out the template H, the radius at the bearing places is that to which the segment is sawn. Generally, the ends can thus be left true enough to joint together, and

Fig. 62.—Segments Tightened with Dog.

even when shooting is required only a small quantity has to be taken off.

If the segments are large and the work heavy, each one of the first course may be screwed from the back of the face-plate, but in many cases it is sufficient to glue paper on the face-plate, and upon this the segments are glued. A pattern of considerable diameter and little depth may be held by a patch of glue at each end of a segment. The joints are drawn together with dogs, as shown in Fig. 62. When the work is finished a chisel is used as a wedge to split the paper and detach the work from the face plate.

A quicker way is to nail all the first course on the plate with fine oval wire nails (well punched in), and when the work is finished wrench it off with a chisel as before. The nails are then pulled through the work and remain in the plate, or if found to remain in the work may afterwards be pulled through with pincers.

The first course is faced flat in the lathe, and the outside and inside are turned down nearly to size. The next course is permanently fixed in place, each segment having

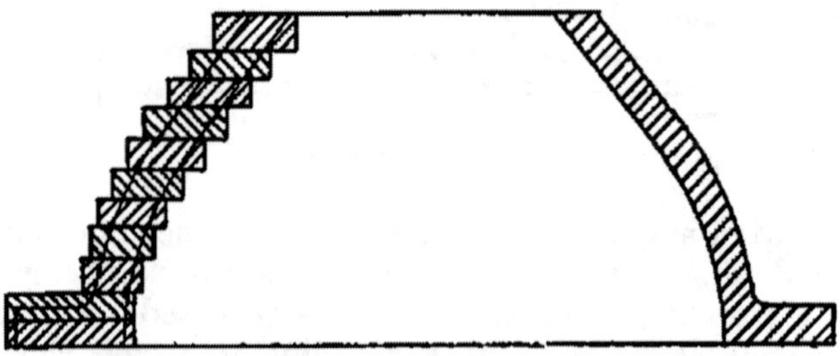

Fig. 63.—Building Pattern of Varying Section.

its centre immediately over the joint between the segments in the course below it (see Fig. 62). These operations are repeated until the pattern is built up, after which it is turned to shape and finished.

For a casting of varying section (Fig. 63), make each course of segments to a diameter obtained by setting out a full-size section. The courses and segments should be numbered. When the section varies slightly, several courses may be sawn of the same diameter. At a flange the segments should be so thick that the greater part (at least) of the adjoining fillet may be formed from them. When segments are to be built up on a wooden disc, as in the pattern shown at Fig. 64, a rebate is turned round the edge of the flat disc to form a bed for the segments. The segments are brought to a joint at A by means of spokeshave or compass-plane.

The joints between the courses are glued, and further secured by screws, nails, or pegs. For straightforward, substantial work screws are best, the heads being well let in to avoid the turning tools. For slighter work nails, well

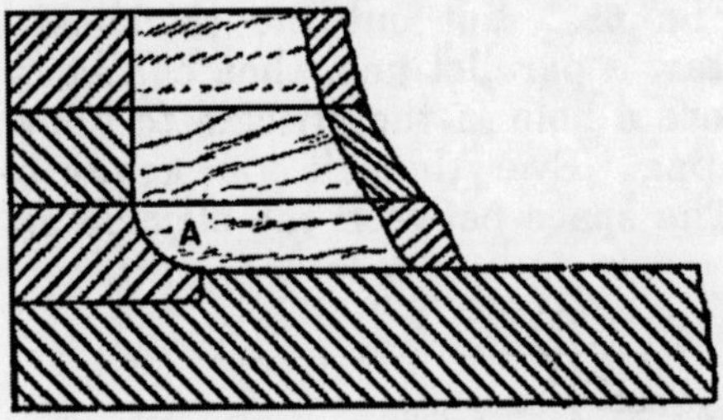

Fig. 64.—Segments Built up on Disc.

punched down, will answer, but, when the contour of the pattern is curved or tapered, it is best to use wooden pegs.

Fig. 65 shows a steel plate for making the pegs circular after they have been split off. The central hole has a cutting edge slightly below the face of the plate to avoid accidental blows from the hammer. The holes at the side are for screws that fasten it to a block, with a central hole through which the pegs fall clear as they are knocked through one by one with a hammer.

Allow all glued joints to dry before boring the holes into which the pegs are driven.

A cheap circular pattern required quickly may be made of plaster. A circular pan with cover (Fig. 66), to fix on a gas fire and enclose a plumbers' ladle, may be taken as an example. The first thing required is a flat board

Fig. 65.—Plate for Shaping Wooden Pegs.

battened on the underside and made large enough to give a margin of, say, about 4 in. round the job to be strickled. Next procure a piece of square stuff and turn it down in the lathe at each end, as in Fig. 67, the length between the shoulders being equal to the depth inside the pattern required. Fix this in the centre of the board by means of the short peg, driving in two or three nails to hold it firm.

The shape of the pan is next set out on a piece of pine about 1 in. thick, working from the centre line, as shown in Fig. 68. Set out the thickness of the metal required, draw a parallel line, then cut away to the inside line, also bore a hole in the strickle to allow it to revolve on the top peg. Everything is now ready for striking up the core. The space between the strickle and the upright

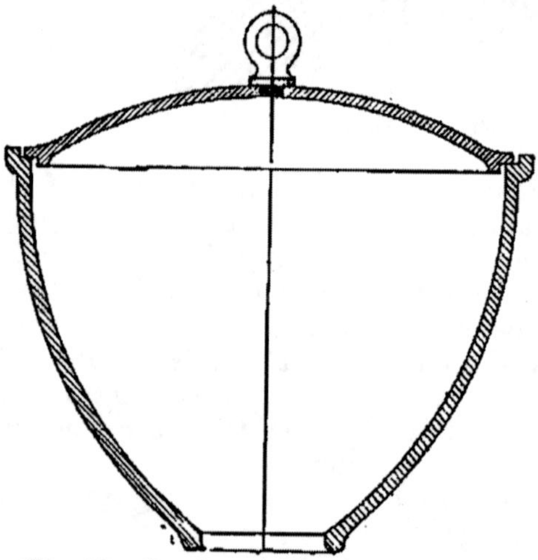

Fig. 66.—Section of Circular Pan, with Cover.

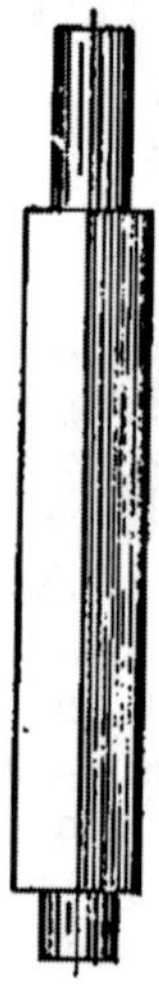

Fig. 67.—Axle for Strickle.

piece forming the core of the pan may be filled in with scrap wood, room being left, however, for a layer of plaster of Paris to finish.

Superfine plaster should be used, well mixed, and all lumps should be thrown out. In laying on the plaster, keep working the strickle round on its centre, the result being a circular core of the shape of the inside of the pan. This must be allowed to set hard and afterwards varnished. While this is drying, cut away the strickle to the second line, and varnish the baseboard where the strickle does not touch. Oil all the varnished parts and again lay on the plaster, keeping the strickle moving round all the time, the result being the outside shape of the pan. Use the plaster fairly thin towards the finish so as to leave the pattern smooth. Allow it to set hard, and varnish it in place. When quite set, the shell can be easily removed from the core and the required pattern is complete. This is very cheap compared with making a similar pattern in wood. The cover for the pan is worked up in the same manner, core first and pattern afterwards.

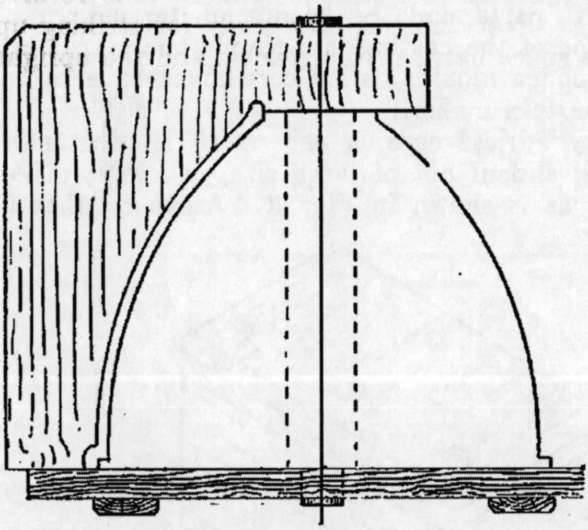

Fig. 68.—Strickling Shell.

Fig. 69.—Edge of Strickle.

Another convenient use for the strickle is found in striking up different forms of mouldings for use on fancy patterns both straight and circular. When a straight moulding is required, nail down a straight edge along which to run the strickle, and if a thin shell is required, strike up the core first as in the circular work, adding, of course, the varnish and oil. A strickle, after being cut to shape, should always be bevelled at the back, leaving the front edge about ¼ in. thick, as shown in Fig. 69.

CHAPTER V.

MAKING CORE-BOXES.

THE sand moulds used in metal casting are almost always constructed with parts made of dried sand, termed cores, unless the shape of the casting is a simple one. To form these cores, wooden moulds called core-boxes have to be made by the pattern maker.

A simple cylindrical core is one which is constantly being required, and, if not of large size, is always made in a box such as is shown in Fig. 70. Assuming that a

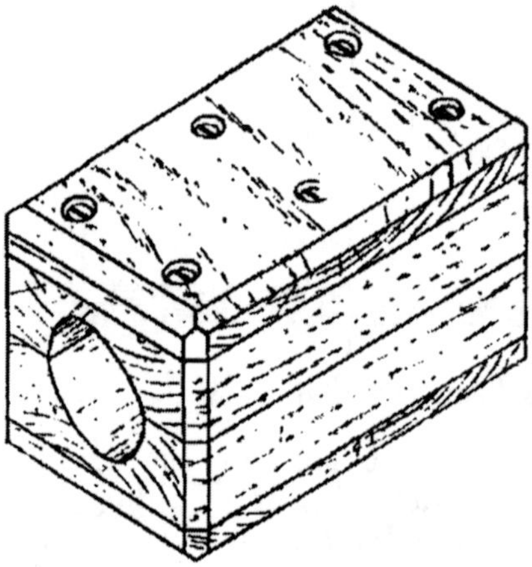

Fig. 70.—Core-box for Plain Circular Core.

core 3 in. diameter and 12 in. long is wanted, two pieces of wood, each measuring a little over 12 in. in length, about 6 in. or 7 in. wide, and 2 in. thick, are dowelled together face to face, the dowels being placed towards the edges of the wood. For a box of this size, dowels would be put in two opposite corners, as in Fig. 71, which is a view of one half of the box. The ends are then squared off, and the length is finished to the required size. On the back of each part, pieces of wood termed "backing" are glued and screwed, with the grain running at right angles to that of the core-box. The backing is generally a very necessary part of the core-box, in order that it may possess sufficient strength and permanence of form.

The core maker raps the backing with a mallet to loosen the core in the box, and to save it as much as possible from the effects of the blows, the backing should always have the edges well chamfered off, and the holes

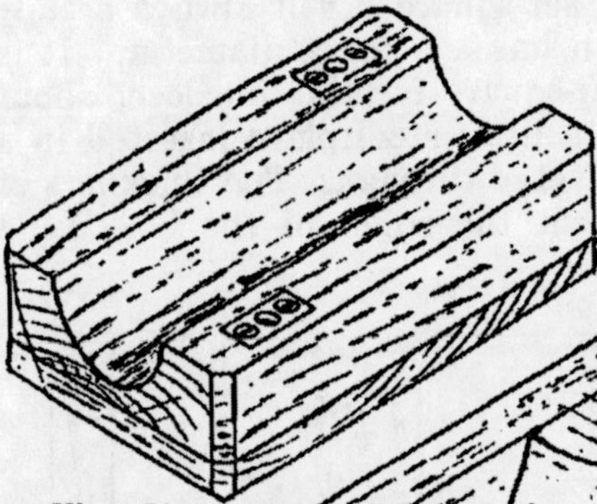

Fig. 71.—Half of Core-box, showing Dowels.

Fig. 73.—Template for Working Circular Core-boxes.

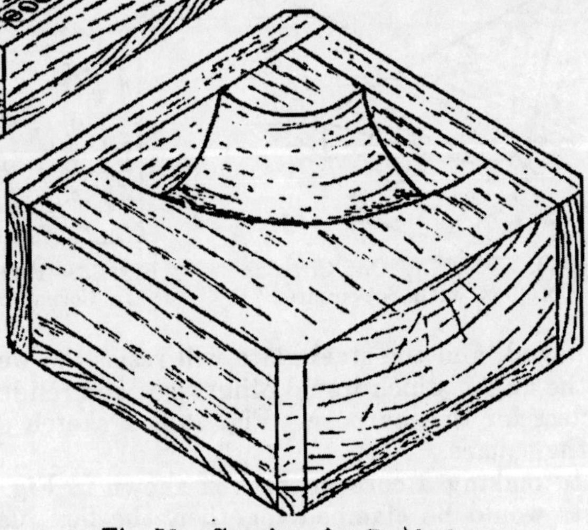

Fig. 72.—Core-box for Bend-pipe.

through which the screws pass deeply countersunk. A 3-in. circle is now struck on one end of the box; and from each point of that diameter of the circle that intersects the joint of the box, gauge lines are marked on one half of the box. Another circle is struck on the other end, and the box is ready to be worked out. This is done by means of gouges and round-soled planes.

If the core-box should be shaped as in Fig. 72, which

shows a core-box for a bend-pipe, planes are not available, and a template or a set-square is necessary to ensure truth of shape. Fig. 73 shows the template, which is used by smearing the semicircular edge with red lead and oil, and trying in the box from time to time as the cutting out progresses. If a set-square is used, it is applied as in Fig. 74, the dotted lines showing varying positions of the square. When the two sides rest on the edges A B, the rectangular corner of the set-square C will always occupy a point in the circle which has A B for a diameter. It is best to make a special set-square for this purpose, about ¼ in. or $\frac{5}{16}$ in. thick, with a little steel plate inserted in a saw-cut (see Fig. 75) and riveted through. The thickness of the square will then prevent the edges of the box being

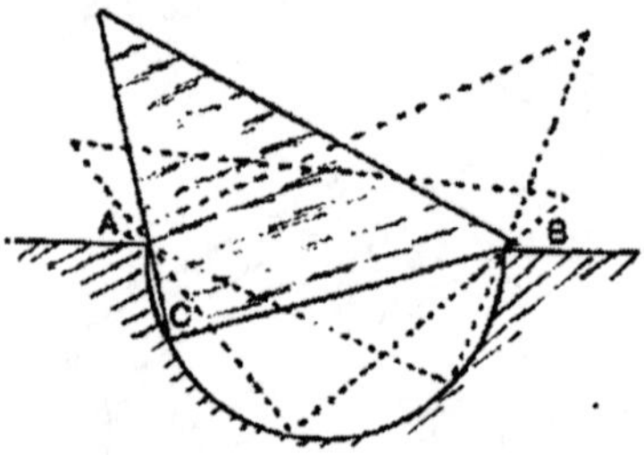

Fig. 74.—Working Out Circular Core-box with Set-square.

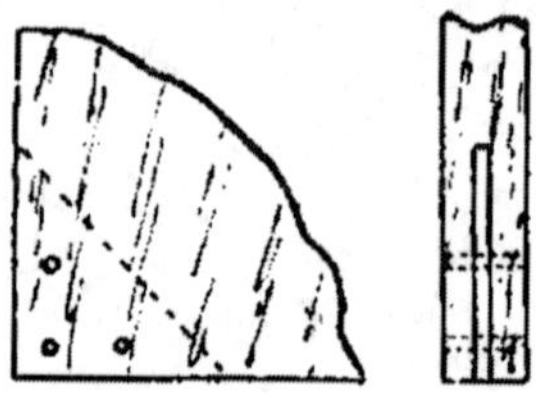

Fig. 75.—Fixing Steel Plate in Corner of Set-square.

damaged, and the steel plate will resist the wearing action at the angle, which would otherwise soon render the square useless for this purpose. Fig. 75 is a sketch of the corner of the square.

In making a core in the box shown in Fig. 70, the two parts would be clamped together, the box placed upright and sand rammed into the cylindrical space. When it is either impossible or awkward to ram the core from the end, as in Fig. 72, the ends are stopped by screwing on pieces of backing stuff, as shown. The two halves of the core are then rammed separately, and the halves of the box are brought together after a wash made of clay and water has been smeared on to fasten together the halves of the core.

When an internal flange is required in a straight box of any considerable length, such as A (Fig. 76), it is usually best to cut through to the greater diameter, and then let in the flange (which is turned in halves) as shown. If, however, a large number of them were required somewhat close together, it would be best to cut through to the

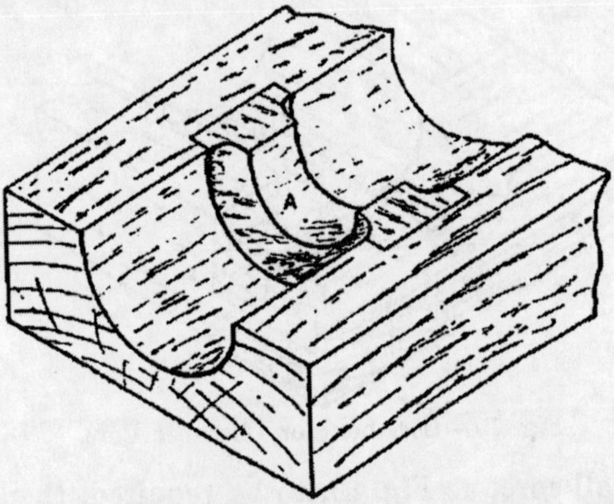

Fig. 76.—Internal Flange Fitted into Core-box.

smaller diameter, and cut out to the larger diameter with gouges.

Cores of the shape of Fig. 77 are called "chamber cores," and are frequently required. If the chambered part—namely, that having the greater diameter—is long, whilst the remaining part is short, a good way of making the box is to cut through to the large diameter, and then,

Fig. 77.—Chamber Core.

cutting away the ends, make up with blocks placed transversely, and cut these through to the small diameter. This is shown in Fig. 78. If the box is required for making a few cores only, it will then be sufficiently strong without backing. If the part having the smaller diameter be very short, a plain piece may be screwed on to the end and worked through, as shown in Fig. 79.

Cores which are rectangular solids, or approximate to being so, are of a shape which is very much required. Sup-

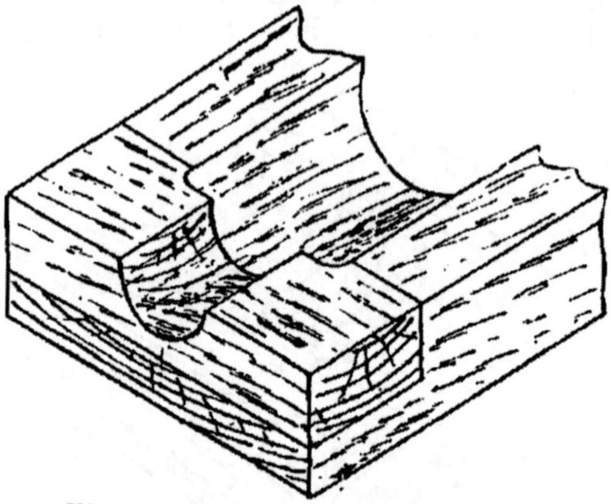

Fig. 78.—Core-box for Chamber Core.

pose a small core, as Fig. 80, to be required, then the box is made as shown in Fig. 81, with one diagonal along the line of the joint. This ensures the box coming freely away from the sand after ramming. In making the core, the two parts of the box are held together, placed on a flat board, and scraped off level after ramming.

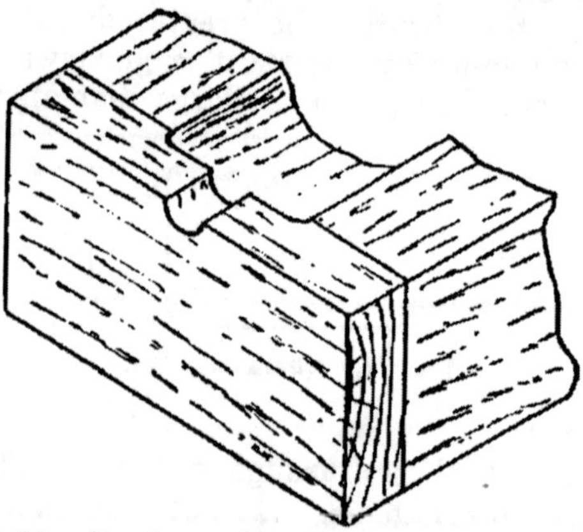

Fig. 79.—Core-box with End of Small Diameter.

Such a method of construction as that shown in Fig. 81 is applicable only to core-boxes which are of the smallest size. For larger cores the construction shown in Fig. 82 is almost invariably used. The ends are housed into the sides, and, when the core is rammed, some of the screws are slackened so that it may be more easily removed from the box as at A. For large boxes, screwed pins and bow nuts are used instead of ordinary wood screws; this is shown at the corner B. Bosses, ribs, or other projections with axes at right angles to either of the sides or ends may be fixed on, and when the fastenings of the box are removed the side or end may be drawn away without disturbing the sand. If bosses are required on the bottom

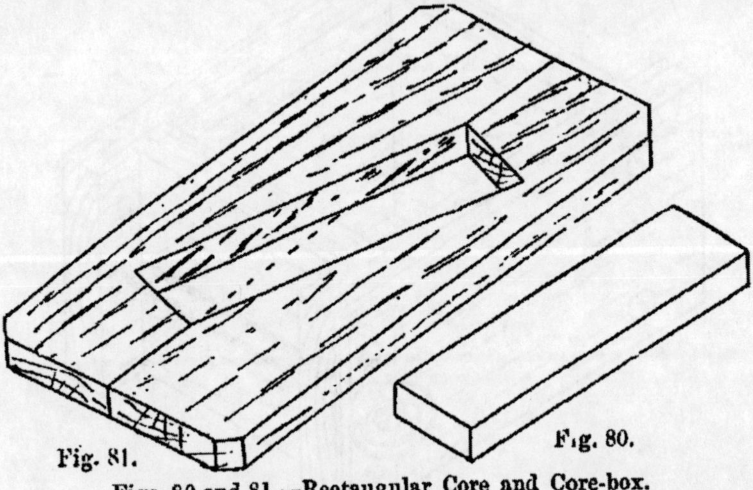

Fig. 81. Fig. 80.

Figs. 80 and 81.—Rectangular Core and Core-box.

of the core, the box is dowelled on to a bottom board upon which the boss or rib may be fastened. A boss may be formed on the top of the core by dowelling across it a narrow bridge-piece, upon the underside of which the boss is fixed. A boss inclined at an angle to one of the sides may be formed by making the boss loose, and withdrawing it after the sides are taken away; or a plug having a shoulder to ensure it being properly placed is passed through the box, and the boss formed upon the end inside the box. This plug is withdrawn from the core before the sides of the box are removed. The centre line of the hole through which it passes is, of course, at the same angle as the boss.

Large round cores are generally formed without using a box at all but in special cases a box is required, and then it is built up as in Fig. 83. A number of lagging pieces are fitted into transverse pieces A, and end pieces B are fitted on after the shape of the box is worked out as at C. In most cases a half box is sufficient, the two half cores, after being made, being fastened together.

Fig. 84 is another case in which a half box may be

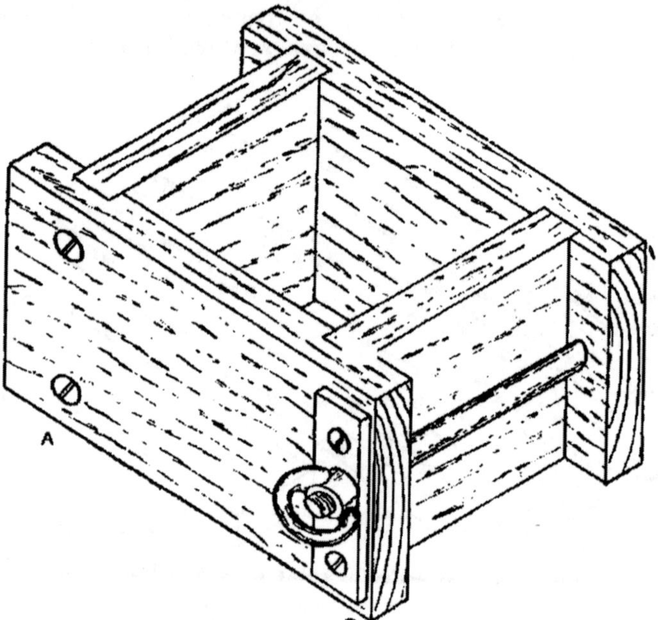

Fig. 82.—Built-up Box for Large Rectangular Core.

used, but for Fig. 85 a whole box would have to be made, for the two halves of the core would overlap each other if placed face to face. Fig. 86 shows the shape of a core which can be made with a half box if provision is made for placing the branch on one half to the full lines, and on the other to the dotted lines. This is done by having two branch pieces cut out, and stopping one off when one half core is made, and the other part when the other half is made.

In moulding flywheels, spur wheels, and large pulleys,

core-boxes such as Fig. 87 are in general use. If the wheel has six arms, a segmental box embracing one-sixth of a circle is built up, and in this a pattern of one-sixth of the wheel is fitted. The sides are made to come apart and

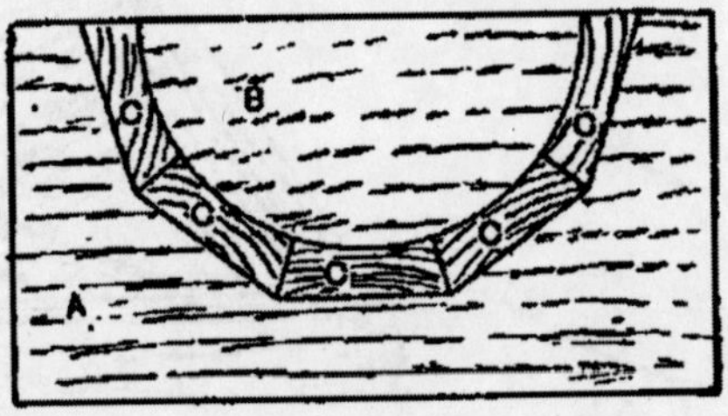

Fig. 83.—Half Box for Large Circular Core.

withdraw separately from the core, leaving the arm in the middle of the core to be withdrawn afterwards. If for a flywheel, the face is made by means independent of the core-box. If for a spur wheel, another segmental box is

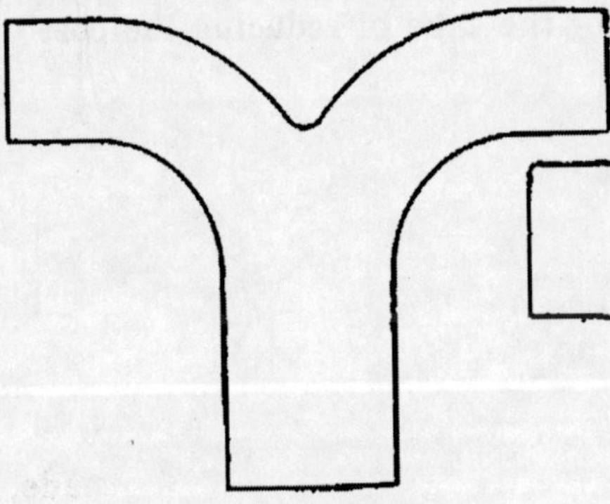

Fig. 84.

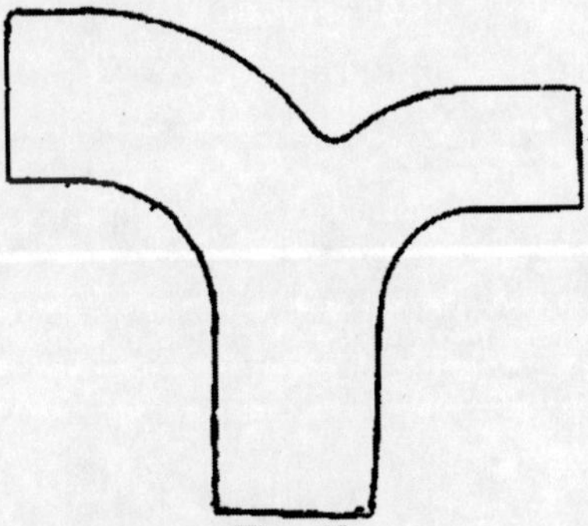

Fig. 85.

Figs. 84 and 85.—Symmetrical and Unsymmetrical Cores.

made for forming the teeth, and the cores made in it are laid in a circle in the mould. Thus a nearly complete mould is formed by laying the cores on a flat bed of sand.

The top is covered up either by making a ring of flat segmental cores, or by covering with a box of sand rammed up and scraped off to a flat surface.

Fig. 86.—Core for Bend-pipe with Branch.

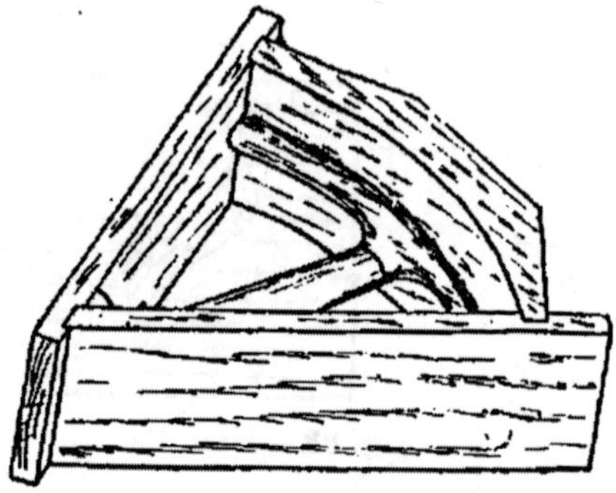

Fig. 87.—Core-box for Making Flywheel.

A complete pattern may, of course, be used instead of core-boxes, and in the case of small castings it is sometimes better to do so, but core-boxes are almost always used for large castings for the sake of reducing the cost of pattern making.

CHAPTER VI.

CORING HOLES IN CASTINGS.

In very many cases the best method of coring a hole is obvious and simple enough; but it is otherwise in a large number of instances. It is proposed to give in this chapter a few examples of this class of work.

Take first one of the very simplest cases that can occur, a plain cylinder cover (shown in Figs 88 and 89). To core the centre hole A for the stuffing-box and piston-rod, a print

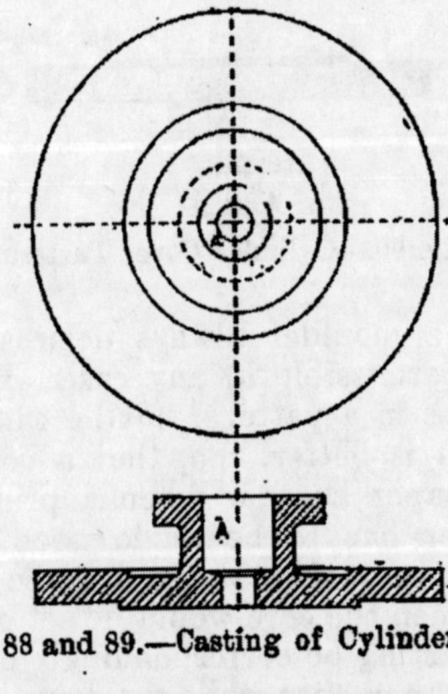

Fig. 89.

Fig. 88.

Figs. 88 and 89.—Casting of Cylinder Cover.

is put on the pattern on the side which goes downwards in the mould. This is shown on the pattern at A (Fig. 90), where the pattern is illustrated in the position in which it is withdrawn from the mould. Since the hole is shouldered, that is, not parallel throughout, a core-box must be made. This is illustrated in Figs. 91 and 92. The core made from this is dropped into the print impression A in the mould, and is thus centred and retained in its correct position. The mould, with its core in place, is shown in section in Fig. 93.

This is a very common illustration of the simplest kind of coring. Almost all holes which pass vertically through castings are formed by the insertion of cores thus set in print impressions in the lower portion of the mould. There are a few special exceptions, as in the case of work for which the cores are so large that they are set in place by measurement alone, since they do not need assistance from the impressions of prints.

All prints which are used for vertical cores are tapered, or coned smaller in a direction away from the pattern face. This is shown in Fig. 90. It is done to prevent the print from tearing up the sand, which a parallel print would almost certainly do on withdrawal. The reason why a larger amount of taper is given to a print than to its

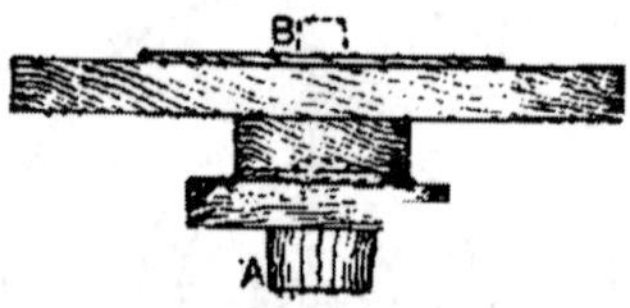

Fig. 90.—Cylinder Cover Pattern.

pattern is that a moulder always desires the maximum taper which is permissible in any case. He cannot have just what he likes in a pattern, but he can in prints, and so he gets it. It is better, too, that a core print should have plenty of taper because when a print tears up the mould, the latter has to be made good again; and if badly broken, it probably would not be mended quite accurately, and then the core would be set out of truth and the hole in the casting be correspondingly out of truth. It may be noted, further, that while the print is tapered there is no taper in the core-box (Figs. 91 and 92) to correspond; consequently, taper has to be filed or rubbed on the core to make it enter and fit the print impression exactly.

When a few castings only are wanted, it is not usual to put the print taper in the core-box; but if many (say twenty and upwards) are required the taper should be formed in the box to correspond with that given to the print. It saves the moulder's time, and reduces the risk of the cores being set out of the vertical, due to more being filed off one portion of the sides of the core than off others.

There is yet another point of importance. One print only is shown on this pattern (that on the bottom), and it is sufficient in the example given. But suppose the length, or height, of the core were double or treble what it is, then one print alone could not be trusted to hold safely the core upright. In such a case a second, or steady, print is put on the top face to make a hole for the top end of the core. This is shown dotted at B (Fig. 90).

Many cases occur in which top prints are absolutely necessary; but, obviously, lengths and diameters are re-

Fig. 91.

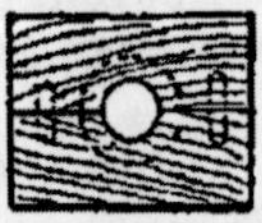

Fig. 92.

Figs. 91 and 92.—Core-box for Cylinder Cover.

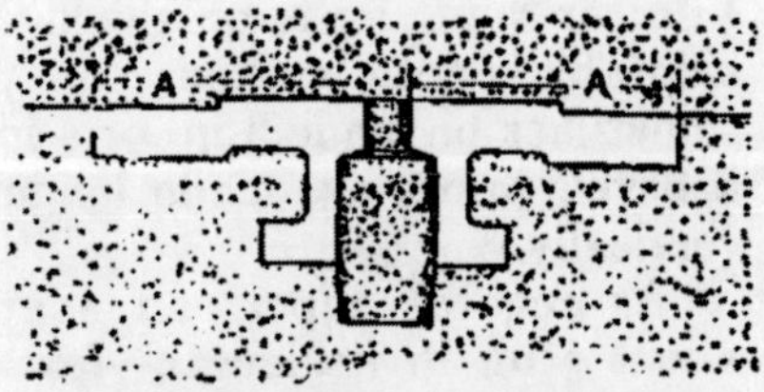

Fig. 93.—Mould for Cylinder Cover.

lative. So that if a core were 4 in. diameter and 12 in. high, it could be set safely in a bottom print alone; but if it were 1 in. in diameter and 12 in. high, a top print would be required. Also, a long vertical core may be held by a bottom print alone if there is a good chance of centering it by measurement right up to the top; otherwise, a relatively short core may require a top print. For example, in Fig. 93 measurement can be taken in the mould from the edge of the core to the edge of the mould, the radius A A being easily taken. Then the question of the securing of the core in the top simply means the thrusting of the core well into its print impression, and the application of the pressure of the cope on the top of the core. Many cases, however, arise in which a large portion of the mould comes up into the top and the core has to pass up into it, and measurement cannot be taken at the top. Then a top print is desirable to guide the core correctly, because the moulder cannot see and measure it. In some later examples attention will again be drawn to this important point.

Cases arise in which top prints cannot conveniently be used. Then the difficulty is often got over by making the bottom print double, or even treble, the usual length, so that it shall form an efficient stay, as well as a guide to the core.

The lengths of these prints and the amount of taper to be given to them vary within wide limits. For bottom prints up to 2½ in. or 3 in. diameter, the length is usually made about equal to the diameter; over these diameters the length diminishes. But, after all, the length depends in the main on the length of core which the print is required to steady; so that for coring through thin plates of metal, prints of 2 in. diameter need not be more than ½ in. or ¾ in. long, or thick. For coring through a considerable depth without top prints, a 2 in. print would sometimes be made 3 in. or 4 in. long. For coring holes at a bevel, prints are made longer than for similar cores set vertically.

As regards taper, an average print will be tapered about ⅛ in. in its length—few less, the larger ones more. Both length and taper are therefore matters to be decided upon according to the requirements of each individual job.

Another matter, very obvious apparently, relates to the length to which core-boxes must be made or cores cut off. This length must always include the length of core required in the casting, plus the length of print on the pattern. That is obvious on comparing Figs. 88 and 93.

When holes have to be cored in horizontal positions in the mould, either two prints or one may be used, but taper is not required in the portion of the print that forms the impression for the core. In the case of what are called "pocket" or "drop" prints, the portions above the part which corresponds with the core are tapered. Two prints are employed when the mould is wide, and only one when it is narrow.

Taking a familiar object, Figs. 94 and 95 illustrate a plain steam cylinder casting in longitudinal and in transverse sections. The central bore A has to be cored with a horizontal core laid in two parallel print impressions. The passages C C B have to be formed with cores laid in bottom tapered print impressions; B will be supported at the other end C (Fig. 95) in a parallel print impression; C C are supported at one end only by prints. At the opposite ends they abut against the main core A. In some exceptional cases core print impressions for C are cut in A, so fulfilling the purpose of top prints; but in general work it is more convenient to dispense with their assistance.

Figs. 96 and 97 illustrate the pattern of this cylinder in the position in which it would lie in the mould. The

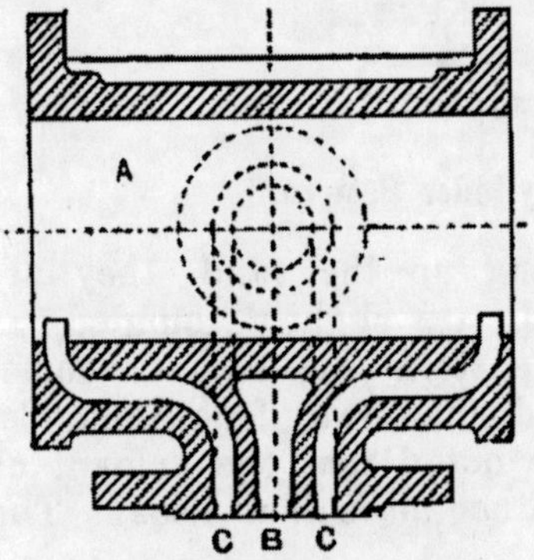

Fig. 94.

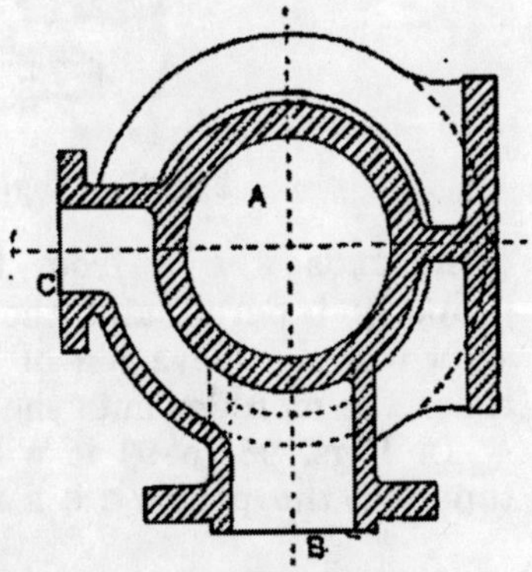

Fig. 95.

Figs. 94 and 95.—Casting of Engine Cylinder.

prints are lettered similarly to the cored portions in Figs. 94 and 95 for convenience of reference and identification. Fig. 98 shows a longitudinal section and Fig. 99 a transverse section of the mould cored up—that is, with the cores inserted in their places.

The reason why taper is not necessary in prints for horizontal cores is now clear. Still, it is not so obvious to those who have not had opportunities of considering pattern-making as it is seen from the standpoint of the moulder. The only reason why prints are made tapering is to facilitate their withdrawal from the mould. As, therefore, these horizontal prints do not withdraw in the direction of their longitudinal axis, taper in that direction would be worse than useless, because that would involve filing the core to correspond. The half pattern bodies are withdrawn in the direction of the arrows seen in the end view, Fig. 97, and the semicircular forms of the prints are all in favour of withdrawal. To prevent the

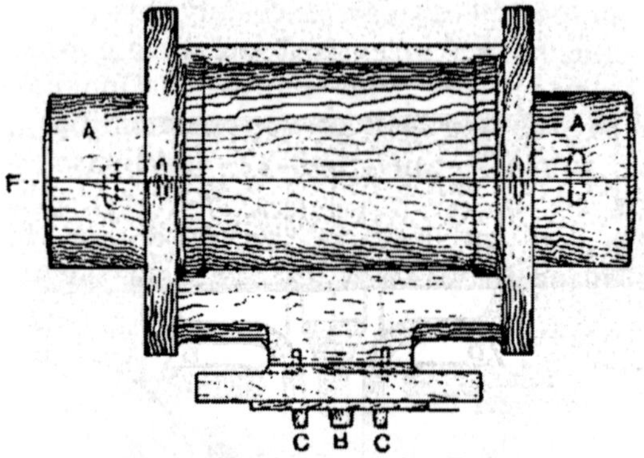

Fig. 96.—Engine Cylinder Pattern.

print ends C C B from tearing up the sand, they are properly tapered and the end are slightly rounded, as shown in the elevation of the pattern (Fig. 96). Or sometimes the moulder cuts the sand clean away from the ends.

In Figs. 96 to 99 it will be noted that the amount of taper on the prints C C B is rather more than usual. The

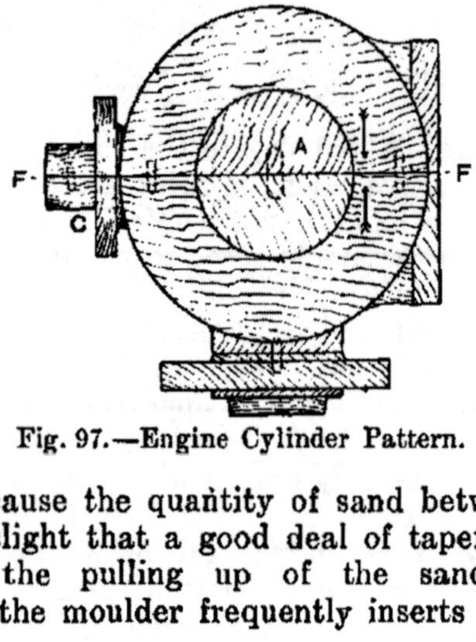

Fig. 97.—Engine Cylinder Pattern.

reason is because the quantity of sand between adjacent prints is so slight that a good deal of taper is necessary to prevent the pulling up of the sand. And not only so, but the moulder frequently inserts slips of hoop iron close alongside the prints, so flanking and reinforcing the weak sand during the withdrawal of the prints and the insertion and securing of the cores. And further, many

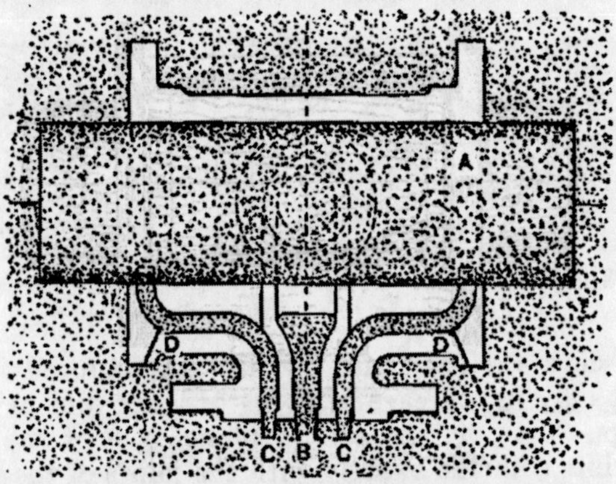

Fig. 98.—Mould for Engine Cylinder.

cylinders are cast, not with three separate passage cores entering into separate print impressions, but with three cores rammed in one and entering into a block print impression common to all three. This is done to avoid the

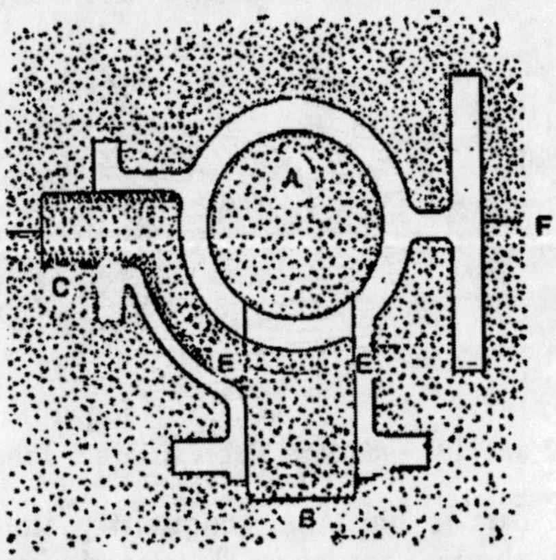

Fig. 99.—Mould for Engine Cylinder.

troublesome separate prints and cores and fixing of the latter.

The reason why print impressions are not necessary

to secure the top ends of the passage cores A A is apparent from Figs. 98 and 99. The cores are supported by one or more chaplet nails D D (Fig. 98), upon which they rest, and E E (Fig. 99), which prevent side movement, while they are prevented from rising by the pressure downwards of

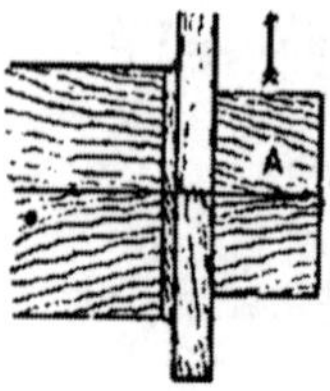

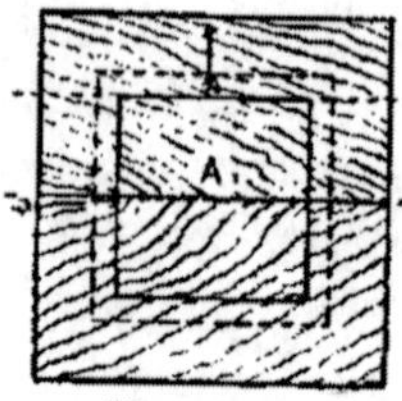

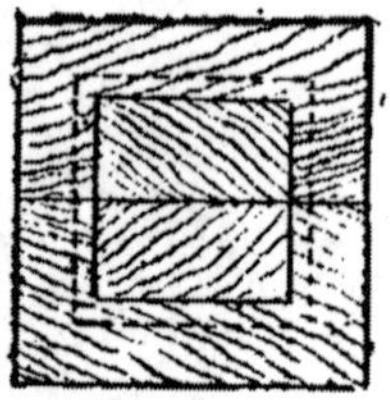

Fig. 100. Fig. 101. Fig. 102.

Figs. 100 to 102.—Square Print.

the main core A. The nails E E are not required in small work, but only in the case of cores of large dimensions.

In Figs. 96 to 99, the centre planes F F of the core A and its prints coincide exactly with the joints of the pattern and of the mould, and these are typical of an immense number of cases which arise. But in an equal number the central planes and pattern mould joints are not coincident, and then prints of other forms are used.

The sides of the main prints for the cylinder bore facilitate delivery and withdrawal, because they are

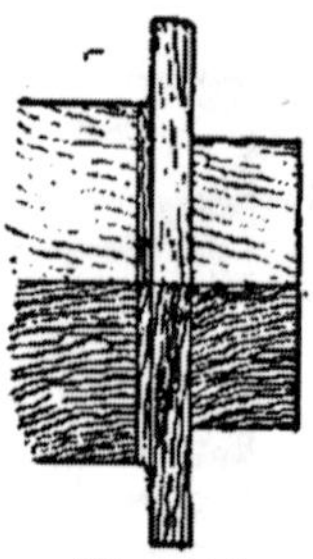

Fig. 103.

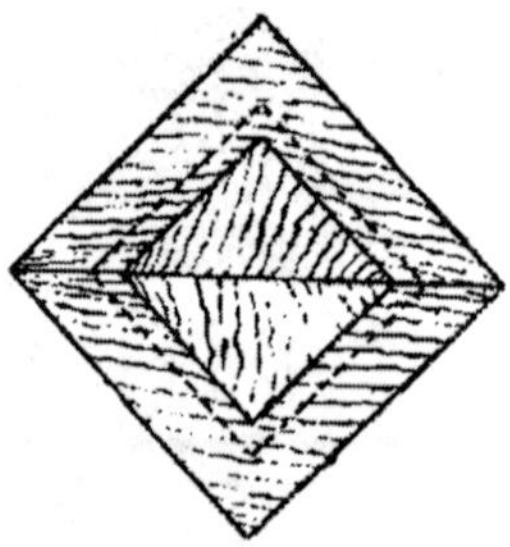

Fig. 104.

Figs. 103 and 104.—Square Print Jointed Diagonally.

semicircular. But it happens frequently that core prints are of such a shape that they do not deliver freely, and then they are made to taper sideways—never, of course, lengthwise.

If a square print A (Figs. 100 and 101) were jointed

diameter-wise as C C (see also Fig. 102), the mould would be vertical, and would probably be torn up during the lifting if the cope were lifted off the pattern. Or the lowering of the cope down by the edges of the core would probably crush the sand or the core. Then two courses are usually open. One is not to joint the print, but to make the mould joint come along the top face B B, and to taper the print slightly downwards. Then the print draws wholly in the direction of the arrows, and there is no risk of the sand in the cope or the core becoming crushed. Another way often practised is to turn the pattern joint round 45°, and with it the print, bringing

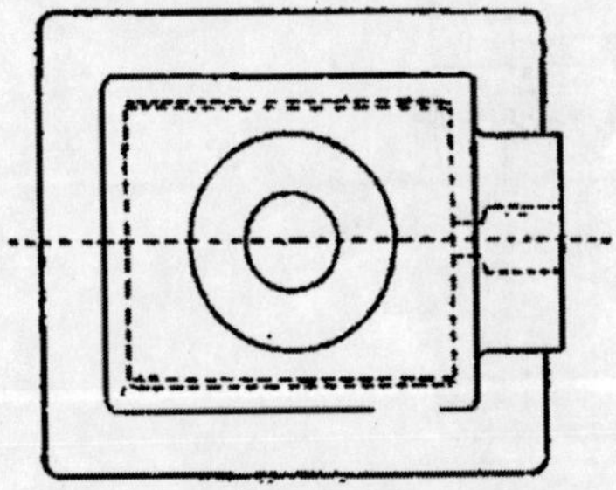

Fig. 105.

Fig. 106.

Figs. 105 and 106.—Steam Chest Casting.

the joint diagonal wise, as shown in Figs. 103 and 104; then there is not the least difficulty either in moulding or in coring up. If, however, the print must be jointed, as at C C, in Figs. 100 and 101, then a common practice is to make the top half wider than the bottom half, and to taper it more freely. The effect of this is to prevent tearing of the sand, and also crushing during coring up. The core fits tightly in the bottom half, and easily in the top; but it cannot shift, because secured in the bottom, and the only disadvantage is the presence of a slight fin between the sides of the core and those of the top print impression but this fin is easily chipped off.

The forms and purposes of prints for vertical and

horizontal cores in which the central plane of the prints generally coincides with the main joints of the pattern, and the mould having been considered, the case of prints for horizontal cores, in which the plane of the print and of the pattern do not agree will now be taken.

In some instances a plain round parallel print is made for use. Two principal cases occur—one in which the moulder can make a sloping joint from the main joint to the centre of the print and core; the other, that in which the print can be drawn back into the mould, and the core be inserted from the interior of the mould. Figs.

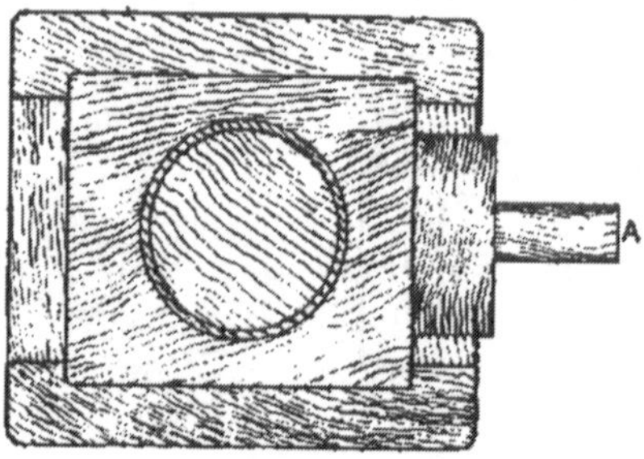

Fig. 107.

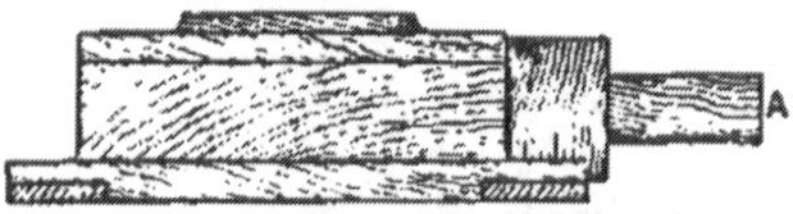

Fig. 108.

Fig. 109.

Figs. 107 to 109.—Steam-chest Pattern.

105 to 110 illustrate a job of the first kind. Figs. 105 and 106 represent a cylinder steam chest, in which it is desired to core the stuffing-box and valve-rod hole A. The pattern must mould flatwise, and the moulder's main joint has to be made along the plane C C (Fig. 106), while the centre of the stuffing-box is in the plane B B. Figs. 107 and 108 show the pattern provided with a long round parallel print A for the core. What is termed a pocket print might be used, but it is not so suitable for the job as the round print shown. The use of a round print entails upon the moulder a little down-jointing. This is objectionable in deep faces, but not so in the case of a shallow face, as in this instance. The slope of the down-jointing is

indicated by the dotted lines on the ends of the pattern in Fig. 109, coming, it will be noted, to the centre of the print A and the plane B B in Fig. 106. The mould is shown in section in Fig. 110. The print is of sufficient length to counterbalance the weight of the core A, thus preventing risk of the core being moved out of truth.

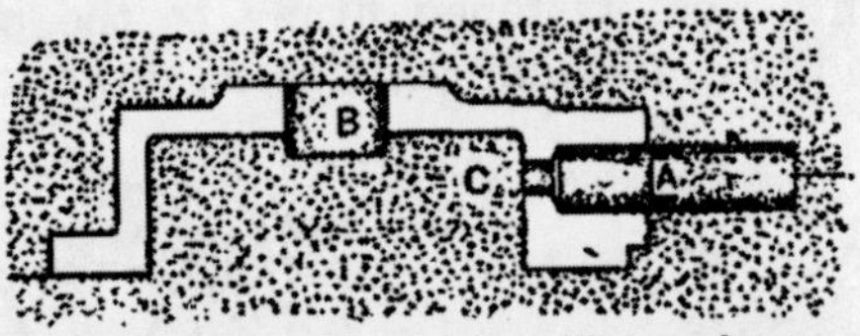

Fig. 110.—Mould for Steam-chest.

If the round core were not made so long, it would be necessary to support the core at the inner end on another print impression (shown dotted at C), which would have to be that of a pocket print. The shallow print for the steam inlet core B affords an illustration of the remark previously made to the effect that prints used for coring through thin plates of metal ed be very thin only.

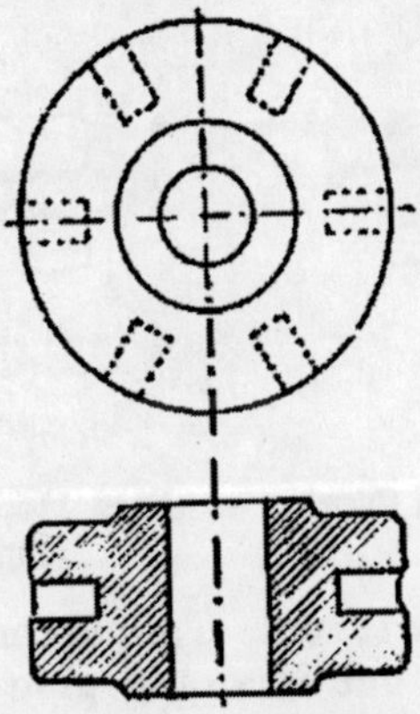

Fig. 111.

Fig. 112.

Figs. 111 and 112.—Casting of Hand Capstan Boss.

Thus, as there is not the slightest risk of the core B toppling over, the print in thickness or length is not above one-fourth its diameter. But the print for the core A, on the contrary, which is liable to fall, is more than twice its diameter in length, being longer than that portion of the core which hangs over into the mould.

Figs. 111 to 116 illustrate the second case named—that in which round prints can be drawn into the mould without down-jointing, and the cores inserted from the interior of the mould. Figs. 111 and 112 show a casting of a small hand capstan boss, used in some machines. It has a central-shaft hole, and six holes cast for the turning bar. If round prints were fastened firmly to the pattern, the moulder would have to make six sloping down-joints, which

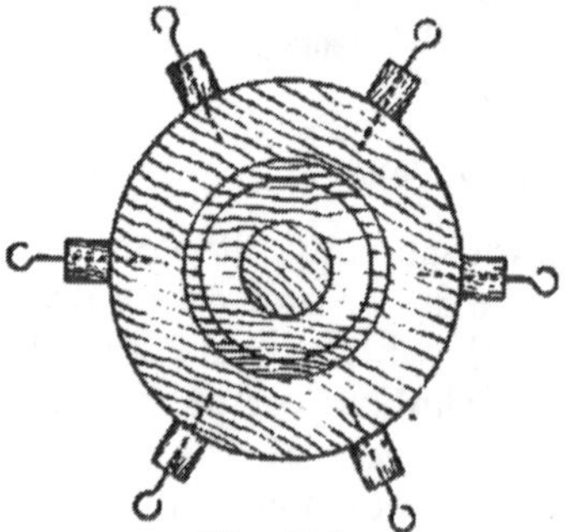

Fig. 113.

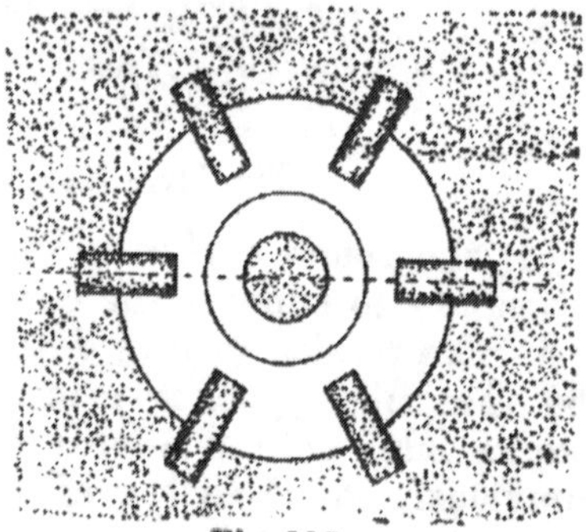

Fig. 115.

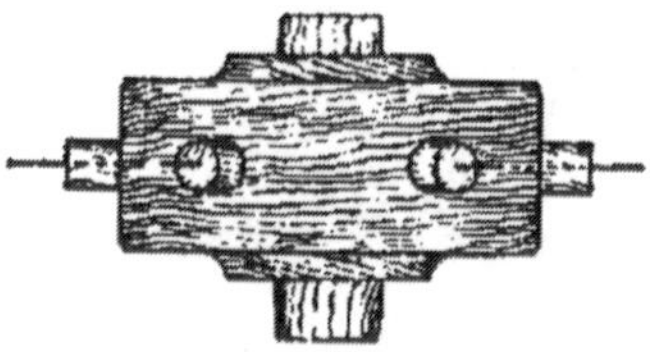

Fig. 114.

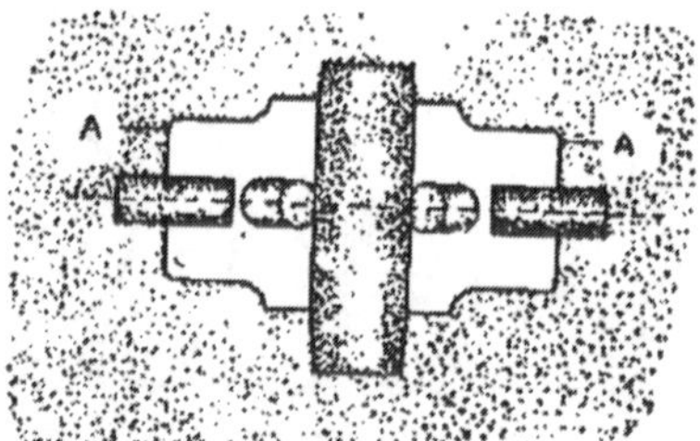

Fig. 116.

Figs. 113 and 114.—Hand Capstan Boss Pattern.

Figs. 115 and 116.—Mould for Hand Capstan Boss.

he would prefer not to do. To put on six pocket prints would prevent this, but it would give him equal trouble in stopping over six cores. But if six round prints are attached loosely with skewers, as in Figs. 113 and 114, which illustrate the pattern, these prints will be all left behind in the mould after the withdrawal of the main portions of the pattern, and then they can be drawn back singly into the mould, each in the direction of its longitudinal axis. This method of withdrawal is practicable only when there is sufficient clear space in the mould.

These prints do not require taper, because as the moulder withdraws each singly, he can by gentle rapping and shaking loosen the front or inner ends of the prints sufficiently to ensure clean withdrawal. The cores are more likely to be inserted truly also than if they had to be filed to fit tapered prints. If a special core box were made, then prints and cores could be tapered with advantage. Figs. 115 and 116 show the mould with the cores inserted. They are all readily put into their print impressions from the interior of the mould, previous to the insertion of the central core. The joint between the top and bottom parts of the mould is in the plane A A.

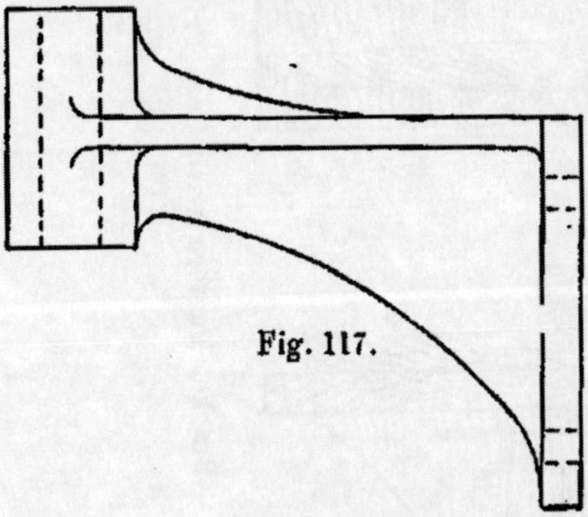

Fig. 117.

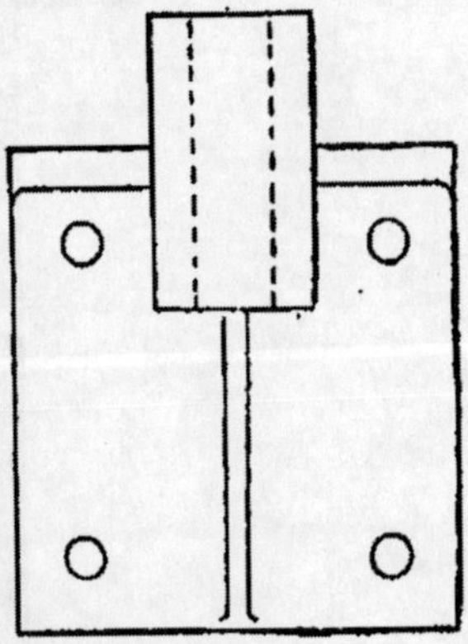

Fig. 118.

Figs. 117 and 118.—Bracket Casting.

Many jobs occur in which the use of round prints for coring horizontal holes is not practicable, and in which the amount of down-jointing would be too great, and in which there is not sufficient open space in the mould to withdraw the prints into. In such cases the pocket or drop print offers the only alternative. This will now be illustrated and described.

The bracket in Figs. 117 and 118, in which holes are cored in the foot, is selected to illustrate the typical pocket prints. The bracket pattern is not moulded as the casting stands when bolted down by the foot, but as in Figs. 119 and 120. Neither down-jointing nor drawing-in of prints is practicable, for this reason the pocket prints, shown in Figs. 119 and 120 or Fig. 121 are employed. Figs. 119 and

120 illustrate one method, in which distinct prints are used for each core; Fig. 121 illustrates a method by which one print does duty for two cores. The latter requires a special core-box, the former needs no core-box. Fig. 122 illus-

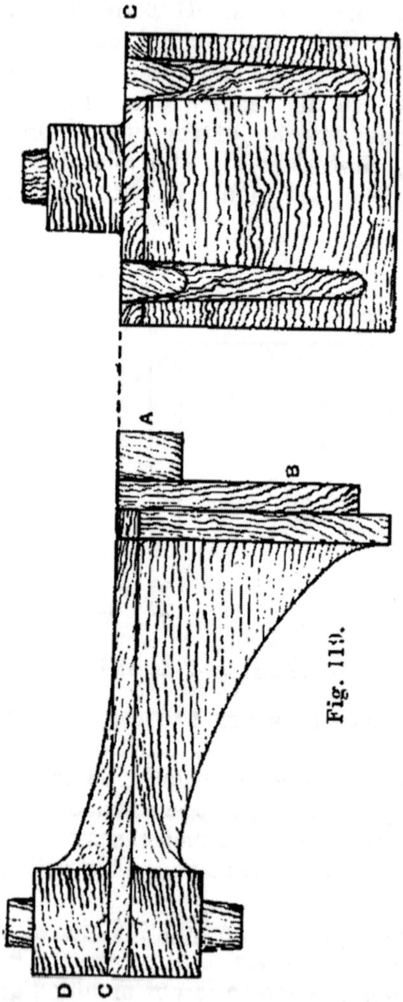

Fig. 119. Fig. 120.

Figs. 119 and 120.—Bracket Pattern with Core Prints.

trates the mould cored up for Fig. 119; Fig. 123 the same cored up for Fig. 121. Everything will be clear on a comparison of the figures.

In Figs. 119 and 120 the prints A, for the holes which

come uppermost, are fastened on the outer faces of the prints B, which core out the lower holes. The first are also thicker than the second. In Fig. 121 there is no indication in the pattern of any provision for coring

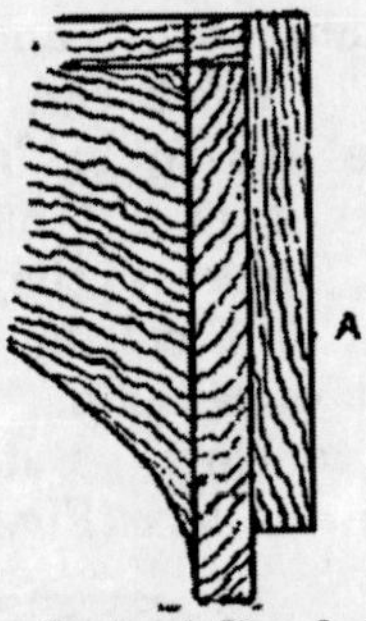

Fig. 121.—Foot of Bracket Pattern.

out the upper holes, one print, A, only being used. In all cases in which a core-box is not provided prints must be put on as shown in Figs. 119 and 120—namely, a distinct print opposite each hole. Then the moulder in-

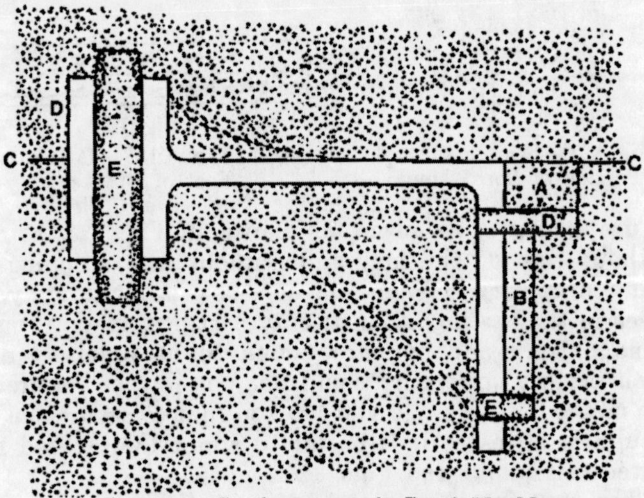

Fig. 122.—Section through Cored Mould.

serts common round cores in the print impressions and stops them over with sand, as in Fig. 122. In all cases in which a single print only is used for two cores, as in Fig. 121, a core-box like Figs. 124 and 125 must be made and sent with the pattern. The latter method ensures a more accurate location of holes in the casting than the former, for the following reasons:—

The prints in Figs. 119 and 120 should be thick enough to counterbalance their cores, and the reason why the top print A is made so much thicker than the lower one B is because its core has to bridge a wider space than the lower one. Then it is not easy to ensure accurate setting of the cores, because they have to be lowered deeply into the mould on the bent end of a cleaner, often by the reflected light of a lamp. In stopping-over, also, the cores are liable to shift. But made as in Fig. 121, with a core rammed in the box (Figs. 124 and 125), the core

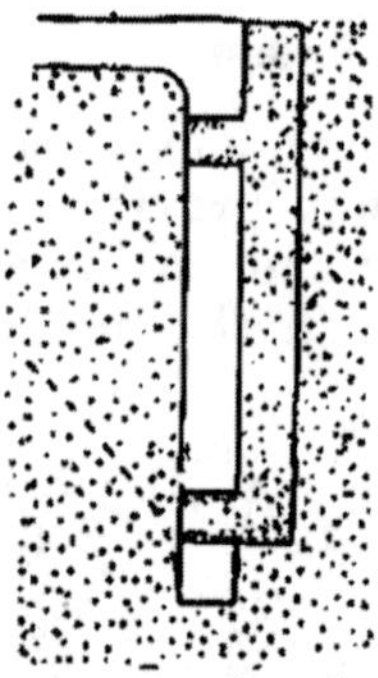

Fig. 123.—Section through Portion of Cored Mould.

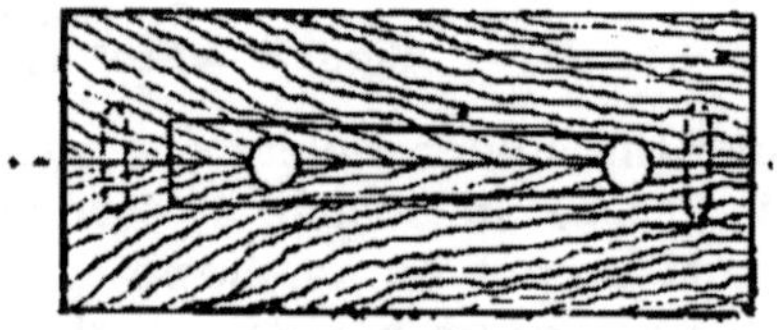

Fig. 124.

Fig. 125.

Figs. 124 and 125.—Core-box for Foot of Bracket.

is dropped into its place, as shown in Fig. 123, at once, without risk of shifting, and without any stopping-over being necessary. When the core-box is made truly, the holes in the casting, or in twenty castings, made from the same pattern and box are bound to be precisely alike. Such perfect uniformity could not possibly be ensured by the method of Figs. 119 and 120; so that to secure the best results in all cases it is better to adopt the method illustrated in Fig. 121 and Figs. 124 and 125.

The stopping-over of the cores is effected by means of a board A (Figs. 126 and 127), cut to a semicircular shape at the bottom, to fit over and rest upon the core. The face of the board is held against the face C of the mould, and the space B left by the print is then filled up and rammed with sand. This completely fills up the print impression, and it is kept from falling into the mould by the face of the board A, which also maintains the filled-in sand level with the vertical mould face of the foot. When the bottom core is thus stopped over, the top one, which goes in the print impression, is similarly treated. In Fig. 122 the cores D E are seen stopped over with the sand which fills up the print impressions A and B. Obviously, the method shown in Figs. 121 and 123 and Figs. 124 and 125 is preferable in all respects.

Allusion has been made to cases in which a rather short core may require the assistance of a top steady print, because of the difficulty of centring it otherwise. Figs.

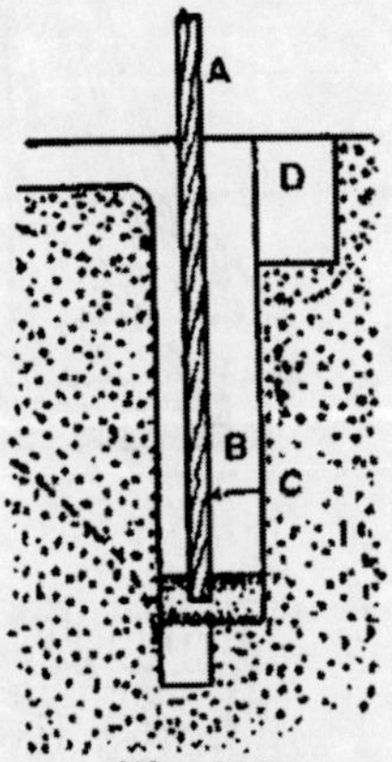

Fig. 126.

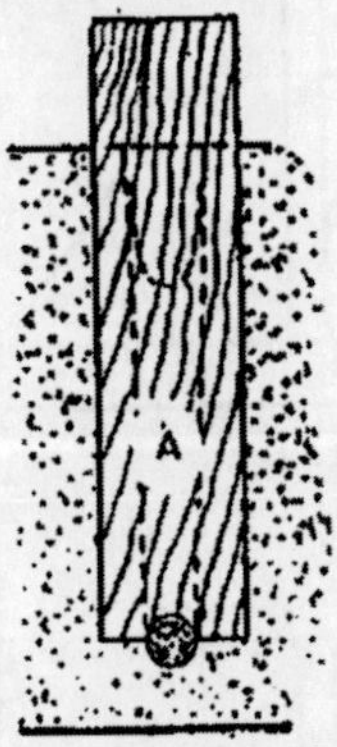

Fig. 127.

Figs. 126 and 127.—Stopping-over Board for Cores.

119 and 120 and Fig. 122 afford a case in point. The pattern and mould are both jointed along the plane C C, so that the upper part D of the boss through which the core E passes is in the top part of the mould, and the core E cannot therefore be checked for truth any higher than the moulder's joint C C. Hence the advantage of a top print in this case—a print which could be dispensed with if the joint of the mould came along the top face of the upper part *d* of the boss.

When a bracket is of the shape shown in Figs. 128 and 129, there are two ways of putting on pocket prints. Here there are four bolt holes, and the shape of the casting is such that the top face of the web—compare with the pattern, Fig. 130—coincides with the moulder's joint between top and bottom flasks, the joint of the pattern B B (Figs. 130 and 131) being also on the same plane. In such a case there are three different ways in which the

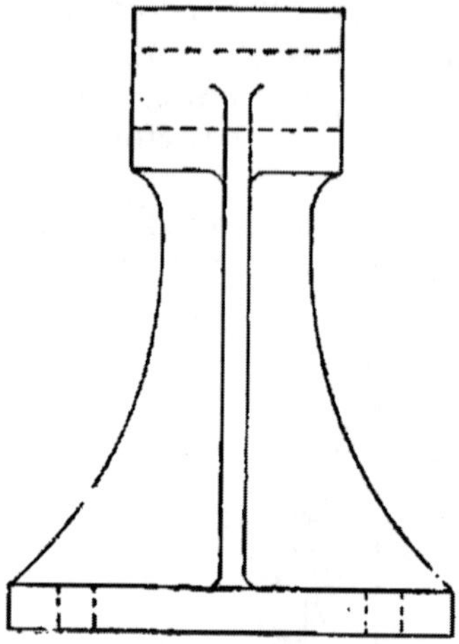

Fig. 128.

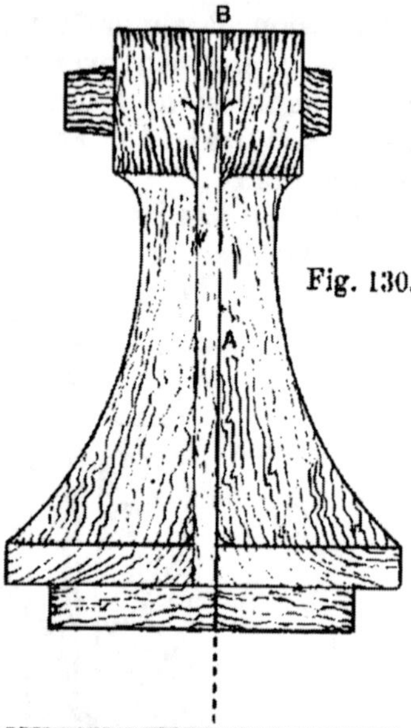

Fig. 130.

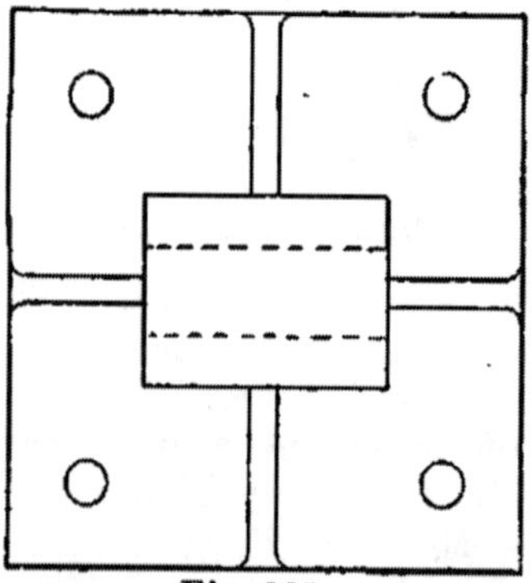

Fig. 129.

Figs. 128 and 129.—Bracket Casting.

Fig. 131.

Figs. 130 and 131.—Bracket Casting Pattern, with Core-prints.

pocket prints may be arranged, and the choice of either depends very much on relative dimensions, degree of accuracy required, moulding flasks available, custom of a given workshop, etc. One method is as follows: First, the foot may be jointed in pattern and mould on a level with the top face A of the web, just as shown in Fig. 130, in which case one portion of the foot will go in the bottom and the other in the top of the mould. Then the pocket prints will be arranged as in Figs. 130 and 131, one print to each hole, the tapering being away from the joint B.

A truer plane face is ensured to the foot of the bracket by leaving it unjointed (Figs. 132 and 133), making only the top rib A loose, so carrying the moulder's joint up to the top edge of the foot, and fastening on the required pocket prints to lift from the top edge, covering both holes, as in Figs. 132 and 133. A third method is to use a single print and core-box, as in Fig. 121 and Figs. 124 and 125 (pp. 73

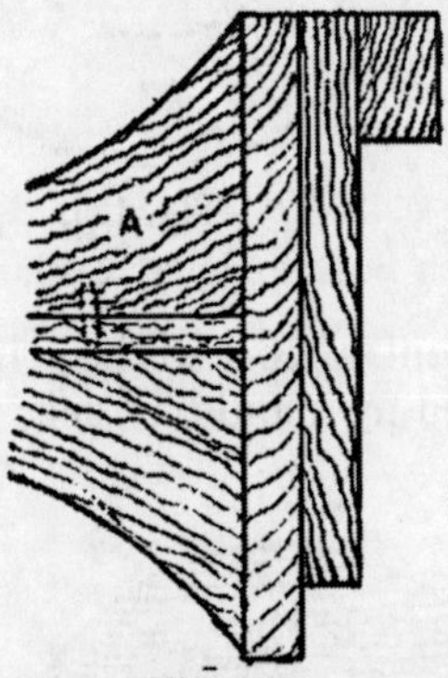

Fig. 132.

Fig. 133.

Figs. 132 and 133.—Alternative Method of Arranging Pocket Prints.

and 74). Whenever practicable, the method shown in Figs. 132 and 133 is the best to adopt, but with a single print only, a more accurate face being ensured than when a moulder's joint is carried across it.

Continuing the consideration of pocket prints, take the case of a piece of pipe in the flanges of which square holes have to be cast (Figs. 134 and 135). The pipe has to be moulded horizontally, and the holes therefore cannot be cored with common tapered prints, but must be formed with horizontal cores. Prints must therefore be of the pocket type, and they need only be fastened on one face of the flange, because they have to bridge but a narrow space. Figs. 136 and 137 show the pattern for one of the flanges fitted with its prints. That the shapes of their ends exactly agree with the corresponding forms of the holes which they have to core is clear on a comparison with Figs. 134 and 135. All the portions of the print impressions above the cores have to be stopped over, and this, of course, is completed

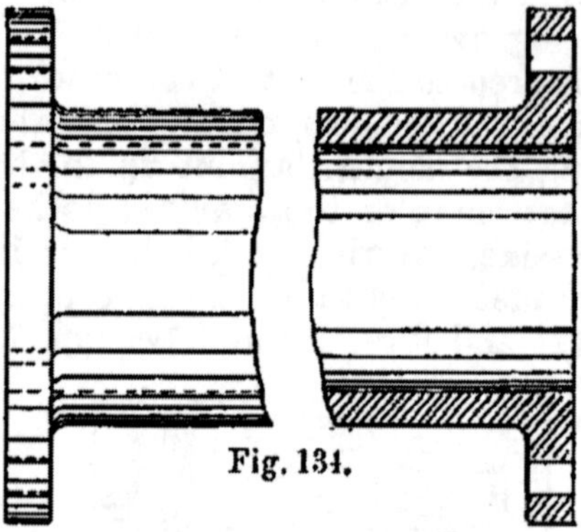

Fig. 134.

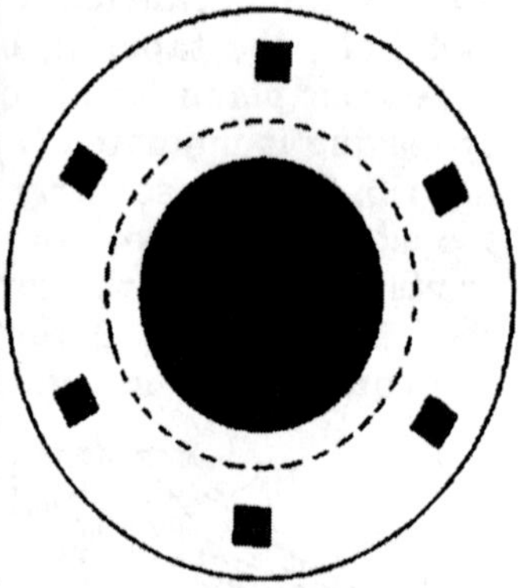

Fig. 135.

Figs. 134 and 135.—Pipe Casting with Square Holes in Flanges.

before the insertion of the main central core in the print impression formed by A. The cored-up mould is seen completed in Fig. 138.

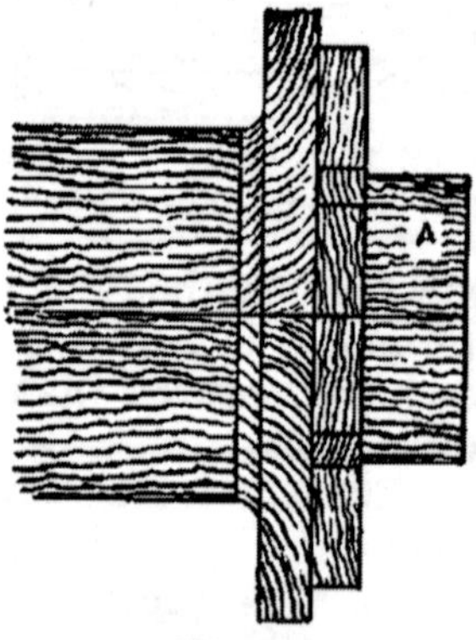

Fig. 136.

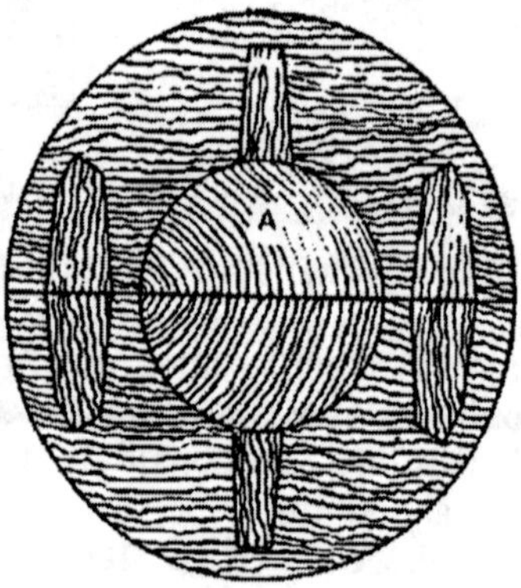

Fig. 137.

Figs. 136 and 137.—Pattern of Flange with Prints for Pipe Casting.

It is, however, common practice to locate the positions of small cores in flanges without the use of prints at all. The cores are then set by means of a gauge or template, called a stopping-over piece, shown in Fig. 139. The cores are lowered down into approximate position by means of the moulder's cleaner, and then set exactly by the lowering down of the stopping-over piece above them. This is illustrated in Fig. 140, A A being cores, and B the stopping-over piece. The cores are retained in position wholly by friction against the faces of the flanges, so that they are made a little full in length. Sometimes a nail is forced into the sand over the cores to prevent the chance of their rising up by the flow of metal. But this is not desirable, nor is it necessary if the cores fit well.

Figs. 141, 142, and 143 show examples of pocket prints

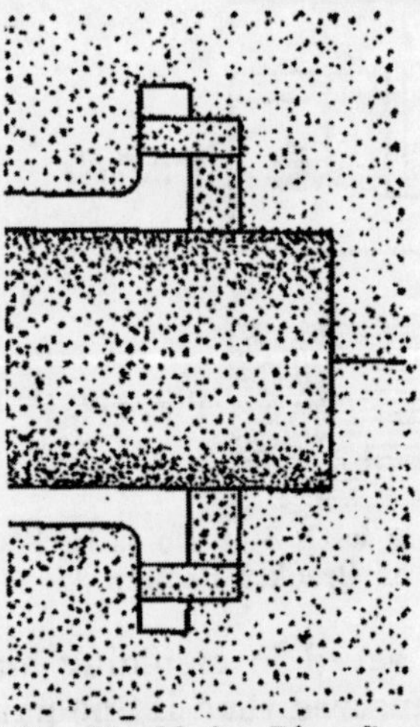

Fig. 138.—Mould for Pipe Casting, with Cores Inserted.

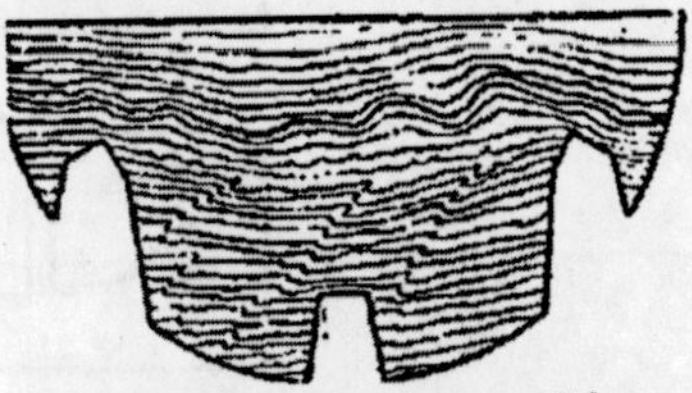

Fig. 139.—Stopping-over Piece used without Prints.

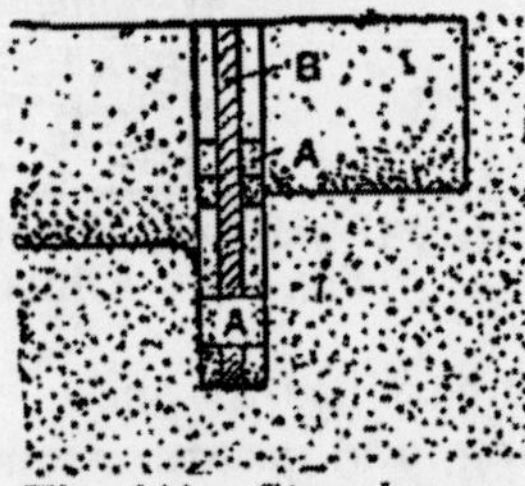

Fig. 140.—Stopping-over Piece in Use.

for coring slot holes. Figs. 141 and 142 are two views of a bracket having slot holes A A cored in the foot. In Fig. 143, the pocket prints A A for these are shown nailed on the bottom of the foot. Here, as in previous examples, it is seen that the shape of the end of the prints coincides with the shape and position of the lower portion of the holes, as the pattern moulds. In this example, too, as in Figs. 136 and 137, the cores may be made of the exact shape of the holes and stopped over. Or the core-box may be so made that the cores shall stop themselves over in the manner previously described.

Cases occur in which horizontal prints which may or

may not be of the pocket form are used to enable several similar small castings to be cored out at once with a single core. Fig. 144 is illustrative of the method. In this case four distinct pieces A A A A are connected with prints B B B B, and one core laid along the whole length cores the

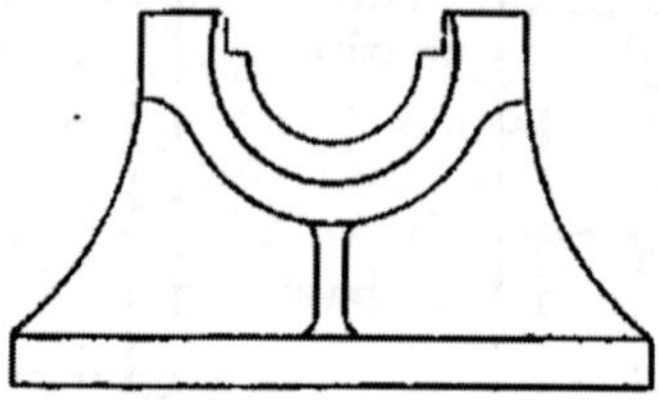

Fig. 141.

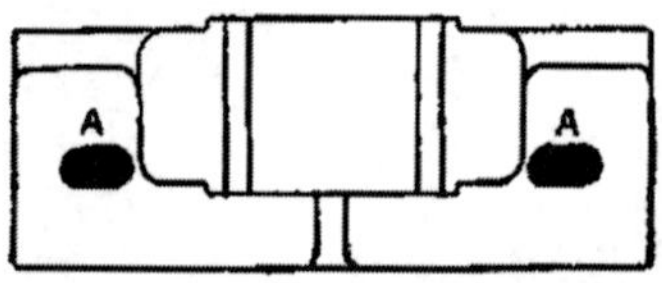

Fig. 142.

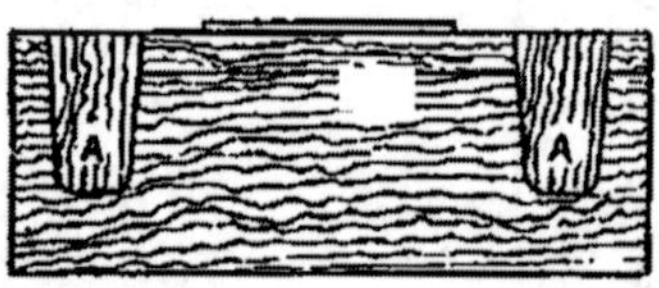

Fig. 143.

Figs. 141 and 142.—Bracket Casting with Slot Holes in Foot.
Fig. 143.—Prints on Foot of Bracket Pattern.

four castings at once. Time is saved in moulding and in coring, and greater accuracy is ensured than if one pattern only were moulded and cored at once. In some classes of patterns, pocket prints would be found most suitable.

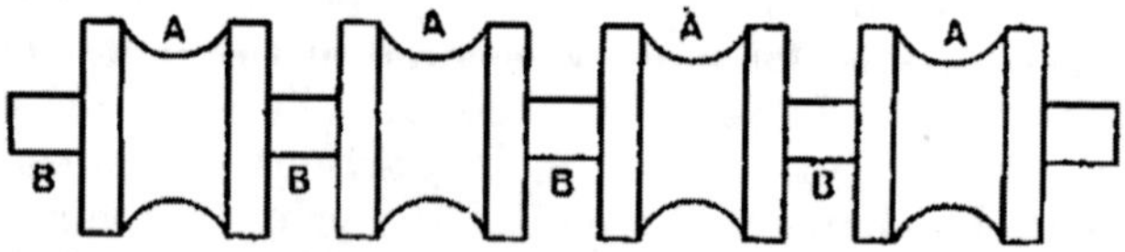

Fig. 144.—Patterns United with Continuous Print.

These and similar examples of coring might be multiplied; one example will be noted, which is of a large type, and in which the reason for coring would not be obvious to a person unacquainted with the details of moulding. This is coring which is not always absolutely necessary, since there would be other possible ways of moulding, but which is most convenient and desirable. Thus the double bracket (Figs. 145 and 146) would be a troublesome job for the moulder if the pattern were made like the casting, because

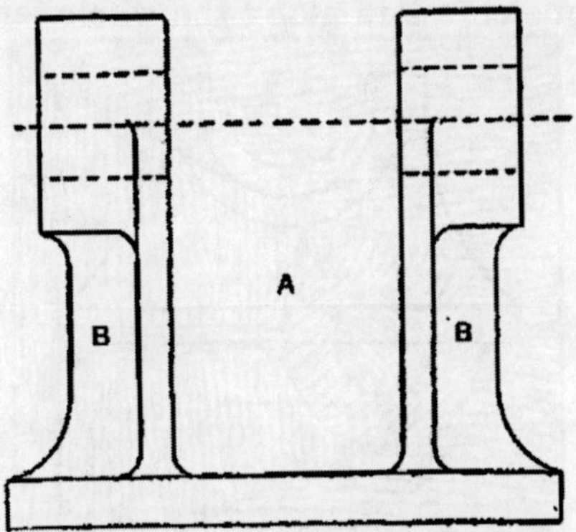

Fig. 145.—Double Bracket Casting.

of the central space A. The best way would be to joint both pattern and mould along the plane A. But if, instead of a central rib B, th : were ribs around the sides at C C, as shown dotted, then the pattern could not be jointed at A. Many such cases occur in which it is

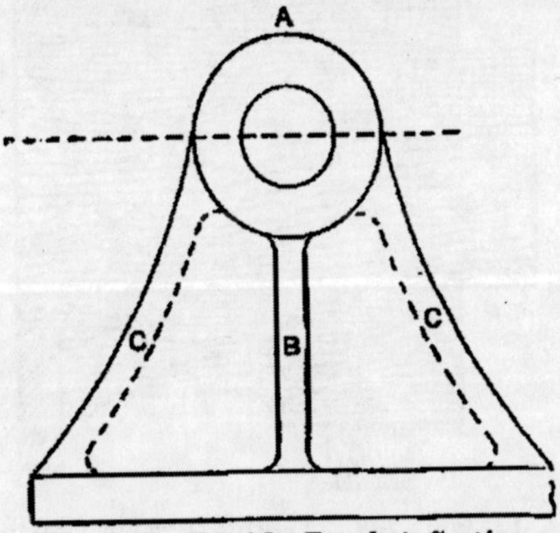

Fig. 146.—Double Bracket Casting..

desirable to take out the central portion A with a core, the pattern being made as in Figs. 147 and 148; the pattern is jointed upon the print A at B B, all above that plane being dowelled to be lifted with the top of the mould. A core-box has to be made to suit the print impression.

The foregoing examples will suffice to indicate the typical methods which are employed for the coring of holes in castings. Not only are small holes cored, but large spaces are taken out in the same manner in order to

Fig. 147.

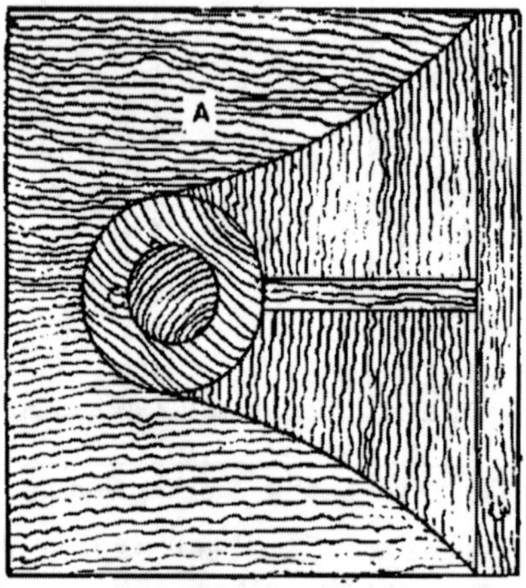

Fig. 148.

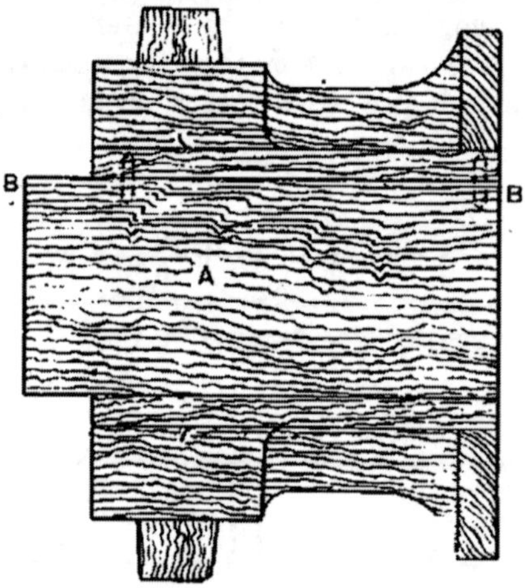

Figs. 147 and 148.—Double Bracket Pattern.

simplify the work of moulding, and to ensure castings more accurate than could be obtained by self-delivery. The principles which have been laid down may be studied with advantage and extended into many details.

CHAPTER VII.

PATTERNS AND MOULDS FOR IRON COLUMNS.

As in the previous chapter, it is thought advisable to give information here on some matters not strictly coming under the particular heading of pattern-making. It was pointed out in the first chapter that the successful pattern-maker must have a knowledge of many operations and processes outside his own special department; and it is with that in mind that the scope of the information here presented has been broadened. Besides the actual making of the patterns, this chapter will give some information on the subsequent processes of moulding and casting.

In the accompanying figures, Fig. 149 is a plan of the complete pattern for an iron column; Fig. 150 is a plan of half the pattern opened in the joint face; Fig. 151 is a cross section through the body taken on the dotted line in Fig. 150; Fig. 152 is an end view of half the print at the large end; Fig. 153 is a similar view of half the print at the small end.

There is no difference in the method of constructing the column pattern when cast horizontally or vertically. It is unusual to cast such columns on end. Large pipes are so cast in the regular pipe-shops, where there are special and costly jigs for the purpose. A column that has to be cast on end is moulded in the same way as a column to be cast horizontally—that is, in an ordinary two-part flask, with round holes at the ends for the core-bar to pass through, and, in addition, two extra holes at the top end, one to pour the metal in, and one for a riser or flow-off gate, the latter being necessary to ensure a clean top face.

If there is anything very special in the specification as to the soundness of the metal, it will be better to add 8 in. or 10 in. of head metal to the pattern. But this is not necessary for ordinary good work. After the pattern is moulded in the ordinary way and cored up, the flasks

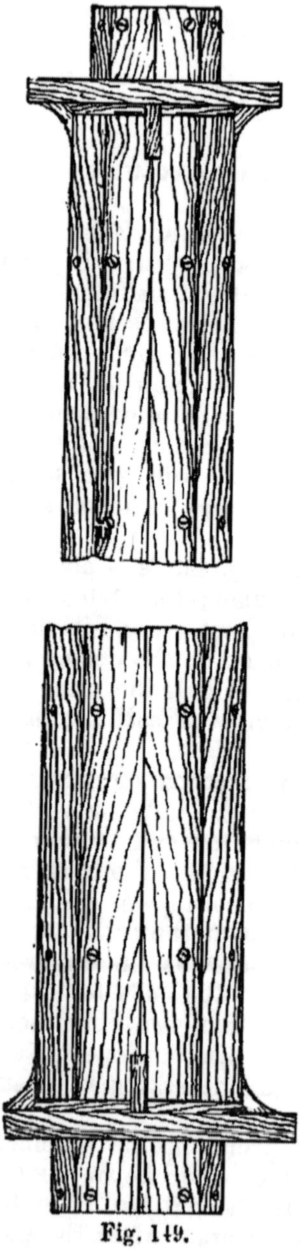

Fig. 149.

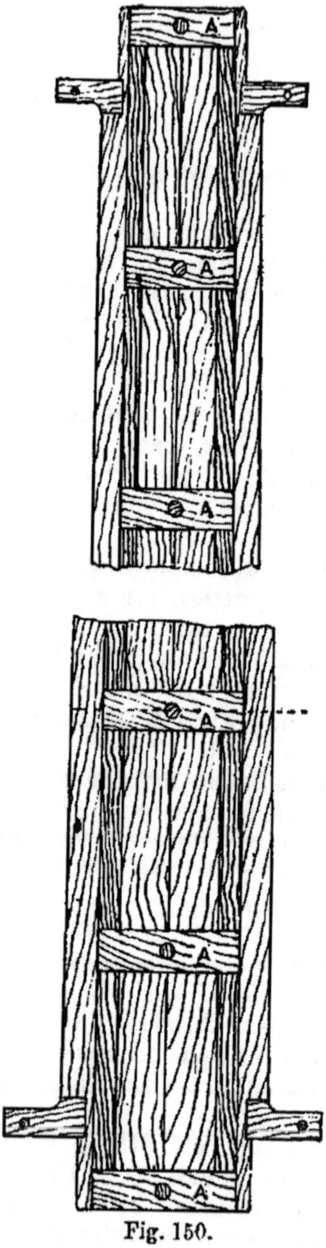

Fig. 150.

Figs. 149 and 150.—Column Pattern and Half Pattern.

are cottered together, lifted on end and lowered into the pit for casting vertically.

The illustrations show a pattern just as it would be made, though, of course, modified methods are practicable. For example, such patterns are sometimes lagged only as

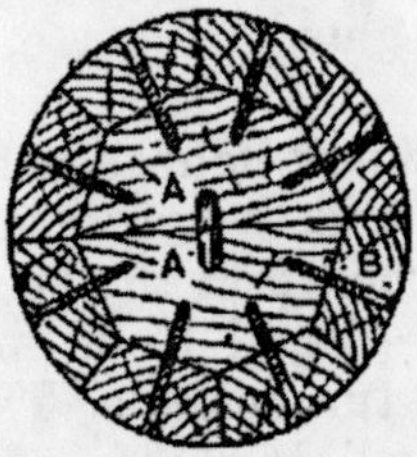

Fig. 151.—Cross Section of Column Pattern.

far as the inner faces of the flanges; these are then screwed directly on the pattern ends, and the prints on those. Slightly thinner stuff may then be employed for the lagging, but it is not desirable to use very thin stuff. Sometimes the pattern, though lagged continuously as shown, has long blocks at the ends instead of the narrow bridges for lagging on. This makes the ends stronger. But the method shown is the best on the whole.

The blocking pieces A (Figs. 150 and 151) are first dowelled together, marked out, and the facets planed. Half the pieces—those with the dowel holes—will then be laid down upon a true bench or plank arranged by means of their centre lines, and at suitable distances apart. Tack them down with brads, checking their truth with a straightedge. Then prepare the lagging strips with saw

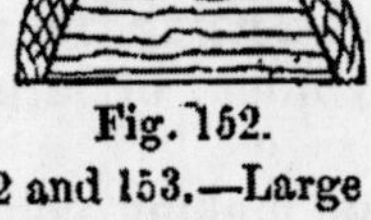

Fig. 152.

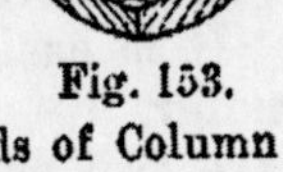

Fig. 153.

Figs. 152 and 153.—Large and Small Ends of Column Pattern.

and plane, and fit each strip to its facet. The two strips next the joint face will be fitted first, and afterwards the two above. Each joint face must be fitted to its fellow, using chalk to check the perfect contact necessary to a good joint, and each is glued to its fellow and also to the facets upon which it lies. The glue joint will be rubbed by two men, one near each end, and a screw will be run through the lagging into each facet of the blocks A. When one half is thus glued up it is lifted off the board, turned on its back, the complementary halves of the blocks A dowelled on, and the remaining half of the lagging fitted and glued—omitting glue, of course, in the joint face of the pattern.

The two halves are now held together with centre-plates screwed in the ends, and the pattern turned in the lathe. The two ends are turned first to the dimensions required, and then one flat is planed from end to end, making a tangent level with the turned ends. This flat being chalked, or rubbed with red lead, is a safe guide for turning down the remainder of the pattern without any guess or trial, involving frequent stoppage of the lathe and trial with a straightedge.

The turning of the prints and the grooves for the flanges follows. The flanges, though rectangular, should have their hollows turned as show This can be done on a face-plate. The stiffening brackets are fitted finally. Those in the joint need not be divided in halves, but made of full thickness and screwed to one half the pattern only. Rapping and lifting-plates, though not shown, should be put in the joint faces. They are best let into the cross-bars.

Figs. 154 to 158 illustrate the moulding of a column 18 ft. long and 14 in. in diameter, with 1½-in. metal. The illustrations are not strictly proportionate, the length being slightly lessened in order to economise space, thus giving larger proportion to the diameter, with clearer detail.

To cast a column of 1½ in. thickness of metal is not so troublesome as to cast one ¾ in. or 1 in. thick, because in the former case there is less risk of getting the metal thin or blown. It is easier to cast a column of large than of small diameter.

There are two or three ways of making columns; the choice depends on the number required. The illustrations show the method employed when only a few castings are required. In this case a pattern is used, jointed down the centre, and rammed with or without the assistance of a bottom or joint-board. The use of the joint-board,

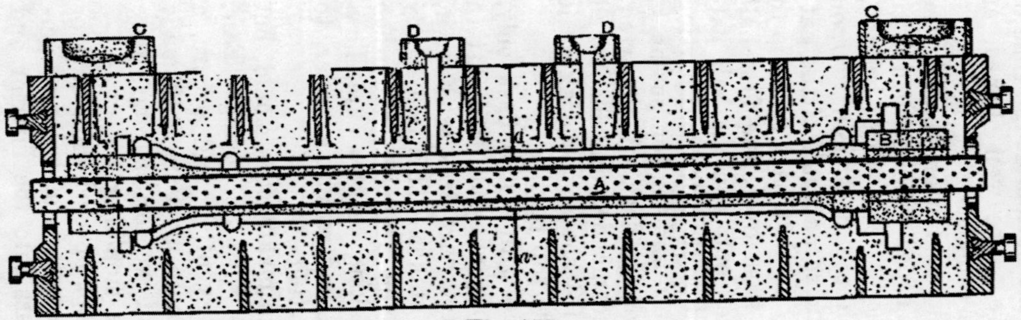

Fig. 155.

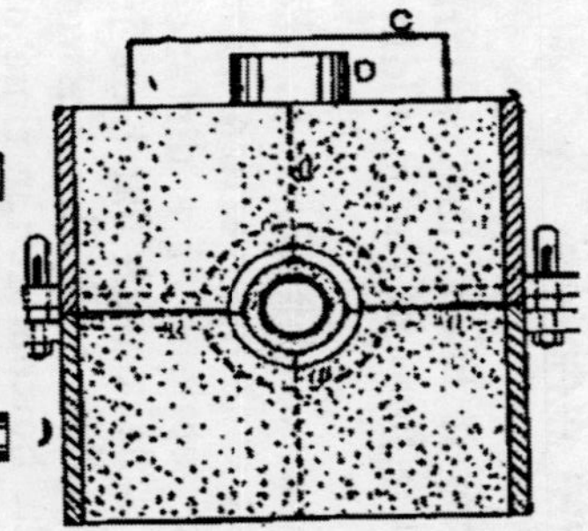

Fig. 156.

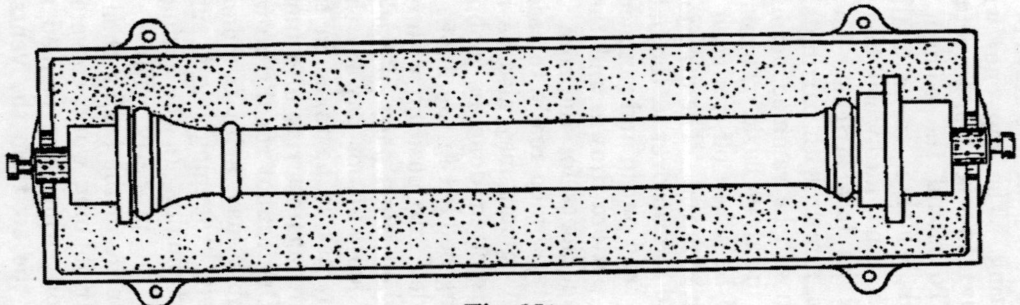

Fig. 154.

Fig. 154. — Drag for Casting Columns. Fig. 155. — Longitudinal Section of Mould for Iron Column. Fig. 156. —Cross Section of Mould for Iron Column.

however, is very desirable, because it keeps the pattern straight, and its joint in line with the joint of the moulding box.

In a proper column box there is no difference in the shape of the top and bottom parts; each has vertical bars or stays cut to follow the column sections at a distance of ¾ in. away from its body. But a flask with flat bars in one half and vertical bars in the other will also answer very well, the flat stays being in the bottom at the time of casting. The top ones will have to be well shaped, as shown in Fig. 155, to retain the sand.

To mould the column without a bottom board, the flask, which is to be finally the cope, will be filled with loose sand, into which one-half the pattern will be bedded, and its face strickled level with the flask joint. Upon this, strewn with parting sand, the second half of the pattern will be rammed permanently in that half which is to be the drag flask. Turning the flask over, the first half will be taken off, its sand knocked out, and the half pattern removed. The drag joint will be strickled and parting sand strewn over it, the half pattern and the top put back, the sand put in and rammed. Then the flask will be parted, the pattern drawn, and the mould mended and blackened in readiness for the core. Fig. 154 shows the drag as it appears when ready to receive the top part.

A column may also be moulded with a half flask only, as is often done in jobbing work, one-half the pattern being bedded in the floor and a top part flask set over it, guided into position with corner stakes. This is a handy method when pairs of flasks are not available, and when the job will not pay for their making. Extra care, however, has to be taken in tucking and ramming under, to guard against risk of a lumpy casting.

One cannot readily go wrong in making the mould, but trouble may arise in connection with its coring. Fair, careful ramming and sufficient venting will secure a good mould. In the coring, the core must be both made and set properly. The causes of waster castings more often lie in the coring than in the moulding.

In jobbing work, cores are swept up on hollow bars or arbors, which are pierced with hundreds of holes to permit the air from the vents to pass into the interior and out at the ends. The relative diameters of bar and core vary considerably. In foundries, bars of many diameters and lengths are stocked, and the one which happens to

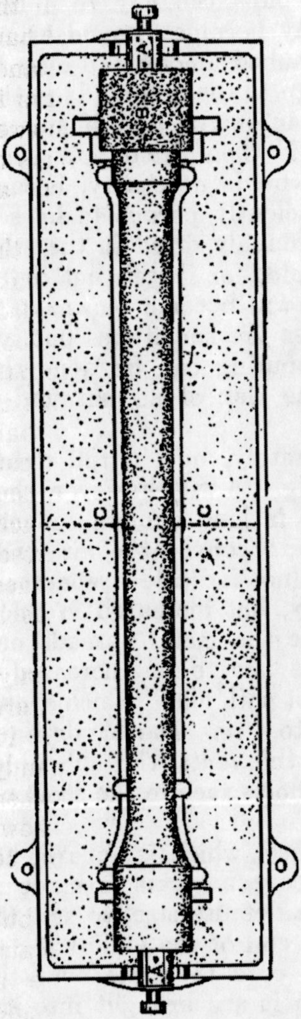

Fig. 157.—Plan of Mould for Columns.

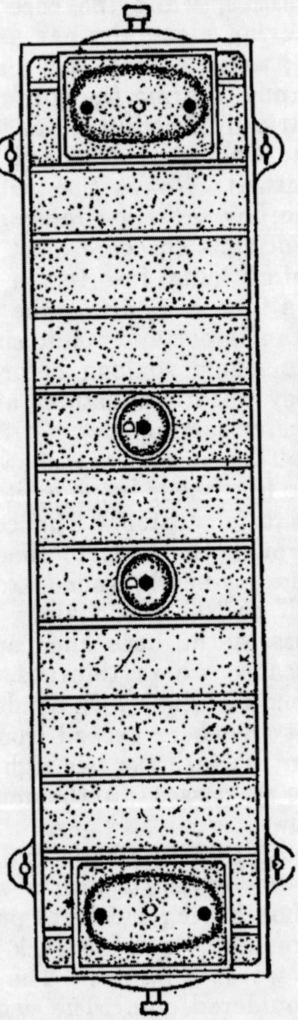

Fig. 158.—Pouring Arrangements.

come nearest to the size required is selected, so that it may often happen that some hay-band is wasted in consequence of the bar selected being rather small. The smaller the thickness of band and loam on a bar the better, bands and the core maker's time being thus economised. From 1 in. to 1½ in. is a minimum allowance.

To sweep up a core, the bar or arbor is revolved on the trestles, while the core maker pulls the hay rope taut, moving along the bar as the hay becomes wound around it; whilst coarse, stiff loam is daubed among and over the bands to bring the core nearly up to diameter. It is then partially dried previous to the daubing on and finishing of the final coat of loam, which is then dried and black-washed. No venting with the wire is necessary, because the hay or straw ropes are sufficiently porous to be self-venting. The core must be thoroughly dried in the stove before being inserted in the mould, for if it is not dry at the time of pouring, the casting will become blown. This is an important point, since cores are sometimes put into the mould so long before the pouring can be done that they absorb moisture, and cause risk of an unsound or waster casting.

The core is not shown separately, nor in full detail, the hay-bands being omitted. Fig. 155 will, however, show what is wanted. The core bar is long enough to come through the ends of the mould, to convey the air away. The hay-bands wound around it (not indicated separately) will be thinly laid along its body, but increased in thickness at the base and cap, where the metal spreads out, because where thickness of core has to be increased it should be done with bands and not with loam, which should not anywhere exceed from ½ in. to ¾ in. The bands lie in contact with the bar right along the vents, through which the air passes into the numerous holes seen in the sectional view.

At the right-hand end, the base, which is square, has to be lightened with a square core B. This is made in a box having a central print of a definite size, to suit the shoulder, which is struck on that end of the main core, as shown in Fig. 155. The square core then fits over the shouldered end. The vents from it are brought into the main core, and so out at the end of the bar.

Fig. 155 is a sectional view of the mould taken in the vertical plane. Fig. 156 is a plan view of the mould opened in the joint, with the core fixed; and Fig. 157 is a cross-section taken in the centre. These illustrate the fixing of the core, and, with Fig. 158, the pouring arrangements.

With reference to the fixing of the core, the print impressions hold it at the ends, and of course they should secure it centrally in the mould. But it is not wise to take this for granted. When a core is inserted in print impressions, the thickness of space must be tried at the top and bottom in two or three places with clays, the flasks being closed on the clays, and on their separation the thicknesses to which the clays will have been squeezed will show the thickness of space between core and mould for the metal. In the joints, the thicknesses at the sides can be measured directly with a rule.

It may seem strange to anyone but a moulder that this measurement should be necessary with a circular core in a circular mould. But inaccuracies creep in whilst the pattern, mould, and core are being made. Prints get out of centre, patterns out of truth circularly and lengthwise, and cores sag by their own weight. The object of checking, therefore, is to afford the moulder a chance of correcting these inaccuracies.

Although the core is secured centrally by the ends, this would not retain it in the central position when the pressure of metal acts upon it, when it would be forced upwards, causing the metal to be thinner in the top than in the bottom; it might also move sideways. Chaplets are therefore used to prevent these movements. These are tinned nails C C, the heads of which abut against the core, and the points against the flask sides, and in top and bottom against stays or plates, or driven into blocks of wood rammed in the sand. In columns having thin metal, these stays must be more numerous than in those of heavier section. In a column with 1½-in. metal, four chaplets at the centre, as shown, are sufficient.

The pouring of columns is done in various ways. If the metal is thin, they are poured from a long thin runner on top, or from a spray or sprays at the sides, as well as from the ends. When the metal is thick, as illustrated, they are poured from the ends. Here, too, the metal can be brought in at the edges of the flanges, or at their ends, or on top. It really matters little which is adopted, and often the question is settled by the presence or absence of bolt cores in the flanges, and of faced or unfaced portions.

In Figs. 155 and 158 the mould is shown poured against the faces of the flanges and at both ends simultaneously, the column being long. Pouring basins C, C are rammed on the top flask to suit runner pins previously rammed up with the pattern. The horizontal runners seen in Fig. 155 carry the metal in an uninterrupted flow between the core and the mould, the streams meeting in the middle before the iron has time to become chilled. Over each flange a riser D is often set, and one or two are set at intervals along the length, their purpose being to relieve the mould of strain, and to take any dirt taken up from the mould.

CHAPTER VIII.

STEAM-ENGINE CYLINDER PATTERNS AND CORE-BOXES.

WHEN steam-engine cylinders of from about 4-in. to 8-in. bore are designed as shown in Figs. 159 to 161, so small a portion of the outer part of the pattern is cylindrical, and the advantage of lagging is so slight, that the method of pattern-making shown in Fig. 162 is best. The half pattern as shown here is built of ten slices, including flanges and core prints. Neglecting the prints, the slices are made to thickness, jointed, and screwed together, glue not being used in these joints. The dowelled joint between the halves is now made, and on one half of the pattern the outline of the section is marked with the line of the joint for the steam-chest flange A (Fig. 162). Fig. 163 is a section on G H (Fig. 162).

The D-shaped outlines of ıe cylinder flanges are marked on the ends, and the positions of the pieces noted by pencilling a letter or number on each part. The centre line of the bore is scribed on each half, the faces A and B (Fig. 160) of the steam inlet and outlet are planed and their shapes struck out, and the whole is taken to pieces afterwards.

By the aid of compasses and square now mark the section of each slice, which may then be brought to shape with band saw or bow saw, chisel, and gouge. Then the slices may be glued and screwed together, a light cleaning-up of the body over the joints being done before the flanges are finally fixed.

The body prints B (Fig. 162) are turned in halves and a flat portion is cut on the lower half, in this case the half attached to the part with the inlet branch. The flat is worked into the circle with a considerable taper, so that the core does not press on the mould until it takes its final bearing. The taper print C (Figs. 162 and 163) is for the core of the inlet chamber C (Fig. 160). The circular print D (Fig. 162) with a stalk is in halves (one for each half of the pattern) for the core that forms the valve

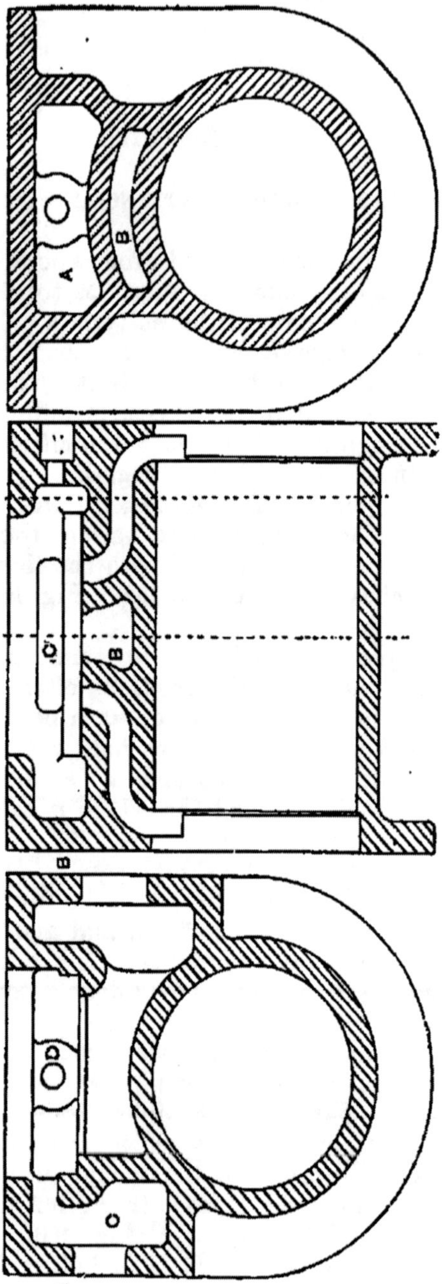

Fig. 161.

Fig. 159.

Fig. 160.

Fig. 159.—Longitudinal Section of Small Steam Cylinder. Figs. 160 and 161.—Cross-sections through Exhaust Port and Steam Passage.

spindle stuffing-box. This print should be long enough to allow the core to lie in position without over-balancing into the mould. The print E (Fig. 162) for the steam-chest core has a sharp taper, so that when the mould is made the top box-part may be lowered upon it, without touching the core until the mould is closed.

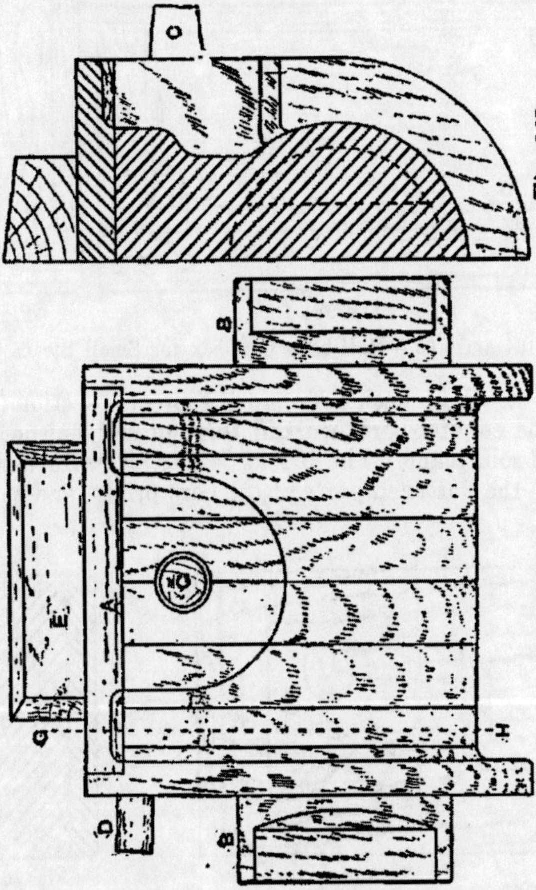

Fig. 163.

Fig. 162.

Figs. 162 and 163.—Half-pattern of Core-box for Small Steam Cylinder.

The pattern may be glass-papered and shellac-varnished, a stiff rapping and lifting plate being let in each half on the joint, and the transverse section marked in black varnish on one half as a guide to the moulder in arranging the cores. The prints should be finished and varnished black before being fastened on the pattern.

The body core-box (Figs. 164 and 165) is built up, dowelled, and stiffened with transverse pieces or backing E (Fig. 165). The ends are cleaned off to length, a centre line is gauged on one half, the bore, less about $\frac{3}{8}$ in. for tooling,

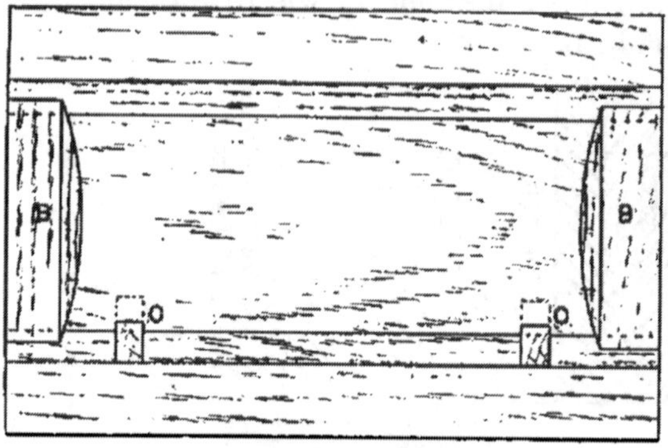

Fig. 164.

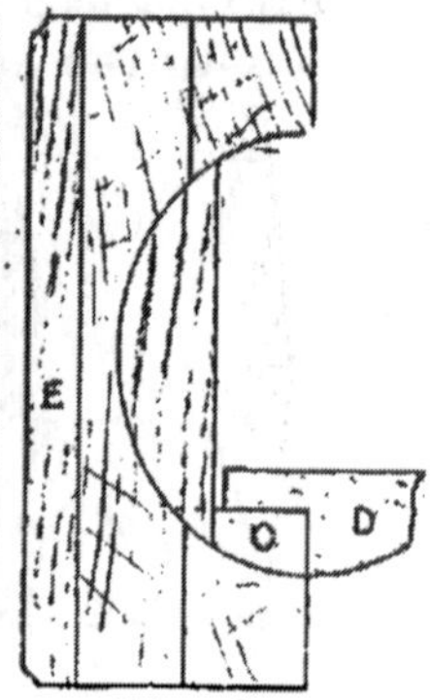

Fig. 165.

Figs. 164 and 165.—Half-body Core-box for Small Steam Cylinder.

being struck on each end, and the circular section (neglecting the counter-bore) worked through and finished with a round-sole plane. The blocks B (Fig. 164) are fitted in to match the flattened parts of the core prints, and the prints

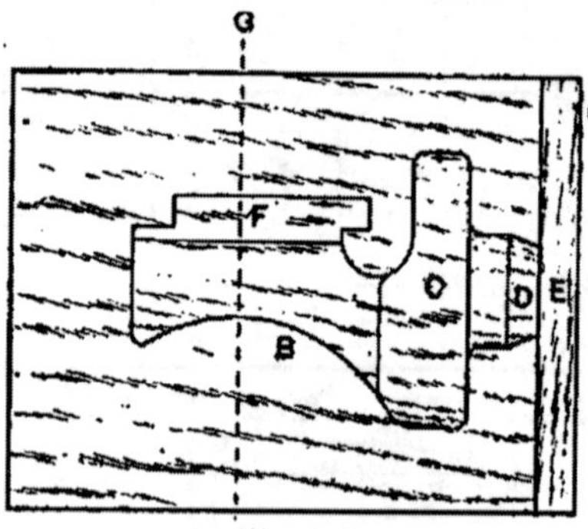

Fig. 166.

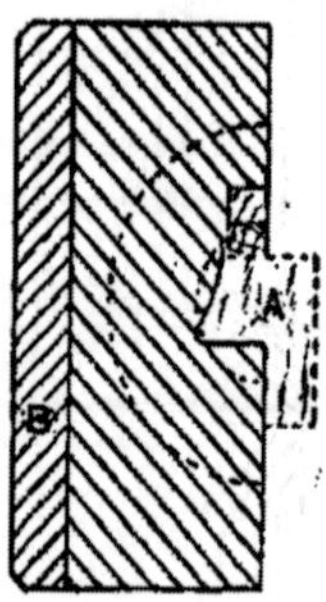

Fig. 167.

Figs. 166 and 167.—Half Core-box for Exhaust Port.

C (Figs. 164 and 165) are attached to give the bearing for one end of the steam passage core. This rests on the impression of the lower part of D (Fig. 165), which is fixed in the half of the box not shown. The bearing part is shown some distance below the joint of the mould, and D will project into the opposite part of the core-box. The latter carries no ends, as it is better to clamp the two parts of the box together, and to ram the core as a whole.

Figs. 166 and 167 show the box for the core to produce

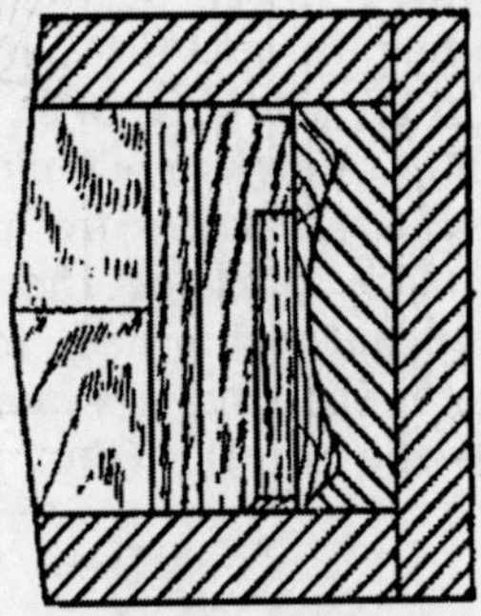

Fig. 169.

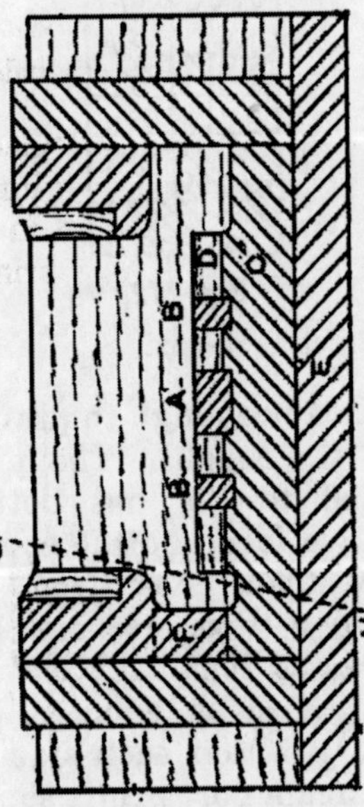

Fig. 168.

Fig. 170.

Figs. 168 to 170.—Steam-chest Core-box.

the exhaust port and passage shown in Fig. 160. Fig. 167 is a section on G H (Fig. 166). A (Fig. 167) shows by dotted lines the template used to obtain the shape of the box corresponding to B (Fig. 159). This template is moved radially around the curve B (Fig. 166). C (Fig. 166) may be circular in section, as shown by the dotted lines in Fig.

167, or D-shaped, like the steam-inlet. The part D (Fig. 166) fits the impression in the top box made by a print on the face B (Fig. 160). The end-piece E (Fig. 166) stops the core-box, each half core in this case being separately rammed, and afterwards fastened together. B (Fig. 167) shows the backing which is glued and screwed on the box.

Figs. 168 to 170 show the core-box for taking out the steam chest, Fig. 169 being a section on G H (Fig. 168), and to understand the part F (Fig. 166), reference should be made to A (Figs. 168 and 170), which is the core print corresponding to this part. The main part of the box consists of a frame, housed together but not glued, for it is necessary to separate the parts after the core is rammed. The upper part of the box matches the print E (Fig. 162),

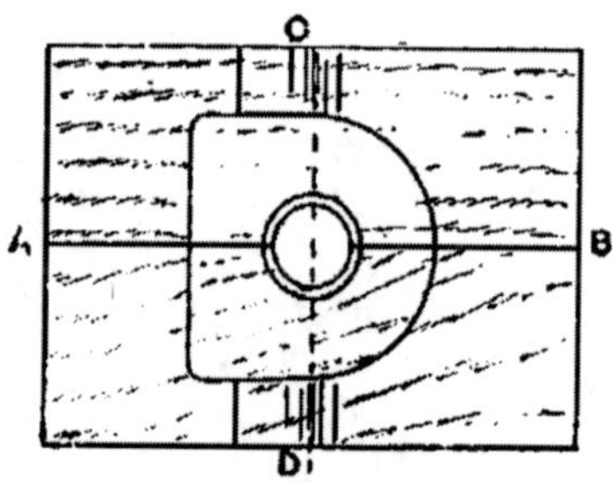

Fig. 171.

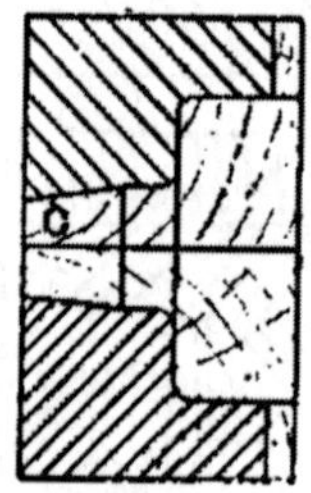

Fig. 172.

Figs. 171 and 172.—Steam-inlet Core-box.

and this part of the core should be heavy enough to prevent the overhanging part falling into the mould. The piece C (Fig. 168), permanently fastened to the flat bottom board E, gives the shapes of the valve face and the convex back of the metal separating the steam chest from the passages, as at A (Fig. 161). A and B (Figs. 168 and 170) are prints fitted loosely into grooves so that each may be drawn separately from the core. A is as wide as the exhaust port, less an amount (say $\frac{1}{16}$ in.) on each side for chipping and filing, while B for the steam-port prints should have similar allowances. One end of each of these prints touches the facing D (Fig. 168), as the port cores are lowered into the mould after the body core and steam-chest core are in place. The other ends are best cut short of the width of the steam passages to obtain increased thickness of sand in the steam-chest core to support the port cores,

The valve face should allow about ⅛ in. for tooling. F (Fig. 168) is an extension of the flange of the steam-chest, and forms a stuffing-box for the valve spindle D (Fig. 160).

Fig. 171, with Fig. 172, which is a section on C D, shows a core-box made of two pieces of wood dowelled on the joint A B. This box is for the steam inlet chamber C (Fig. 160). The part C (Fig. 172) corresponds to the print C (Figs. 162 and 163). From C (Fig. 160), which gives a

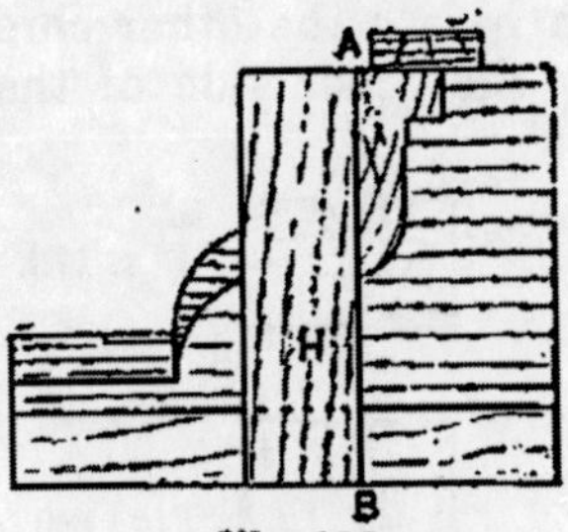

Fig. 175.

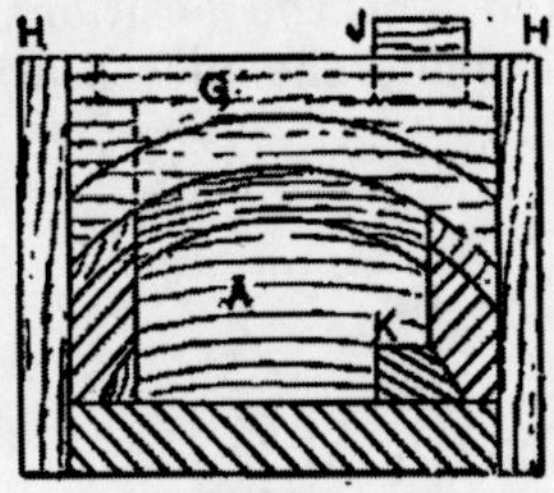

Fig. 174.

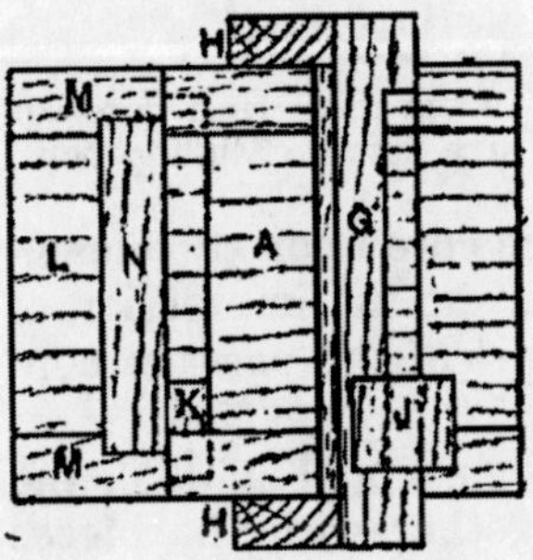

Fig. 176.

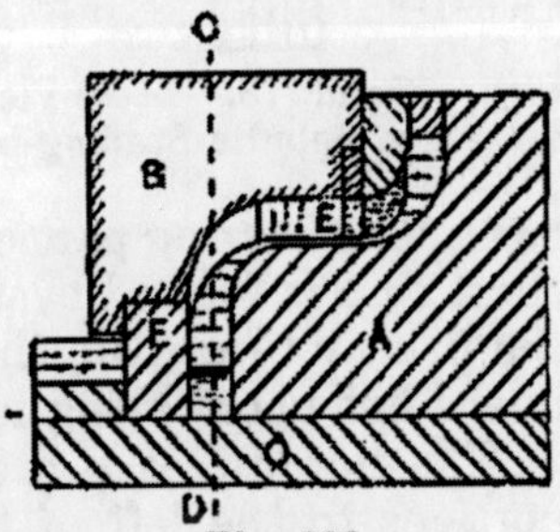

Fig. 173.

Figs. 173 to 176.—Steam-port Core-box.

section of the core at right angles to that of Fig. 172, the contour of the upper face of the core-box may be obtained. This contour is transferred to the core by drawing a straight strickle across the box after the ramming is completed. One part is in contact with the steam-chest core, and this part cores out the oblong opening C (Fig. 159).

Figs. 173 to 176 show the steam-port core-box, Fig. 174 being a section on C D (Fig. 173). A block A (Figs. 173, 174, and 176) has an upper surface corresponding to the convexity of the steam passage B (Fig. 161). The core is rammed upon this, and the upper surface of the sand brought to shape by drawing the strickle B (Fig. 173) across two guiding surfaces E and F (Fig. 173). G (Figs. 173 to 176) partly forms the steam-port core, and is fastened to the two vertical pieces H (Figs. 174 to 176) screwed on M (Fig. 176). Both the steam-port cores are made from this box, but as they are not exactly similar, two loose pieces J and K (Figs. 174 to 176) are provided. J is also shown in Figs. 177 and 178. One core is rammed with J and K in the positions shown; then before the other core is made the pieces are changed to the other side of the

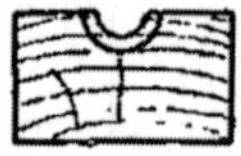

Fig. 179.

Fig. 177.

Fig. 180.

Fig. 178.

Figs. 177 and 178.—Loose Piece for Valve Spindle Stuffing-box.

Figs. 179 and 180.—Half Core-box for Valve Spindle Stuffing-box.

box. The bearing part of the passage core upon the steam-chest core is formed by J, and this enters the impression of the print B (Fig. 170), the bearing part of the passage core in the body core being formed by K.

The side pieces M are divided along A B (Fig. 175), the portions to the left of this line together with the pieces N and G (Fig. 176) being connected to form a frame which is fitted loosely over the block A. L (Figs. 173 and 176) is a small block fitted to the backing O (Fig. 173) to keep this frame in place whilst the core is rammed. Finally, Figs. 179 and 180 show the core-box for hollowing out the valve spindle stuffing-box.

CHAPTER IX.

WORM WHEEL PATTERN.

To make accurate patterns for worm wheels, it is almost necessary to have the worm cut first. It is possible, at a great expenditure of time, to mark off the teeth directly from a drawing which shows a section of the thread of the worm, and to work to the lines so struck. But such time is grudged in the shops, neither is the method so accurate in practice as the one about to be described. It is to have the worm cut, and to make it the gauge for checking the correspondence of the wheel teeth therewith in all positions of the worm and wheel during their movements.

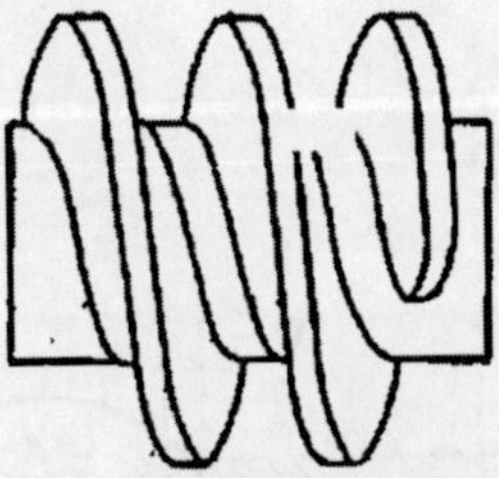

Fig. 181.—Worm Casting.

The method in principle is precisely that which is adopted for cutting or "hobbing" the metal teeth of worm wheels. In this method a steel worm is made, and then the thread is serrated at intervals, and backed off behind each serration, much like a master-tap; and this, when hardened, is used to cut the worm wheel. There need be no trouble experienced in getting the worm made before the wheel is made; for it is always necessary to fix the dimensions of the worm before the wheel can be marked out, and if the worm is cast it can be cast first; if forged, it can be cut in the lathe first.

Having the worm, or its dimensions, the wheel must be marked out in section therefrom, and the angles of the teeth are also fixed by it, as follows: There are three principal dimensions on the worm (Fig. 181), the pitch diameter P (see Figs. 182 and 183), the pitch Q, and the

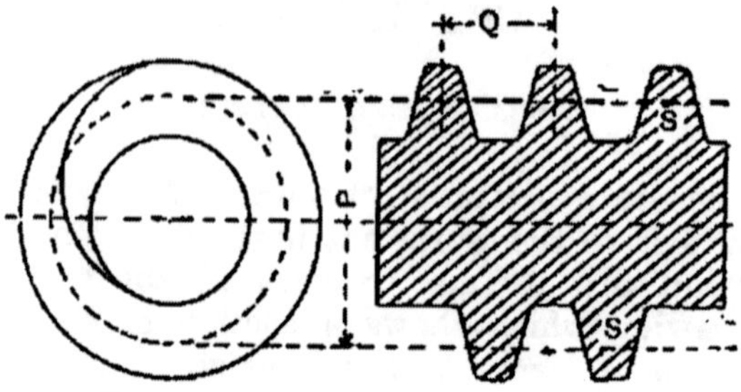

Fig. 182. Fig. 183.

Figs. 182 and 183.—End View and Section of Worm Casting.

tooth section S. P and Q together govern the angle of the teeth on the worm wheel; P governs the sectional curves of the teeth, Q the tooth centres, and S the tooth forms.

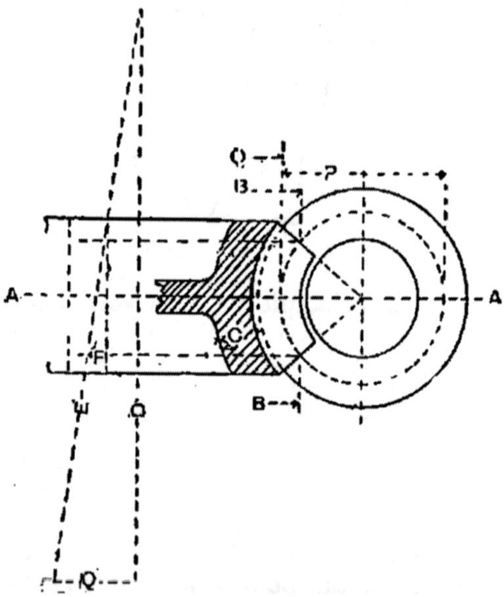

Fig. 184.—Marking Section of Worm Wheel.

It may be noted that the sections of the worm tooth should always be those shown—namely, sloping like the rack teeth for involute wheels. The points and roots are very slightly rounded, only just to avoid sharp angles.

Fig. 184 shows the methods of using the worm to get the leading dimensions of the wheel. First as to the section of the wheel. The pitch diameter P of the worm

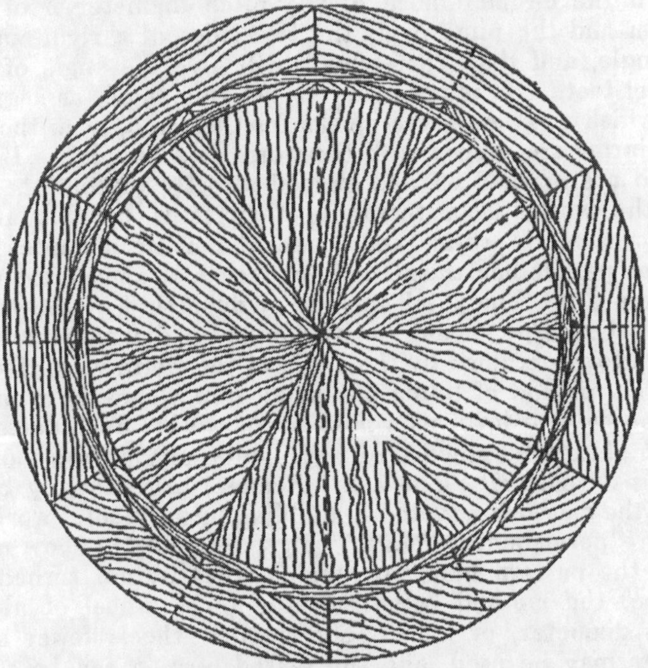

Fig. 185.

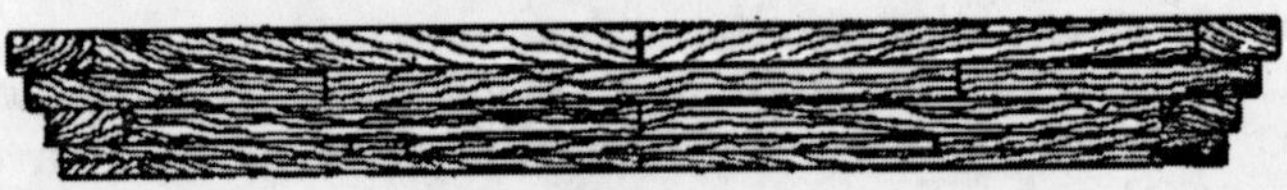

Fig. 186.

Figs. 185 and 186.—Half-pattern of Worm Wheel Body Glued up Roughly.

comes in contact with the pitch diameter of the wheel Q on the central plane A A, so that the diameters measured from B B are not the true pitch diameters, but are larger, and are regulated by the radius of the worm. The sectional curves of the wheel teeth, allowing for clearance, are struck from the centre of the worm, as shown, and the ends of the teeth radiate from the centre. The thickness of the rim C, equal to the tooth thickness, is added, and the curve for that also struck from the centre of the worm. The angle of the wheel teeth is obtained by laying down the circumference of the pitch diameter D of the worm and the pitch Q, as the two sides of a right-angled triangle, and the hypotenuse E will give the angle of the wheel teeth. It is necessary to get this angle, as a guide by which to glue on the blocks for the teeth, even though the latter are shaped with the worm as a template. If the teeth are marked off and shaped directly without the aid of the worm as a template, then it is by this angle that the teeth are marked round at definite distances out of the perpendicular on the joint face A A, and on the diameters B B. The total amount of departure of the teeth from the perpendicular on the extreme diameters B B is equal to F, obtained by the angle of the worm wheel teeth.

The method of lining out being now clear, the making of the pattern involves a neat bit of work. Such patterns must always be glued up in segments, and always parted along the central plane A A. Readers have already been told the methods adopted in building up segmental work to ensure permanence of form. Figs. 185 and 186 show one-half the pattern built up roughly, that is, not turned to shape, the method being suitable for a wheel of about 2 ft. diameter, or more. For smaller wheels fewer segments may be used, and the plated portion can be solid instead of being formed in two thicknesses as shown. The illustration explains itself.

There are two methods of jointing the halves, shown in Figs. 187 and 188. In the first the plate is built in one, either with or without segments, and the top part of the pattern is jointed as a ring to it. This is not so durable a method as the one shown in Fig. 188, in which each half ring is glued to half the plate thickness. The loose unstayed ring in Fig. 187 is apt to go out of truth in time; but in Fig. 188 both rings are supported alike with a half thickness of plate.

After the rings are glued up, the curve of the rim upon which the teeth are to bed is turned by template A (Fig. 189) made from the drawing. This curve, and the joint faces of the two halves, are the parts to be turned first, because they are the most important. Afterwards the halves can be re-chucked by the central stud B and corresponding stud hole, and the edges, the inner rim curves, and the outer faces of the rim turned. In addition to the central stud, it is necessary to insert a dowel

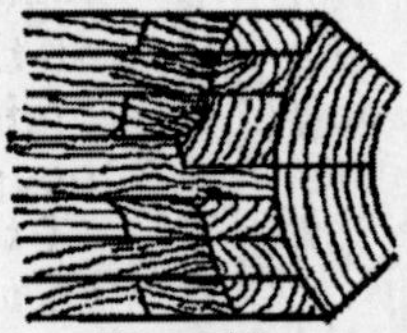

Fig. 187.

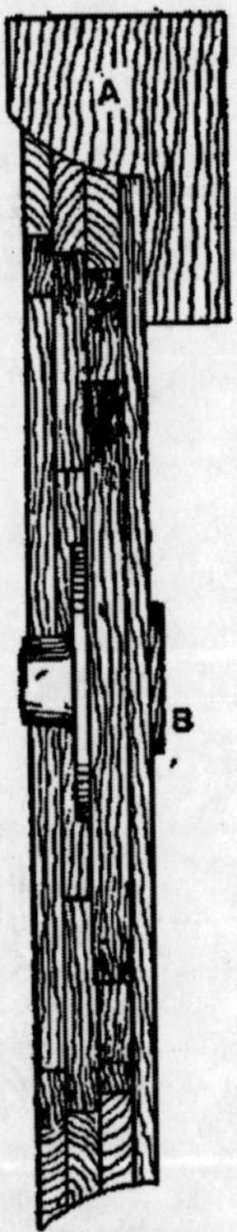

Fig. 189.

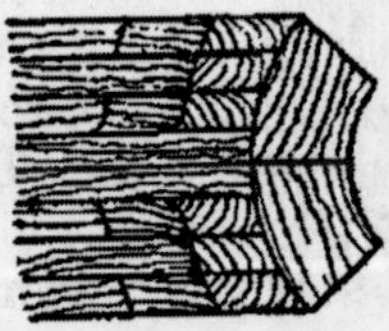

Fig. 188.

Figs. 187 and 188.—Jointing Worm Wheel Pattern. Fig. 189.—Turning Outside of Wheel Rim by Template.

between the two halves of the pattern to preserve the two halves always in the same position in relation to each other, so that the edges of the teeth shall always coincide precisely.

Before re-chucking, the blocks for the teeth ought to be fitted and glued on, otherwise time will be wasted. The half-lengths of the teeth, with turning allowances, are fitted with a chisel at approximate angles to the turned seatings, which are chalked to show points of contact. They will have the appearance seen in Fig. 190. They are then faced and turned to the form in Fig. 191 with template A, after which the re-chucking before alluded to will follow

Fig. 190.—Tooth Block Glued on Wheel Rim.

Fig. 191.—Turning Tooth Points by Template.

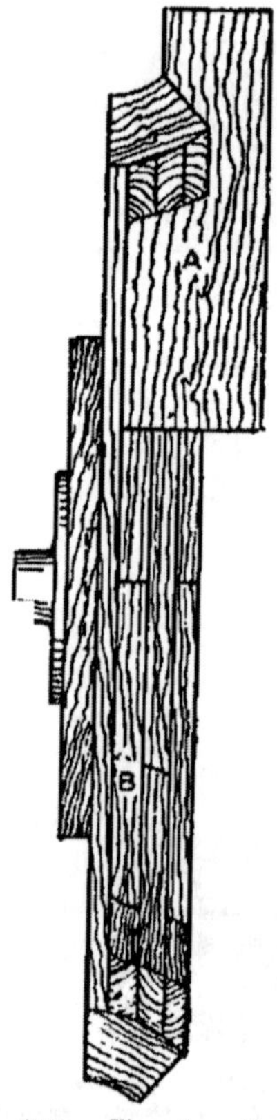

Fig. 192.—Turning Inside of Wheel Rim by Template.

(Fig. 192). Then the face B will be skimmed over to the required thickness, and upon it a template A will be set for checking the turning of the inside of the rim and its edges and the ends of the teeth. This is shown clearly by the illustrations, so that more detailed explanation is not required.

The centres of the teeth are now to be pitched along

the joint face A A (Fig. 184) on one half of the pattern. To obtain the forms of the teeth, see Fig. 193 and 194. For all involute teeth there is a base circle A (Fig. 193), as well as the pitch circle B, which is used for convenience. The base circles of a pair of wheels coincide approximately with the

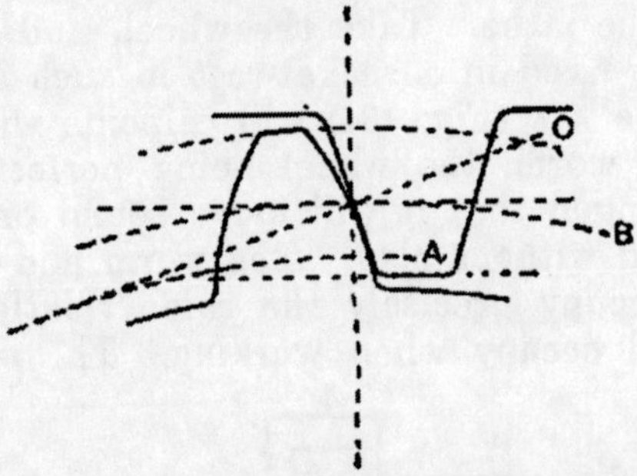

Fig. 193.—Forms of Teeth on Worm and Wheel.

roots and the points of the teeth C. A line drawn tangent to both base circles is the pitch circle or path of contact of the teeth. In a worm tooth, as in a rack, the tooth flanks are at right angles with the tangent line (Fig. 193). In the wheel tooth the movement of the tangent line on the base line A gives the curve for the flanks. This is done in practice by laying a slip of wood carrying a needle-point against a template, cut to the radius of the base line, and moving the slip around it, the needle-point then marking the tooth curve (Fig. 194). The

Fig. 194.—Template for Marking Tooth Curves.

angle of obliquity usually adopted for rack teeth is 75° with the line of centres.

The teeth should all be marked out in the joint face of one half the pattern, and cut in a little way with the chisel. The teeth on the other half of the pattern can be marked from them, and cut or set in. That is all the marking out that is really necessary. The two half patterns are screwed together, chalking the outlines set in, to prevent risk of cutting into the tooth forms in the subsequent work. Take the worm and place it truly between centres in the lathe. Take the wheel, and mount it on a pin or pivot fixed in a socket-rest in such a way that its central plane A A (Fig. 184) will coincide with the central axis of the worm, the wheel being perfectly horizontal, and so arranged that it will move round on the pin with freedom, and without play. The worm and wheel pattern will then occupy precisely the same relations which the castings will occupy when working. The only difference

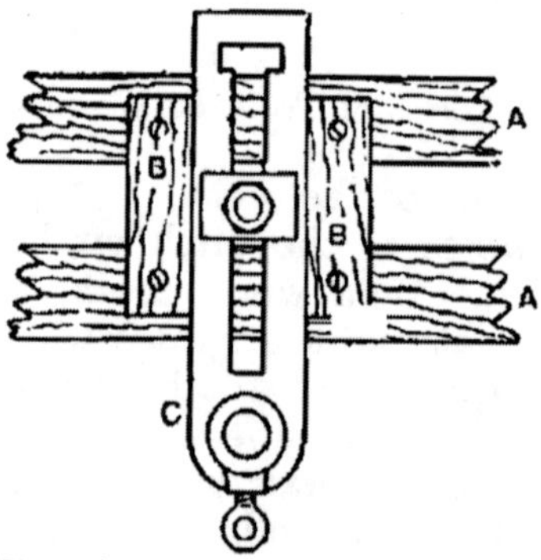

Fig. 195.—Cutting Wheel Teeth.

will be that the T-rest socket must be set and guided by a couple of parallel strips screwed across the lathe-bed, so that it can be slid to and fro, putting the wheel into and out of gear with the worm. Fig. 195 shows a suitable arrangement in plan, A A being the lathe bearers, B B parallel strips, and C the T-rest socket.

It is now easy to see that the wheel teeth can be cut carefully and tested until they make a perfect gear with the worm. When cutting the teeth, the T-rest socket is drawn back. To ascertain the amount of contact and accuracy attained, it is thrust forward, and the worm is revolved by hand, carrying the wheel round a portion of a circle, and leaving marks of contact on its tooth flanks, the worm being smeared with red lead and oil for the purpose.

If the rig-up is steady and due care is taken that the

tooth forms set in on the middle plane are not cut below, there is no need to mark the tooth forms on the outer faces B B (Fig. 184). Still, it is safer on the whole to do so. After working, therefore, three or four teeth carefully, the forms on the outer faces B B will be developed—differing, of course, from those on the joint face A A (Fig. 184)—and their widths and the location of the radii of their flanks can then be taken and set out round the remainder of the wheel. The time of marking out is not wholly lost, because, after marking, all the teeth can be cut in by the lines nearly to shape without any trial in the worm until the final corrections are necessary.

If these directions are followed carefully, the result will be a more perfect gear than can possibly be attained

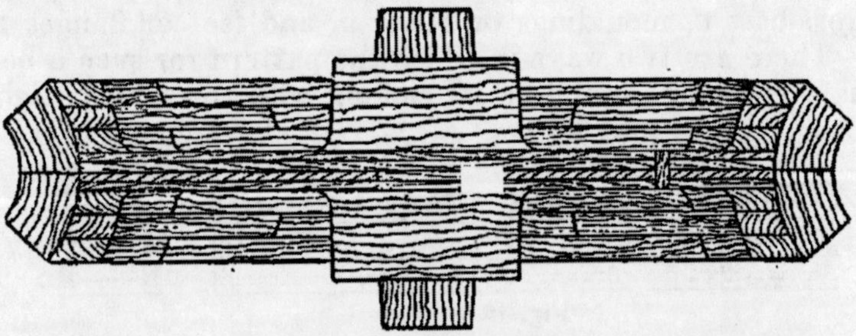

Fig. 196.—Cross Section of Finished Worm Wheel Pattern.

by any method of marking out direct from a drawing of the tooth forms. The conditions being precisely those which exist in actual gear, the rest is a matter of care on the part of the workman.

Fig. 196 shows the wheel complete in cross section, with teeth, central stud, dowel, bosses, and prints in place. The bosses may be screwed or studded on. The latter is more favourable for subsequent alterations in bores, if such are likely to be required. Fig. 196 shows the central web built up, each half in two thicknesses, as in Figs. 185 and 186; but some of the illustrations show one thickness only of solid stuff. In adopting the latter method, however, it is always best to make open joints, if a wheel is over 10 in. or 12 in. in diameter. The segments will hold together the strips which form the plate.

CHAPTER X.

LATHE-BED PATTERNS.

THIS chapter will describe first the pattern for a lathe-bed (Figs. 197 and 198), a plain bed for a hand-turning lathe without slide-rest. Fig. 199 is a cross section. Dimensions are not given, and are not necessary, but the figures are drawn proportionately for any lathe of from 3-in. to 7-in. or 8-in. centre, and the method here described for constructing the pattern will be correct for any lathe bed of that type. Its parts are, sides A, sliding ways B, cross-bars C, mouldings or fillets D, and feet or flanges E.

There are two ways in which the pattern for such a bed may be made—first, like its casting with some very slight

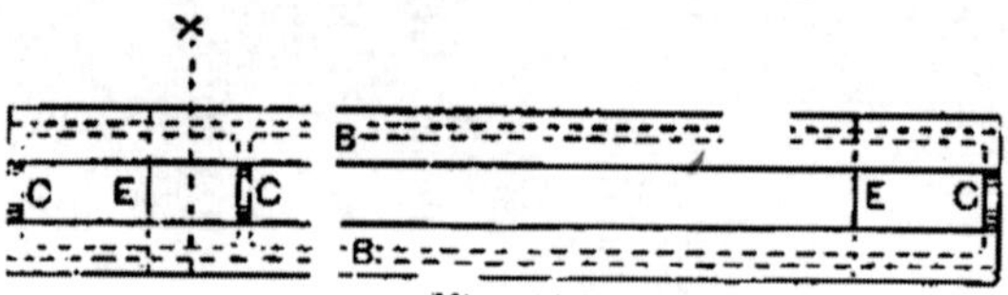

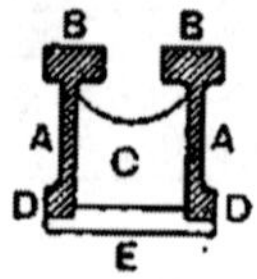

Fig. 199.

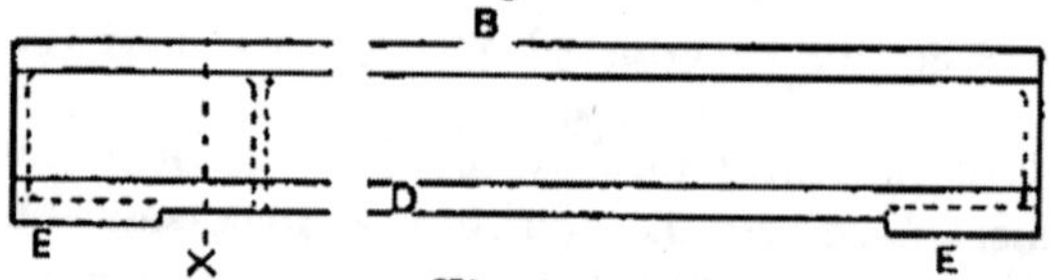

Fig. 198.

Figs. 197 to 199.—Lathe-bed Casting.

differences; or it may be made so that only the outer faces correspond with the form of the casting, and the interior portions are represented by core-prints only, core-boxes being required in this case for coring out. The first method is much preferable in the case of the bed in question.

In moulding any lathe-bed, it must be remembered that the sliding faces must be cast downwards with the object of securing clean metal there. So this settles the way in which the pattern shall be tapered and which portions are to be kept loose.

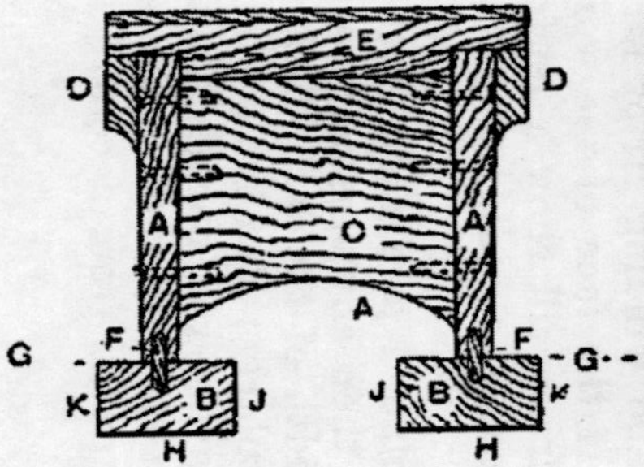

Fig. 200.

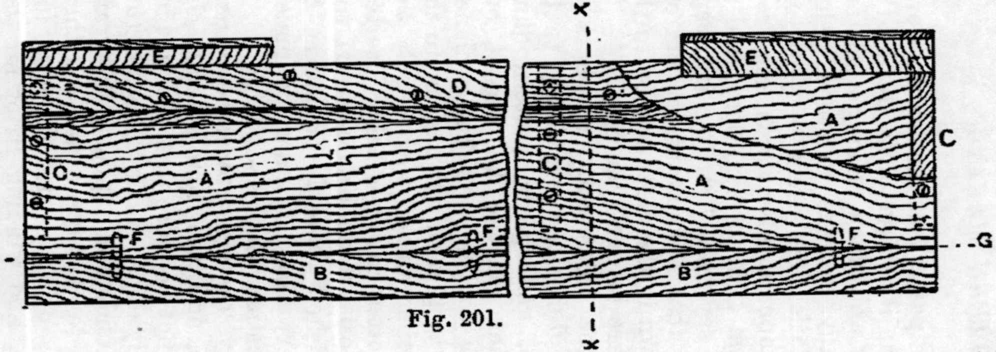

Fig. 201.

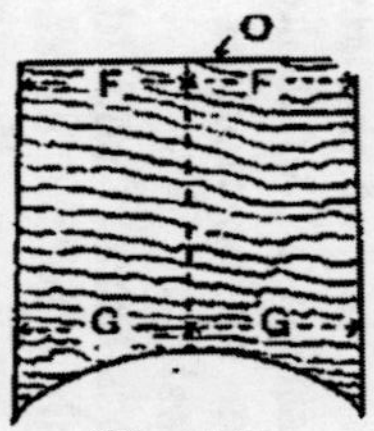

Fig. 202.

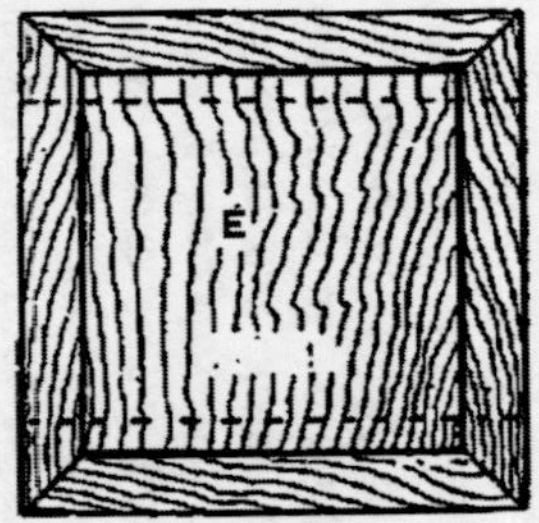

Fig. 203.

Figs. 200 and 201.—Section and Elevation of Lathe-bed Pattern. Figs. 202 and 203.—Cross-bar and Foot of Lathe-bed Pattern.

Figs. 200 and 201 show the pattern of the bed in elevation and cross section, just as it is laid down during the operation of moulding. It is well when making a pattern always to picture it mentally just as it stands when being moulded, and the details then seem to work out naturally. The sides A are tapered downwards, say from $\frac{1}{16}$ in. to $\frac{3}{32}$ in. in beds of from 4 in. to 6 in. deep, and as much as $\frac{1}{8}$ in. in deeper beds, say from 7 in. to 8 in. deep; that is, they are thinner by that amount at the bottom than at the top edges, as shown in the cross section to the left hand. The cross-bars C are tapered similarly.

When putting together the sides and cross-bars of such a pattern as this two difficulties are likely to be encountered. One is that of getting the pattern quite straight lengthwise, the other that of keeping it out of winding. The first is due to the stuff being planed crooked, the second to its being planed winding, or to the ends of the cross-bars not being planed to precisely the same bevels, and also to the cross-bars not being inserted precisely alike, as regards position up or down. If the pattern is winding when finished there is no means of getting the winding out afterwards. It must be pulled apart and corrected, or the casting will be winding.

To prevent such inaccuracy, the sides must be planed truly first, straight lengthwise, and free from winding. In thin stuff like this, which will not be more than $\frac{1}{2}$ in. or $\frac{5}{8}$ in. thick in any case, it is not easily done. Jack plane the stuff all over first, removing the outside and exposing the grain to the air; let the job stand for a day or two and then finish with the trying plane, using a straight-edge for checking the truth lengthwise, and winding strips for the twist or winding of the stuff. If the face of the work is true, the strips when looked across will show a perfectly level plane, no portion of the edges standing any higher than the rest.

The cross-bars C should be planed preferably with the grain running across as shown, then any shrinkage which may occur will not affect the width of the lathe-bed as it would if the grain ran perpendicularly; also the pattern is stiffer than it would be if the grain ran perpendicularly. To ensure symmetry and prevent risk of winding, the ends of the bars should be planed tapered from a centre line, as in Fig. 202, the dimensions F being equal, and G also equal, the difference between F and G being exactly the same as that due to the taper on the inner faces of the sides A. Then having one cross-bar planed correctly, mark the others from it with a scriber, and plane accurately to the scribed lines. Then if the cross-bars are all screwed between the sides with their edges O exactly level with the edges of the sides A, there will be no risk of winding occurring.

The sides are screwed to the cross-bars, and need not be removed during moulding. The top strips B, however, must not be fastened, yet they have to be secured in place during ramming up of the pattern. This is done by the use of dowels F (Figs. 200 and 201), which retain the strips in place, but which permit of the taking away of the main body of the pattern from the strips after the moulding is completed. The mould is jointed along the plane G and then, after the removal of that portion of the mould which contains the main body of the bed, the strips B are left exposed in the bottom part to be withdrawn from the sand separately.

On these strips an allowance for planing the casting has to be made. The allowance need not exceed $\frac{1}{8}$ in. on each planed face unless the bed is exceptionally long, or unless the foundry where it is made turns out rough castings, and then $\frac{3}{16}$ in. will not be too much. The faces to be planed are the top H (Fig. 200) for the poppet, etc., to slide upon; the inner face J for the headstock and poppet to fit between; and the outer edge K for good appearance. These strips must be dowelled accurately upon the sides. If they do not lie parallel and in winding with one another some of the planing allowances will have to be used in getting the casting true, and if the inaccuracy amounts to much it may happen that the casting will not hold up to desired dimensions.

The strips being dowelled on very narrow edges will not lie very steadily on them, but that will not matter; if put on truly, they will be all right and steady when laid upon the levelled bed of sand upon which the pattern will be moulded.

The filleting D is prepared in separate strips; it is screwed, and it may also be glued, along the sides. These

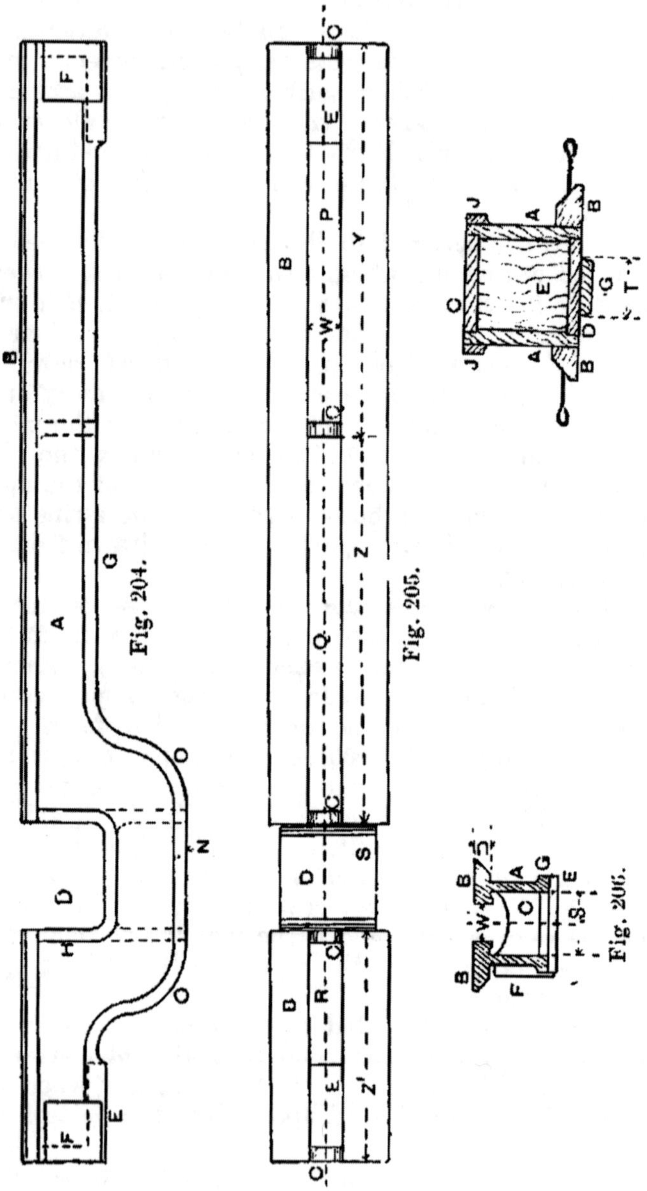

Figs. 204 to 206.—Gap Lathe-bed Casting. Fig. 207.—Cross Section of Gap Lathe-bed Pattern.

strips act as material stiffeners to the pattern, as they also do to the casting.

The feet E by which the bed is bolted to its standards, may either be screwed on or dowelled on, it matters little which. They are shouldered to fit within the sides A. Their faces may be planed all over, or narrow strips may be used as shown. Fig 203 shows the under side of one of these pattern feet. The strips will save some labour if the lathe builder prefers to chip instead of planing.

It will facilitate the moulder's work if the pattern is well glasspapered across the grain, along the width of the stuff, and on the sides and ribs, using a rubber for the purpose. This will remove the plane marks and make a nice smooth surface favourable to delivery. When the pattern delivers freely from the mould, there is tolerable certainty that the casting will be just like the pattern; but when the moulder has to mend up, elements of uncertainty and inaccuracy come in. Two applications of clear shellac varnish will suffice, each being rubbed down when dry with fine glasspaper.

In reference to shrinkage allowances, these may almost be neglected in small beds. If the bed is 4 ft. long the difference in length due to shrinkage will be about $\frac{3}{8}$ in.; if the bed is 5 in. wide over the strips the shrinkage in breadth will only be in theory a full $\frac{1}{32}$ in., and will probably amount to nothing at all, because the moulder will rap the pattern to that extent.

The making of a pattern for a gap lathe-bed is different from that just described for a plain bed which was made to deliver without cores. The one shown by Figs. 204 to 206 will be better if cored out, because the cutting out of the gap would render a pattern for self-delivery very flimsy. That such is the case is evident from a glance at Figs. 204 and 205, where it is seen that the cutting out of the gap would break the continuity of the wood in the side webs A, and there is nothing to reinforce their rigidity. The pattern would therefore twist, especially in small beds of light scantlings, say with sides A only $\frac{1}{2}$ in. or $\frac{5}{8}$ in. thick. The pattern is also rather too deep at the gap for easy delivery. Likewise, in many instances, as in Figs. 204 to 206, the bottom of the gap is bridged over with metal, and that necessitates an awkward lift of sand in

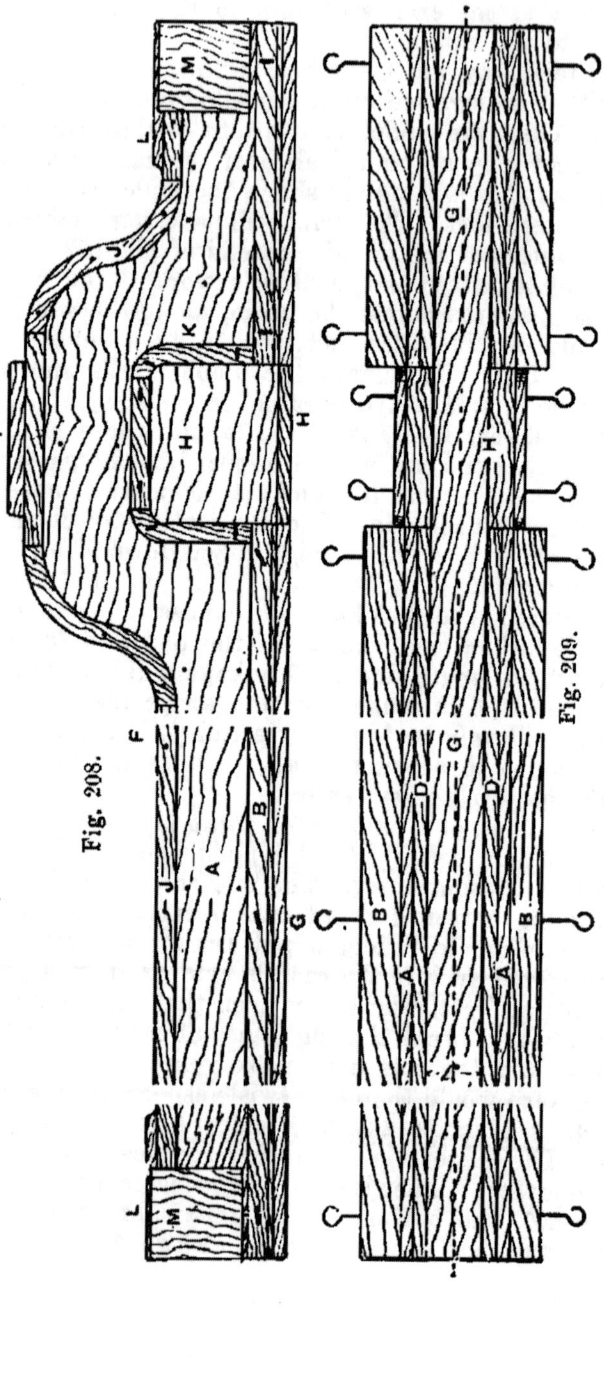

Fig. 208.

Fig. 209.

Figs. 208 and 209.—Gap Lathe-bed Pattern.

the top N above the bridged part—that is, "top" as the pattern moulds. Then there are deep lifts at O adjacent, which would require a good deal of taper in the pattern there.

Another good reason for coring such beds in a machine-maker's shop is that, as lathe-beds for poppets of similar centres often have to be supplied of different lengths to suit customers, it is easier to alter the length of a solid pattern provided with core-prints and core-boxes, than one made to deliver itself without coring.

There is little more difficulty in this job than in the last, but there is more work involved. The type of bed and proportions shown in the illustrations would be suitable for a lathe of from 3½ in. to 7 in. centre.

In Figs. 204 to 206 A shows the sides; B, the bearers; C, the cross-bars; D, the gap; E, the feet; F, facings for the brackets for the leading screw; G H, fillets.

The main body of the pattern is made, not from solid stuff, but by "boxing up," by which the pattern is prevented from warping to any important extent. Boxing up occupies more time than cutting from solid stuff, but it saves timber, and produces a better job. The method of boxing up is shown in Figs. 207 to 211, the pattern being drawn in those figures in the position which it occupies during moulding—that is, upside down. Fig. 207 is a cross section through the main body of the pattern, showing the method of building up; Fig. 208 is a longitudinal elevation; Figs. 209 its plan, looking down on the bearers; Fig. 210, the plan of its under side; Fig. 211, a longitudinal section to show the cross-bars.

The rectangular section is built up of two vertical sides A, A, running the entire depth (Figs. 207 to 209), including the thickness due to the undercut bearers B, B, plus ⅛ in. for planing, and cut to the vertical outline of the bed (Fig. 208). Between these and the top and bottom portions C, D, which complete the rectangle, cross-bars E are fastened by nailing or screwing. At the curved portions F (Figs. 210 and 211), blocking is inserted, sufficiently thick to permit of the cutting out of the curves. The sides A, A, and the ends of the pattern are tapered, the amount varying with the depth of bed—say, from $\frac{1}{32}$ in. to $\frac{1}{16}$ in. on each. If the gap has a solid bottom, as in Figs. 204 and

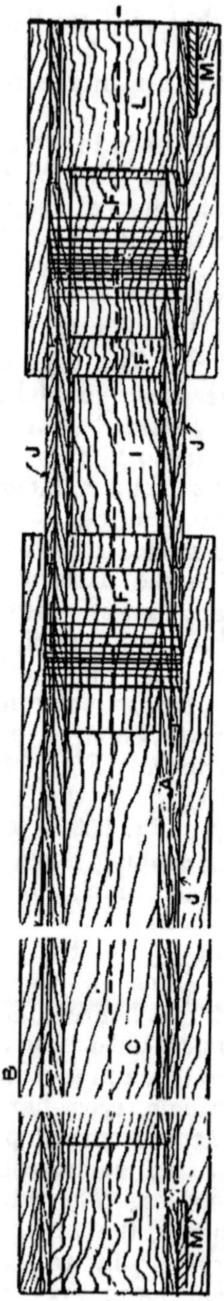

Fig. 210.

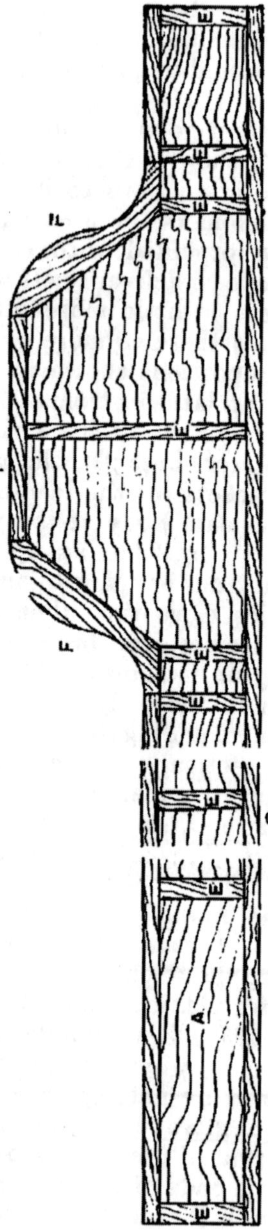

Fig. 211.

Figs. 210 and 211.—Gap Lathe-bed Pattern.

205, it may be either cored out or cut out in the pattern. The work will be lessened and the pattern strengthened by coring it out. If the gap goes right through—that is, without a solid bottom—it will be cored out. It is here assumed that it will be cored out.

On the outer faces of the pattern, those portions of the bearer B with the strips which stand beyond the faces, will be skewered on (Figs. 207, 208, 209, and 210), or else fitted with easy-fitting dovetails (Fig. 212). The skewers are just as good as dovetails, and do not occupy so much time in fitting. Dovetails are neater, and if well fitted are very good. They are adopted in good work to prevent risk of the loose pieces becoming shifted out of place in the mould. Note that extra allowances for planing the castings will have to be made all over the surfaces of these bearers; from $\frac{1}{8}$ in. to $\frac{3}{16}$ in. is usually given.

For coring out the interior, narrow prints G (Figs.

A

B

Fig. 212—Fitting Bearers with Dovetails.

207, 208, and 209) are nailed or screwed along the centre of the pattern. They will be of the same width as the tenons on the under side of the heads, minus the planing allowances between the bearers. Thus, if the space between the bearers is 2 in. in the finished casting, the print G will be $1\frac{3}{4}$ in. wide. From $\frac{1}{2}$ in. to $\frac{3}{4}$ in. thick will be suitable for these prints. H (Figs. 208 and 209) is the print for the gap-core. It is made of the same width over as the sides A, A (Figs. 204 and 205). This leaves the fillets K around the gap standing beyond the print. If the print comes out to the faces of the fillets, the core could not be got in unless the sides of the mould were taken away. At I (Figs. 208 and 210) is shown the print for coring out the metal underneath the gap.

The fillets J (Figs. 207, 208, and 210), shown at G in Figs. 204 and 205, go round the lower edges of the ribs A, stiffening them, and will be fastened on permanently with nails or screws. The method of their fitting is indicated by the timber shading. The fillet K in Fig. 208, which runs round the gap, corresponding with H in Figs. 204 and 205, is skewered on loosely. If these fillets were fastened per-

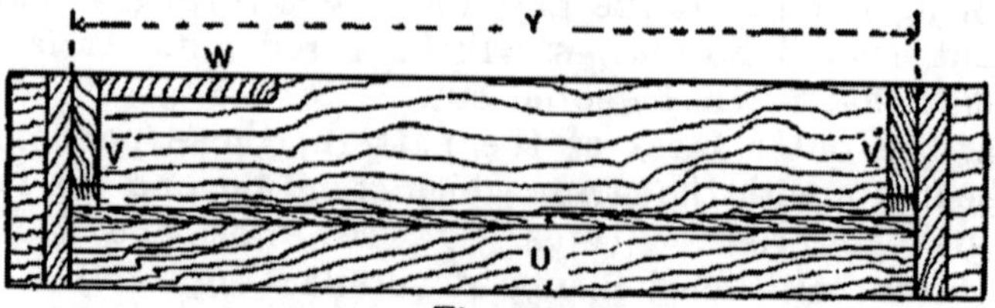

Fig. 213.

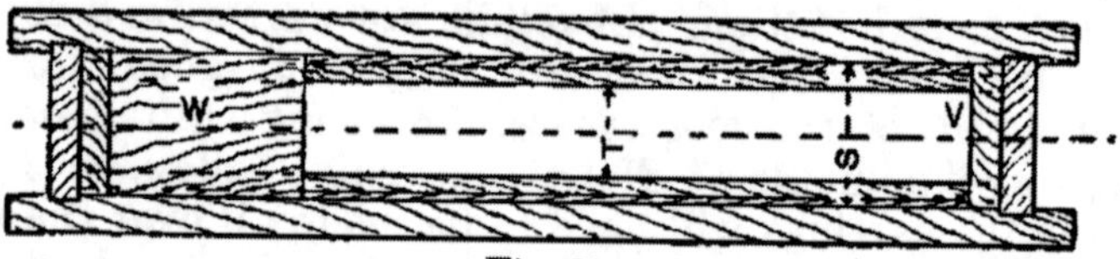

Fig. 214.

Figs. 213 and 214.—Core-box for Taking out Portion of Gap Lathe-bed.

manently they would prevent the withdrawal of the pattern from the mould.

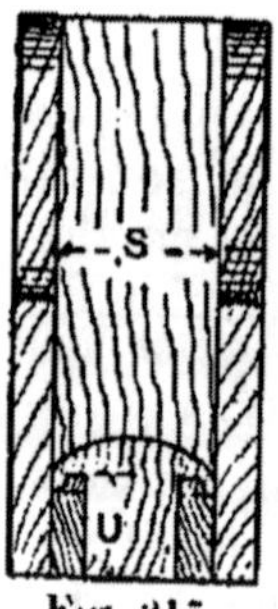

Fig. 215.

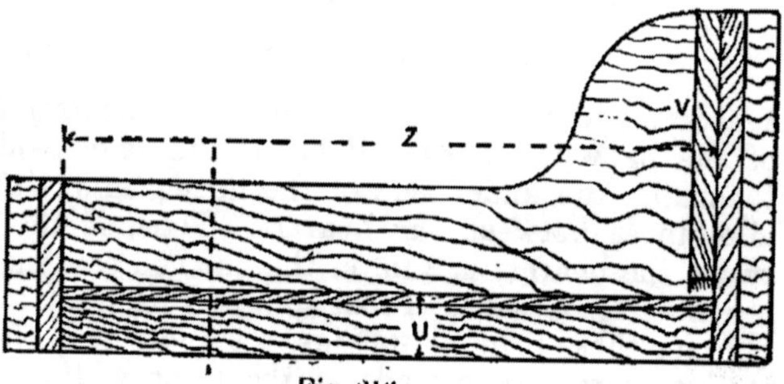

Fig. 216.

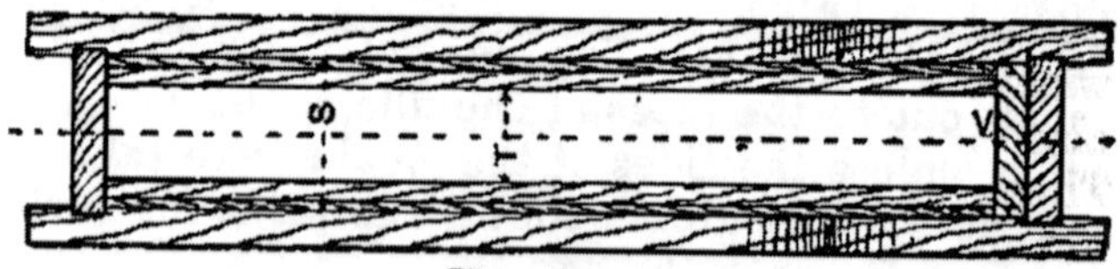

Fig. 217.

Figs. 215 to 217.—Core-box for Taking out Portion of Gap Lathe-bed.

The feet E (Figs. 204 to 206), which receive the standards, are fitted differently from those illustrated in Fig. 201, p. 111. In the present case part of their thickness,

L L (Figs. 208 and 210), is nailed on the pattern. The remainder, or supplementary portion, which comes within the bed, seen dotted in Figs. 204 and 205, will go in the core-boxes. The facings F (Figs. 204 to 206) for the brackets which carry the leading screw are nailed on permanently at M (Figs. 208 and 210). These complete the pattern for a gap lathe-bed; but the core-boxes have now to be made.

It is obvious that the cross-section inside of the core-boxes must be the same as that of the inside of the

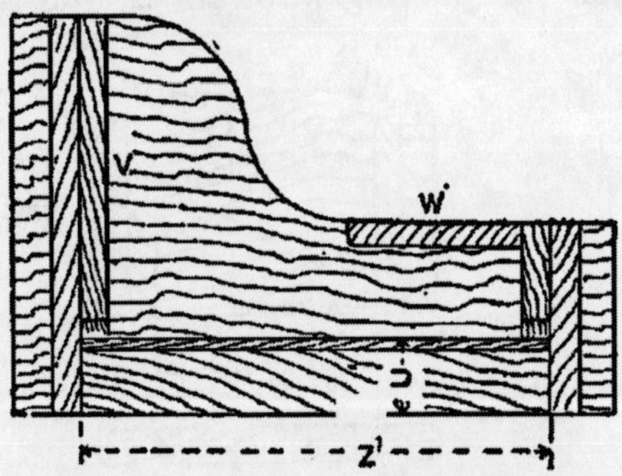

Fig. 218.

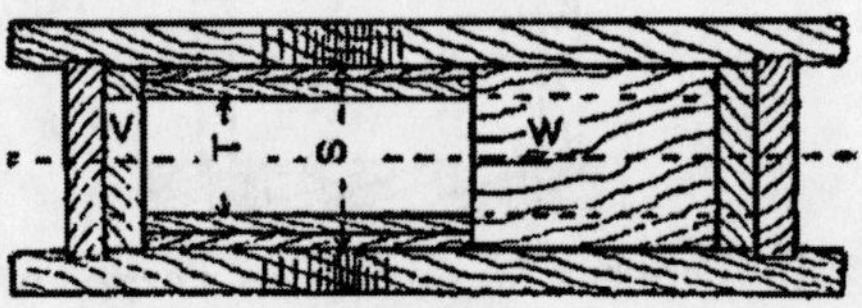

Fig. 219.

Figs. 218 and 219.—Core-box for Taking out Portion of Gap Lathe-bed.

bed casting, and that their outlines and dimensions lengthwise must correspond with the outlines of the bed, and also that of certain dimensions measured lengthwise. These core-boxes are shown in Figs. 213 to 223, with dimension reference letters corresponding with similar lettering on the casting (Figs. 204 to 206) and pattern (Figs. 207 to 210). They are drawn in the positions in which the cores are rammed and placed in the mould—that is, upside down.

Figs. 213 and 214 show the core-box for coring out the portion P of the bed (Figs. 204 to 206); Figs. 215 to 217 that for coring out Q; Figs. 218 and 219, that for R; Figs. 220 and 221, for the gap D; Figs. 222 and 223, for the recess N. A cross-section of one main bed-box is shown at the left-hand of Figs. 215 to 217. That is also correct for Figs. 218 and 219, and the lower portion of it also for Figs. 213 and 214.

Taking the sectional dimensions of the main boxes first: the distances S (Figs. 213 to 219) correspond with the distance S between the ribs A (Figs. 204 to 206), the distance T with the distance W between the bearers B, B in Figs. 204 to 206, minus the planing allowances, the actual distance

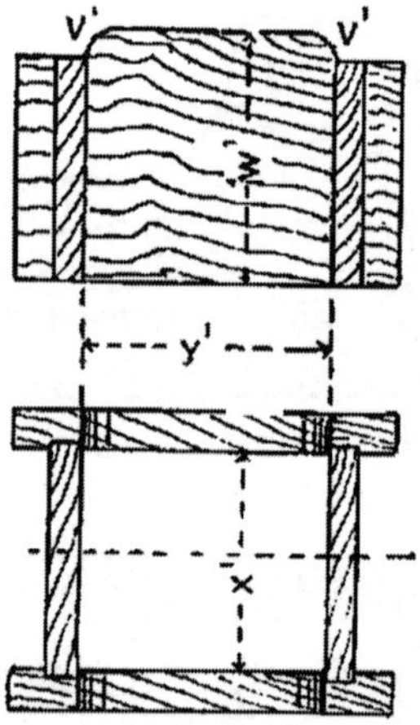

Fig. 220.

Fig. 221.

Figs. 220 and 221.—Core-box for Coring out Portion of Gap Lathe-bed.

corresponding with the width T of the prints G, in Fig. 207. The total depth of the boxes will equal the total depth of the bed pattern, plus the planing allowance on the faces of the bearers B, B, plus the thickness of the prints G. The thickness of the internal bearer strips equals the thickness U of the bearers B, B (Figs. 204 to 206), plus their planing allowance on their top and under faces, plus the thickness of the prints G (Fig. 207). The curved outlines of the boxes (Figs. 215 to 219) correspond with the curved outlines of the pattern of the bed below the gap (Figs. 204 to 208).

The cross ribs C, in the casting (Figs. 204 to 206), are seen formed in the core-boxes (Figs. 213 to 219) at V, and the positions of these ribs in the casting determine the lengths of the boxes; each core ends against the face of a rib. They could also be made to end over the centre of a rib. Or alternatively the entire interior of the casting could be taken out with a single core, but there are objections to this. The method shown in Figs. 213 to 223 is the most suitable. In Figs. 213 to 219, the lengths Y, Z, Z′ of the boxes respectively coincide in each case with the lengths Y, Z, Z′ shown in the casting (Figs. 204 to 206). The box (Figs. 213 and 214) includes two cross-ribs; Figs. 215 to 217, one; Figs. 218 and 219, two.

In the boxes (Figs. 213, 214, 218, and 219) facing pieces

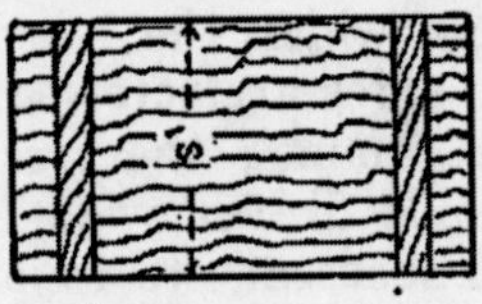

Fig. 222.

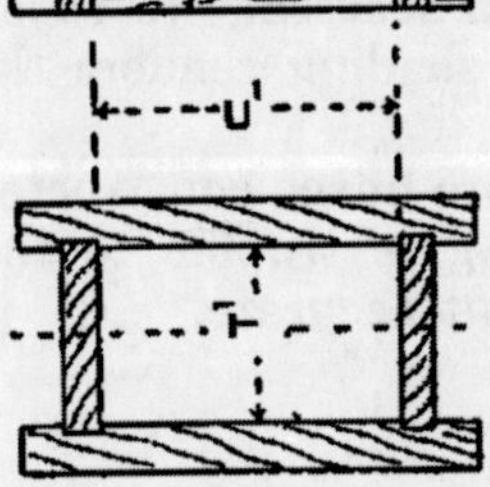

Fig. 223.

Figs. 222 and 223.—Core-box for Taking out Portion of Gap Lathe-bed.

W are seen inserted next the ends. These form the supplementary thicknesses of the facings E cast on the bottom of the bed (Figs. 204 to 206), the remaining portions of which, L, are put on the pattern (Figs. 208 and 210).

In Figs. 213 to 219 each core-box is shown made as a distinct and separate box. They would not be made thus in the pattern-shop, unless a good many lathe beds were wanted all alike. If only two or three beds were required one core-box would be made to do duty for Figs. 215 to 219, then after one core has been made for Figs. 215 to 217, the necessary alterations in length and in regard to the supplementary facing-piece and cross-rib would be made to adapt the box for Figs. 218 and 219.

The box (Figs. 220 and 221) is for coring-out the gap, the core dropping into the impression of the print H (Figs.

208 and 209). The length Y′ corresponds with the length of the gap, X′ with the width over the ribs A in Figs. 204 to 206, W′ with the depth plus the print thickness which stands above the bearers (Fig. 208). The convex edges at V′ (Figs. 213 and 214) form the radius at the bottom of the gap.

Figs. 222 and 223 show the box for coring out the metal underneath the gap. Its length U′ coincides with the length of the print I (Figs. 208 and 210), its width T′ with the width of the print, and its depth S′ with the depth of the recess, plus the print thickness.

The method of construction of the core-boxes is rendered clear by the drawings; grooved sides and ends form the framework within which the bearing-strips and cross-ribs are fitted. The sides are screwed to the ends, so that when the cores are rammed the screws can be removed and the sides and ends drawn away from the cores. For this reason it is not necessary to taper the interior of the boxes at all. The shading renders the disposition of the timber apparent.

A pattern and core-boxes constructed according to these directions will not give trouble to the moulder, and the casting will come out accurate.

CHAPTER XI.

HEADSTOCK AND POPPET PATTERNS.

PATTERNS for fast headstocks, suitable for small lathes of types operated by treadle or by power, will be described first in this chapter. There is no need to give any dimensions, or to show the castings as distinct from their patterns. Three types will be illustrated, the forms and proportions of which will be adapted for all lathes suitable for light turning, for centres ranging from 3 in. up to 6 in. or 7 in.

Figs. 224 to 226 illustrate a pattern for a headstock with back-gear, suitable for hand- or for slide-rest turning, and intended to take hardened steel cone collars for the mandrel. There are three ways in which this could be moulded. One is upside down, the collar bosses being in the bottom of the mould and the flat foot in the top. Then the sand above the projecting lugs C would have to be carried on drawback plates, and this is not desirable for small headstocks. The second way is to make the pattern solid, and to mould upon its side, with the back-gear bearings C in the bottom. This necessitates a moulder's awkward down-joint, running coincidently with the curved edge in the top half, down as far as the centre plane of the head, and this method is not recommended. The third and also the best way is to joint the mould exactly along the central plane H H of the pattern, having one half then altogether in the top, and one half altogether in the bottom. To facilitate this method of moulding, it is desirable, though not absolutely necessary, to joint and dowel the pattern in the same plane H H, and this is the way in which the figures show it to be done. Then the only portions which have to be left loose from the main body of the pattern are the bosses I I for the back-gear, and these are retained in correct position during ramming by means of a central skewer thrust through them to the pattern body.

The strongest method of construction is indicated in Figs. 224 to 226. The base A planed up in two widths and dowelled, receives the two uprights B, each also, of course, in two widths. The base is rebated to take the uprights, or the uprights may be dovetailed into the base. The horns or bearing portions C for the back-gear tenoned into the uprights B are shown as separate pieees. This is to prevent the possible warping or shrinkage of those por-

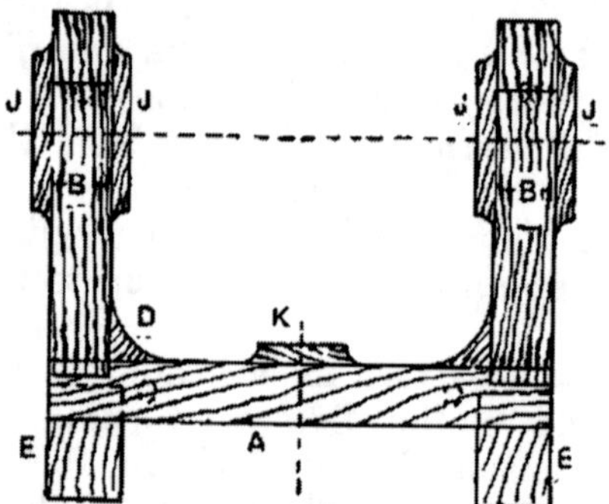

Fig. 224.

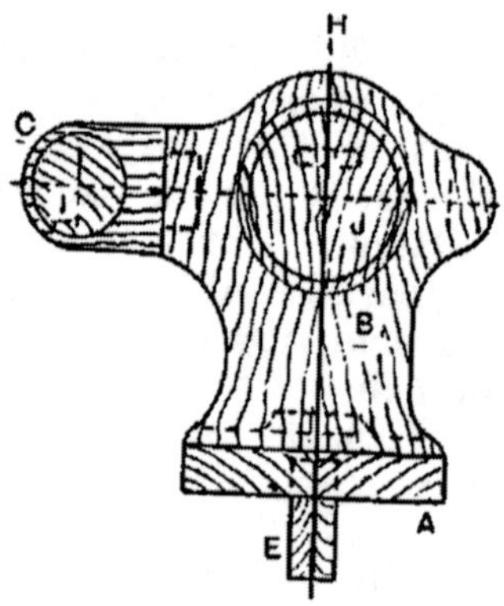

Fig. 225.

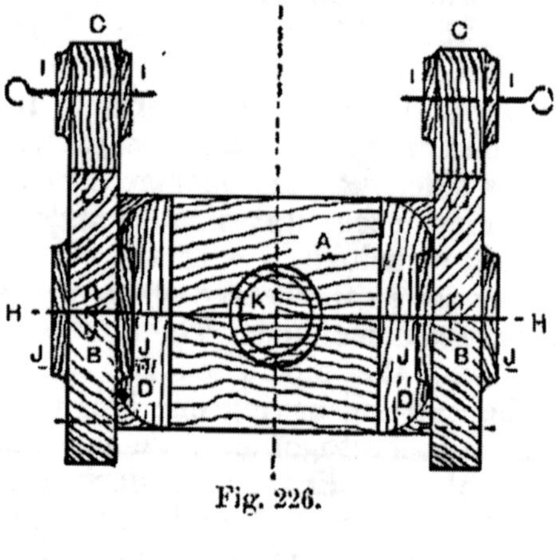

Fig. 226.

Figs. 224 to 226.—Back-geared Headstock Pattern.

tions of the pattern out of truth, which might happen if the horns were cut from the solid with the uprights. After the rebating is done, and the uprights cut to their outlines, they are glued and screwed to the base. It is better then to glue in the hollows D as square blocks, after the glue is dry, and then to plane the hollow portions, than to plane them before insertion. The pieces E used for the setting of the headstock on the bearers, may be tenoned into the feet as shown. The bosses J which have to be bored for the collars, are turned in halves and nailed on the uprights; so also is the boss K for the holding-down bolts. Bosses to be cut in halves should not be turned solid and sawn through the middle—at least not in the best work, though it is often done for rough patterns. They should be planed to make a joint previous to being turned, and then fastened to the face-plate with the joint in the centre, and so turned. The bosses I I are solid and loose.

The holes are not shown cored as it is better not to core holes in small headstocks because castings are frequently unsound and spongy near to cored holes; and if holes

Fig. 227.—Round Parallel Prints.

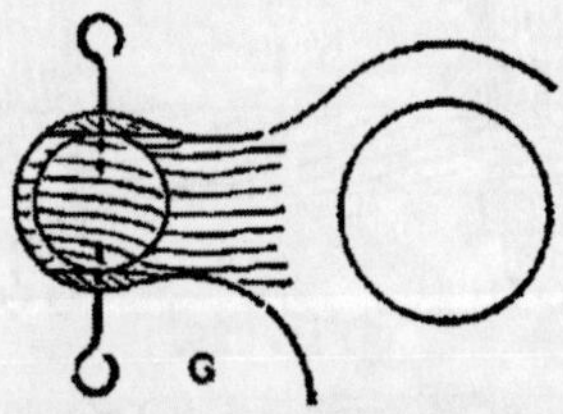

Fig. 228.—Curved Horn for Mandrel Bearings.

are cast out of centre they give much more trouble in boring than if boring is done out of the solid. In no case should the holes be cored in the back-gear bosses, that being a troublesome job, involving the use of deep drop prints. If holes are cored for the main mandrel collars, then plain round parallel prints must be put on in the manner indicated at Fig. 227. But even then the cored holes should give ample margin for boring say $\frac{3}{8}$ in. in diameter.

The horns for the back-gear mandrel bearings are shown running parallel outwards, but they are often curved as shown in Fig. 228. In that case the portions of the boss that stand out beyond the width of the narrowest part of the neck must be skewered on loosely as shown, to be drawn back into the mould after the removal of the main body of the pattern.

The headstock pattern shown in Figs. 229 to 231 is of a type much used for small hand-lathes with gut-driven pulleys. The method of putting the parts of the pattern together is similar to that shown in the previous example, but this has been drawn to show how such a pattern should be made if unjointed. It would be preferable to joint and dowel it like the last, but many small patterns

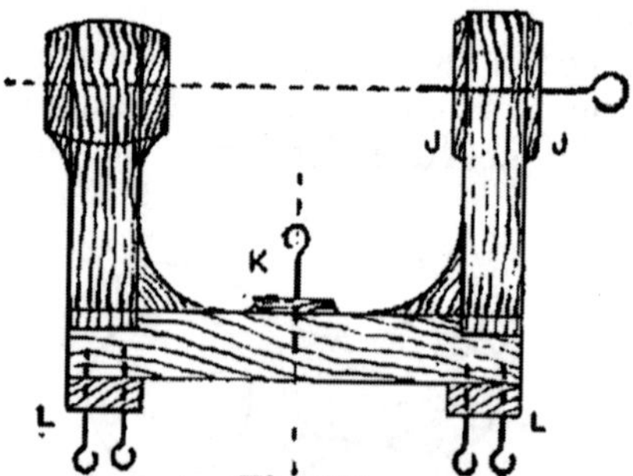

Fig. 229.

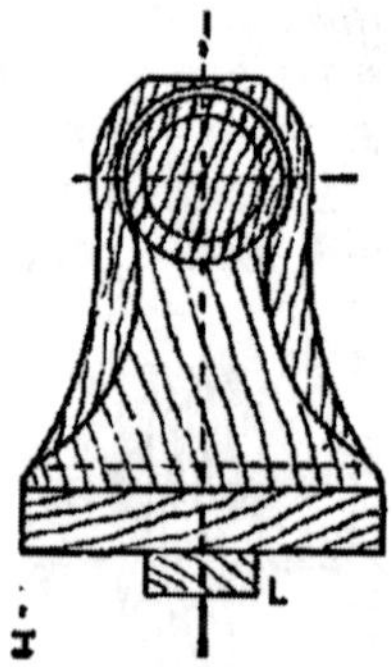

Fig. 230.

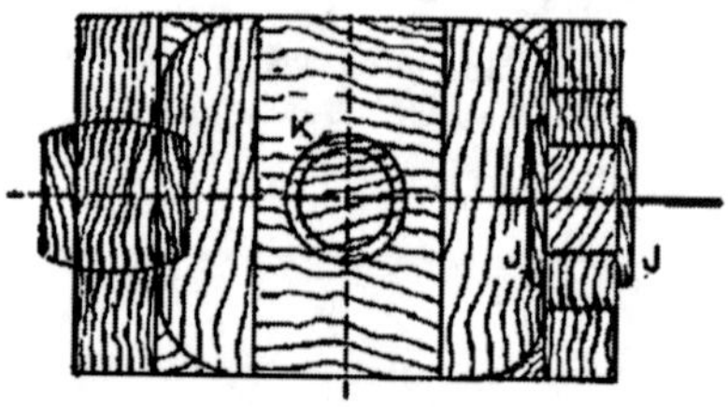

Fig. 231.

Figs. 229 to 231.—Small Headstock Pattern.

are made solid. The pattern will mould on its side, and the moulder's sand-joint will run from H to I round the upper curved edges of the uprights. Then it will be necessary to skewer on loosely the bosses J, the boss K, and the guides L, in the manner shown. The timber shading indicates the various pieces used and the best direction of the grain.

Figs. 232 to 234 show another head suitable for a hand-turning lathe, but made for divided brass bearings in the front instead of for steel cones. The pattern must be jointed along the centre, H H. The seating for the brasses is cored out, the prints being shown at I, a plain square core-box, shown in Figs. 235 and 236, being made to correspond. The uprights are shown not rebated

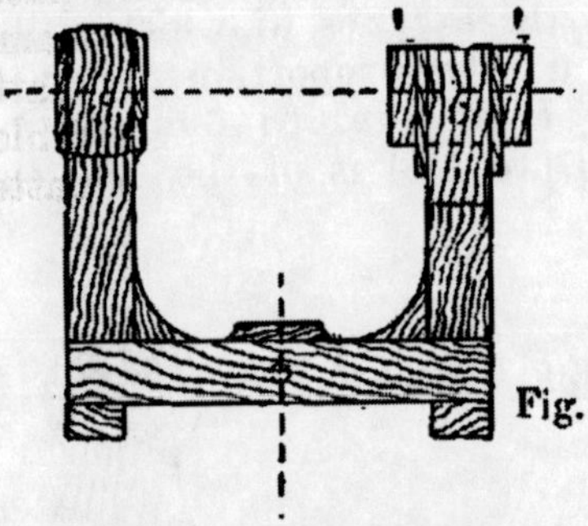

Fig. 232.

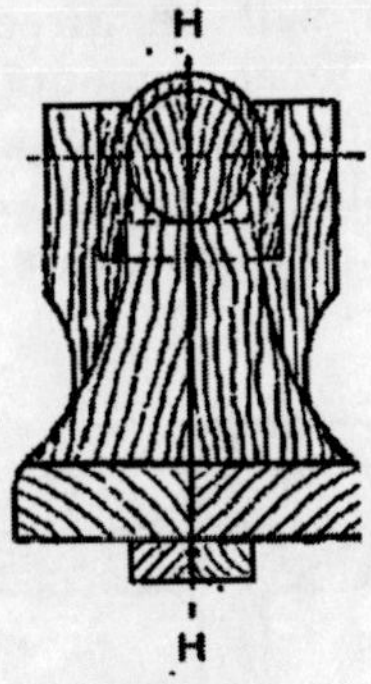

Fig. 233.

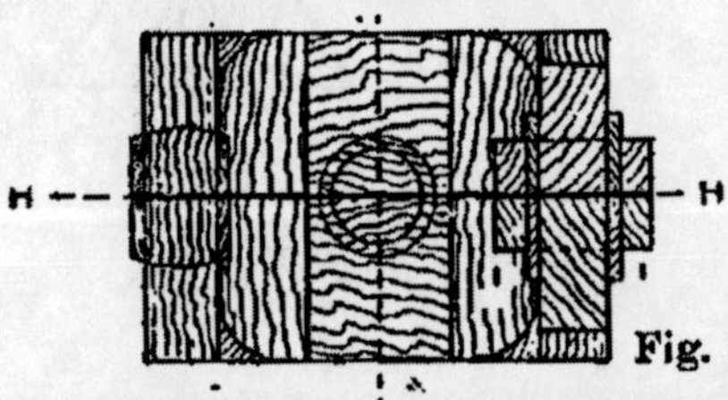

Fig. 234.

Figs. 232 to 234.—Small Headstock Pattern with Split Bearing.

into the foot, but simply butted to it. This is good enough in small patterns, because the gluing-in of the hollows serves to keep the uprights from becoming knocked out of place during moulding. In Figs. 232 to

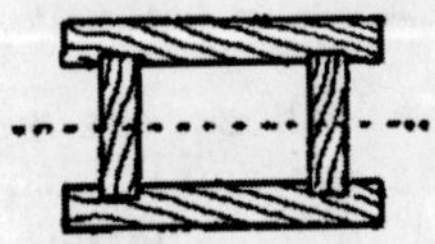

Fig. 235.

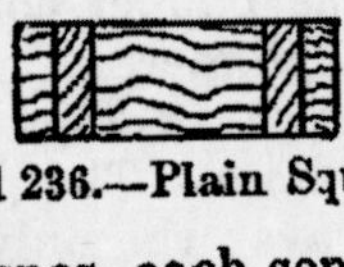

Fig. 236.

Figs. 235 and 236.—Plain Square Core-box.

234, as in the former ones, each separate piece is indicated by its appropriate sectioning.

The taper on these patterns is so slight that it may be almost neglected. If the pattern parts are made thinner by the difference of two or three shavings only on the sides which are lowermost in the mould than on the higher sides, that will be sufficient to afford ready delivery.

The fast heads of lathes having been described, attention will be directed to the construction of patterns for the loose or poppet heads, three types of which will be discussed. Each one is suitably proportioned for the smaller size of lathes, of from 3-in. to 6-in. or 7-in. centres. The first (Figs. 237 to 243) is of the type used

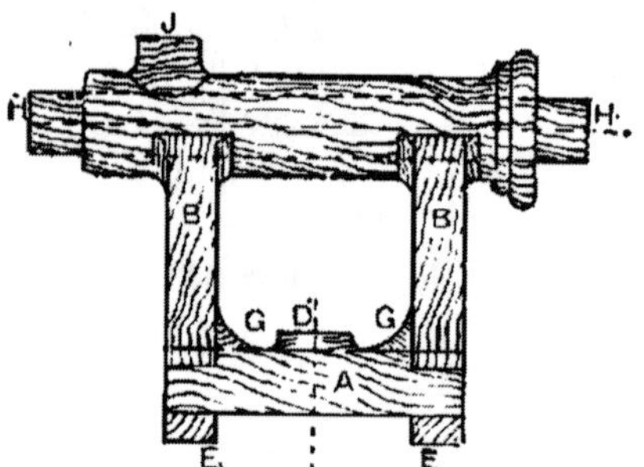

Fig. 237.

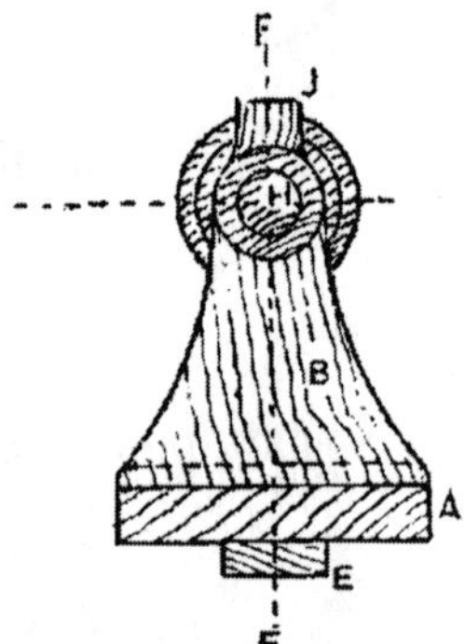

Fig. 238.

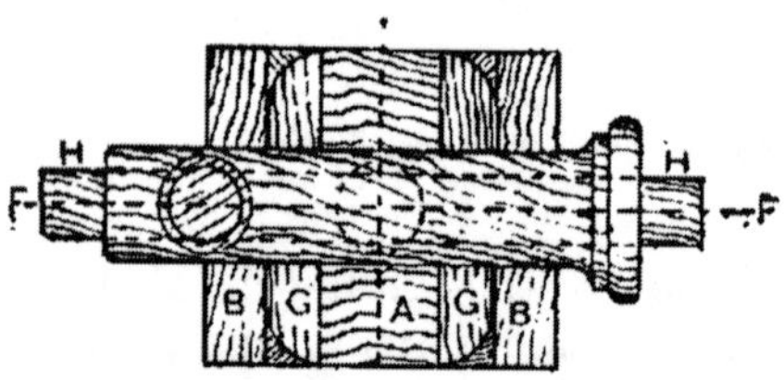

Fig. 239.

Figs. 237 to 239.—Heavy Lathe Poppet Pattern.

for the larger class of lathes; the second (Figs. 244 to 246) is more often made for small lathes; while the third (Figs. 247 to 249) is of a rather simpler type, formerly used more than at present, the poppet consisting of a pointed screw only instead of a cylinder.

The poppet-heads shown in Figs. 237 to 243 may be moulded in one of three ways. The pattern may be made solid and moulded sideways; the only pieces which would then have to be left loose are the hold-down boss D and the guides E, and these would have to be skewered on. The objection to this pattern is the awkward down-jointing and lifting where the barrel is united to the vertical webs B.

Another way is to make the barrel loose from the rest of the pattern, the pattern then moulding as shown at Figs. 240 and 241, in which figures the barrel is shown

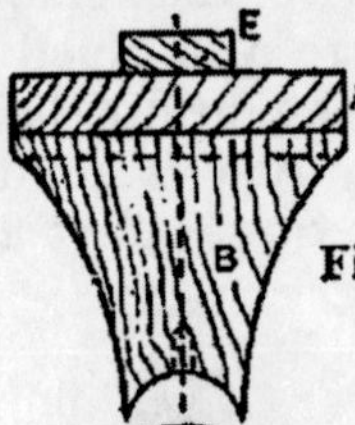

Fig. 240.

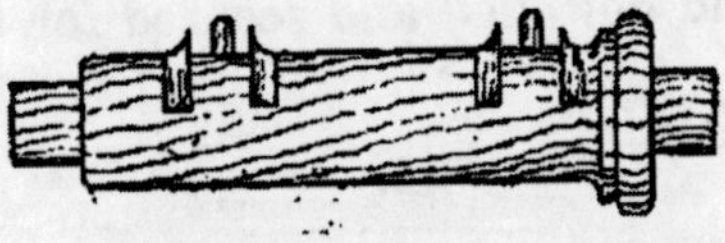

Fig. 242.

Fig. 241.

Figs. 240 and 241.—Moulding Barrel for Lathe Poppet. Fig. 242.—Barrel for Lathe Poppet, with Dowels and Hollows.

away from the uprights, in order to indicate how the two portions of the pattern are fitted and dowelled. Of course, in that case the small fillet seen in Fig. 237, where the vertical ribs B meet the barrel, must not be attached to the verticals, or they would prevent the withdrawal of the pattern from the sand. If introduced in the pattern at all they must be fitted round the barrel as shown in Fig. 242. They may be let in grooves as shown, or fitted round with a gouge, and glued, or flexible hollows may be fitted round. But it is not necessary to fit small hollows like these to the smaller class of patterns, because the moulder will sleek the angles if told to do so. For

Fig. 243.—Turning Poppet Barrel

standard repetition work they should, however, be always inserted. This is a very good and common way of making these patterns, and it ensures sound metal about the barrel, where it is most wanted. It is the method illustrated in Figs. 237 to 239.

Another method equally good is to joint the pattern along the central plane F F (Fig. 238). Then no part is left loose, and everything is in favour of easy moulding. The foot A will be prepared first in two pieces, jointed and dowelled along the plane F F, and the uprights B B will be either rebated into it, as shown, or made to abut simply, then glued and screwed. The hollows G are also glued in. The barrel is turned with its prints H, the prints being made parallel. The barrel is in halves, and is jointed and dowelled and secured for turning—not turned first and

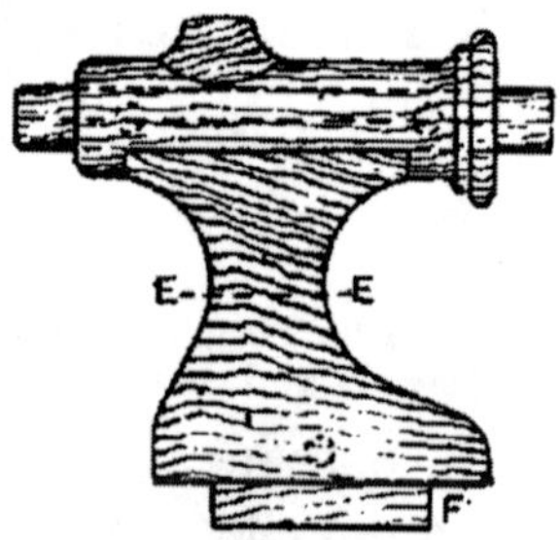

Fig. 244.

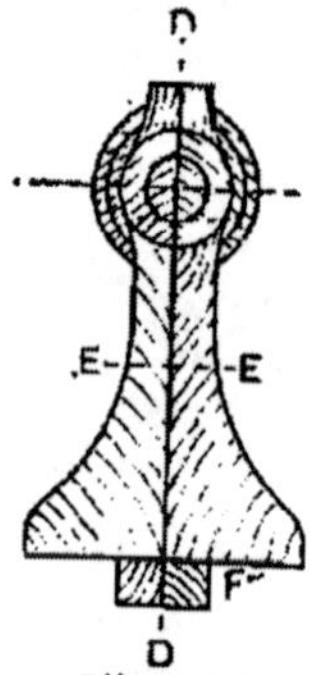

Fig. 245.

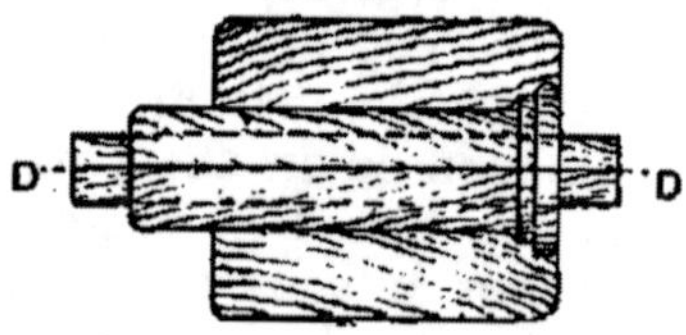

Fig. 246.

Figs. 242 to 246.—Well-designed Lathe Poppet Pattern.

sawn through afterwards. In a small piece of work like this, clips need not be used for securing the two halves during turning; instead, common wood screws are inserted in the roughly-prepared stuff a little way beyond the ends of the prints, as illustrated in Fig. 243, which shows the turned barrel, with its prints, leaving only the ends into which the screws are driven to be sawn off. The barrel is fitted to the uprights B either by the cutting-out of the latter to fit the barrel, similarly to the method shown at Figs. 240 and 241; or the ends of the uprights may be left straight, and grooves cut across the barrel to receive them. In either case the uprights are glued to the barrel.

Hollows like those shown may be glued in, strips of leather being as good as anything. The boss J may be fitted round the barrel in halves, and worked to shape by hand. The nailing on of the boss D and the guides E completes the pattern.

The poppet shown in Figs. 244 to 246 is one of the neatest and stiffest in use for small lathes. It must be moulded on its side, and may be unjointed; but it is better to joint it along the plane D, as shown, because the outline

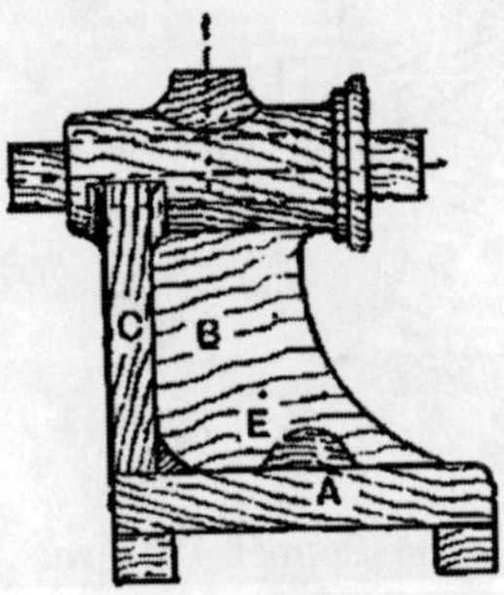

Fig. 247.

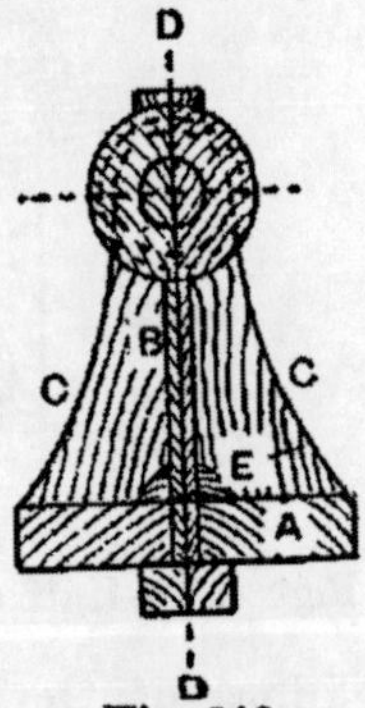

Fig. 248.

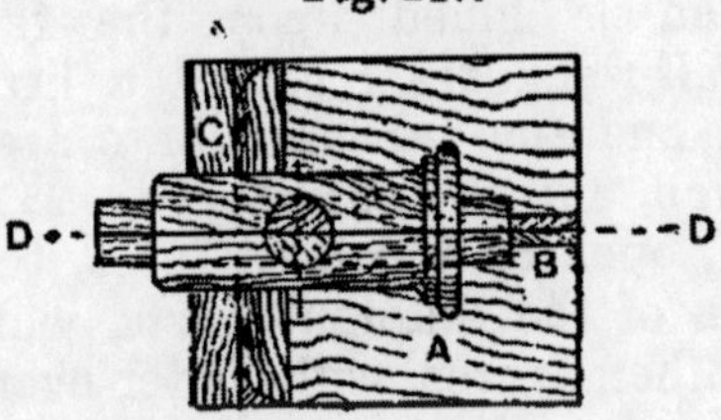

Fig. 249.

Figs. 247 to 249.—Plain Lathe Poppet Pattern.

can then be marked off in the joint of the pattern. The barrel may be worked by hand solid with the body, in which case the beading should be turned separately, and nailed on. Or the barrel may be turned and the body fitted to it, as shown, either by fitting it to the curvature, or by leaving the top part of the body flat and cutting out a portion across the barrel to receive it. The section across the centre of the body E is rectangular, with corners well rounded. The shape of the sides in Fig. 245 will be worked through by the aid of a template, and the angles rounded into the curved ends, which are marked from the joint faces. The guide-piece F is nailed on the bottom, completing the pattern. The timber graining shows the best disposition of the grain. A cross section at E E is shown below Fig. 245.

Fig. 247 to 249 illustrate a plain poppet, easily made and readily fitted up. The pattern must be moulded upon its side, and should be jointed in the plane D as shown. The foot A is made in two pieces, less than the full width

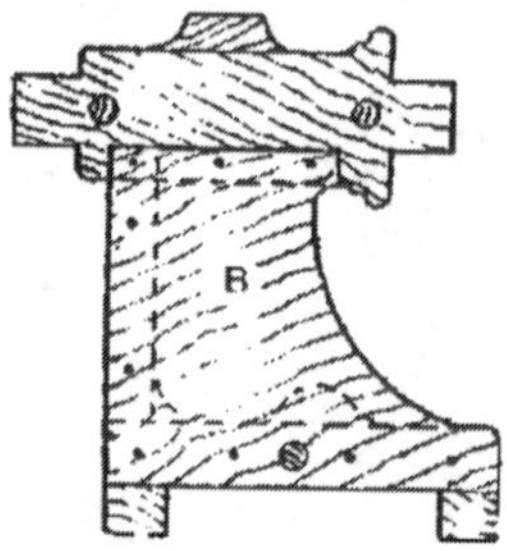

Fig. 250.—Half of Lathe Poppet Pattern.

by the thickness of the vertical web B, which is made in two thicknesses and is glued upon the feet. At the upper part, the half-webs are recessed a little way into the turned barrel, and the vertical ribs C are fitted between the foot, the web, and the barrel. Fig. 250 shows one half of the pattern, open on the joint faces, to assist in illustrating the union of the different parts, which, by a comparison with the other figures, will render everything clear without further explanation; E indicates the boss which provides metal over the hold-down bolt.

CHAPTER XII.

SLIDE-REST PATTERNS.

THE illustrations accompanying this chapter represent the pattern work for an ordinary type of lathe slide-rest, beginning with the saddle and proceeding upwards. The castings are not shown separately, but in the case of cored portions the forms of the cores, as they would appear in the castings, are indicated by means of dotted lines. This is mentioned to avoid confusion, for these dotted lines have no meaning in the patterns themselves which the figures represent.

The saddle pattern is shown in Figs. 251 to 255. Fig. 251 is a plan view as the casting stands on the lathe; Fig. 252 is an underneath plan showing the pattern as it lies in the mould; Fig. 253 an end view at the front; Fig. 254 an end view at the rea and Fig. 255 a side view from next the headstock.

A saddle pattern of large area should be framed together in three pieces, with half lap joints. Small saddles of from 12 in. to 15 in. in length can be cut from solid stuff, and the core prints will serve to keep the main plate true. The most suitable disposition of the grain for this mode of construction is shown in Figs. 251 to 255. In Figs. 253, 254, and 255 the thickness of the main piece is seen, with various fittings on both sides, while the plan views of these pieces are shown by Figs. 251 and 252. On the top face there are prints, and on the bottom face (Fig. 252) are broad facing pieces, which are planed to slide on the top of the bed, strips for the guiding edges, a bracket for the back shaft, and blocks for the attachment of the apron.

In these figures, A is the print for coring out the recess for the cross traverse or surfacing screw. The core-box is shown in Figs. 256 and 257. All the patterns and core-boxes here illustrated are to an exact and uniform scale, so that comparisons between the corresponding dimensions of prints and boxes can be easily made, while the dotted

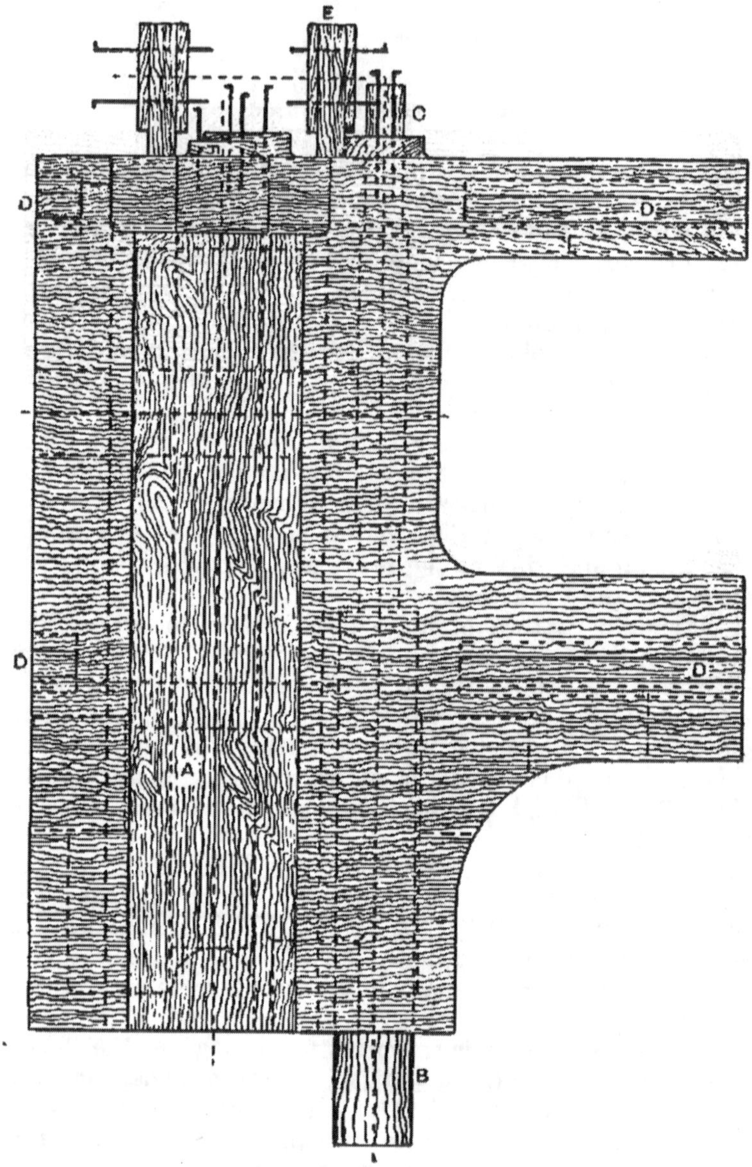

Fig. 251.—Plan of Slide-rest Saddle Pattern.

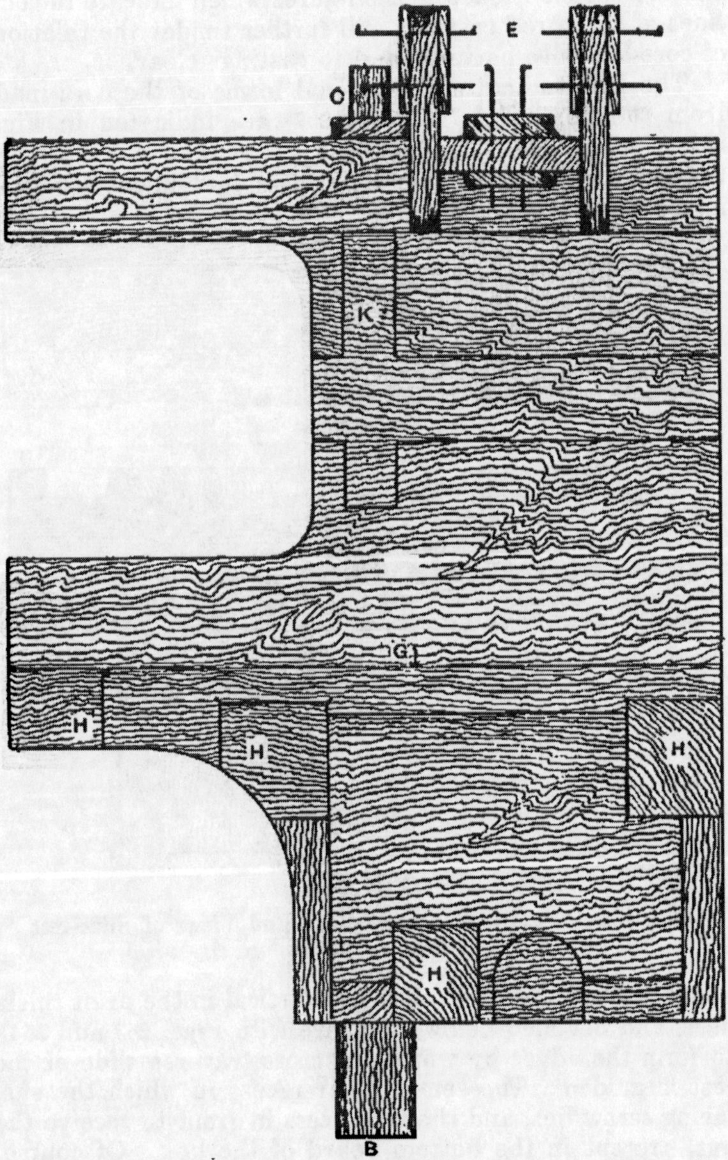

Fig. 252.—Underneath Plan of Slide-rest Saddle Pattern.

lines before mentioned in the figures which indicate the outlines of the cored castings will further render the relations of core-boxes to patterns and to castings clear.

The longitudinal and sectional forms of the core made from the box (Figs. 256 and 257) are indicated in Figs. 251, 253, and 254. The box in Figs. 256 and 257 is framed together with grooved ends, and is laid upon a bottom

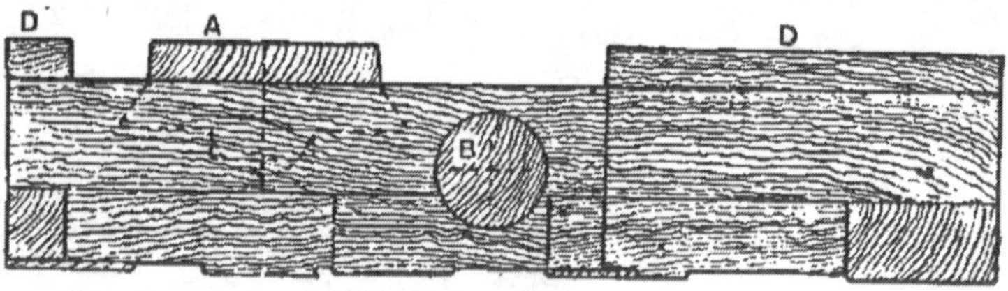

Fig. 253.

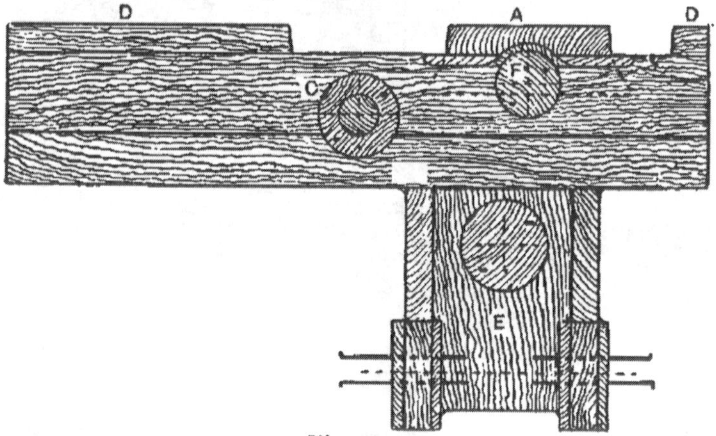

Fig. 254.

Figs. 253 and 254.—Front and Back End Views of Slide-rest Saddle Pattern.

board. The sides of the box are vertical in the print thickness, and bevelled below (compare with Figs. 253 and 254), to form the edges by which the cross traverse slide of the rest is guided. The semicircular recess in which the surfacing screw lies, and the flat recess in front to receive the nut, are cut in the bottom board of the box. Of course, the box framing is not fastened to the bottom board in any way, because that would prevent delivery of the core. It is simply retained truly in relation to the board by

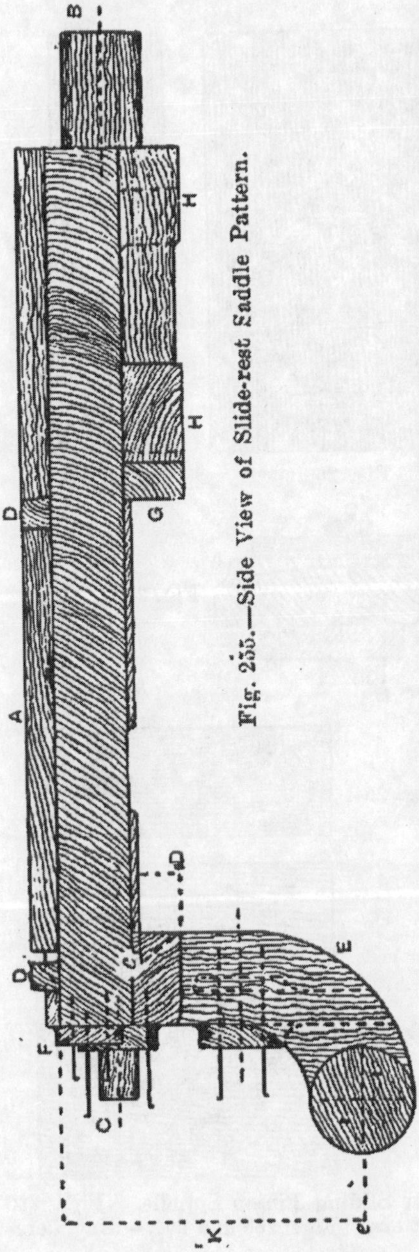

Fig. 255.—Side View of Slide-rest Saddle Pattern.

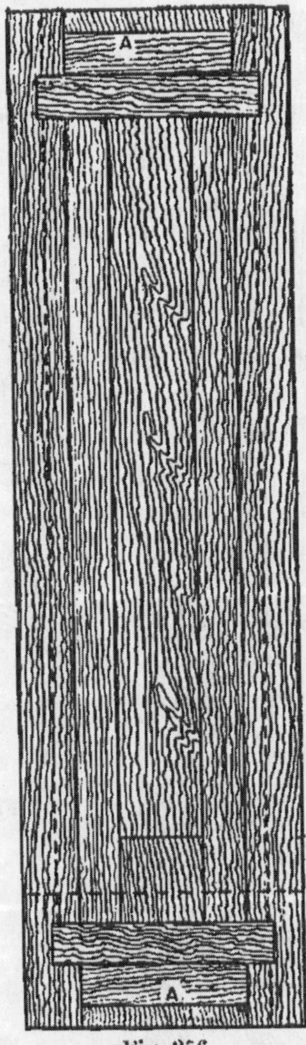

Fig. 256.

Fig. 257.

Figs. 256 and 257.—Core-box to Form Recess for Surfacing Screw.

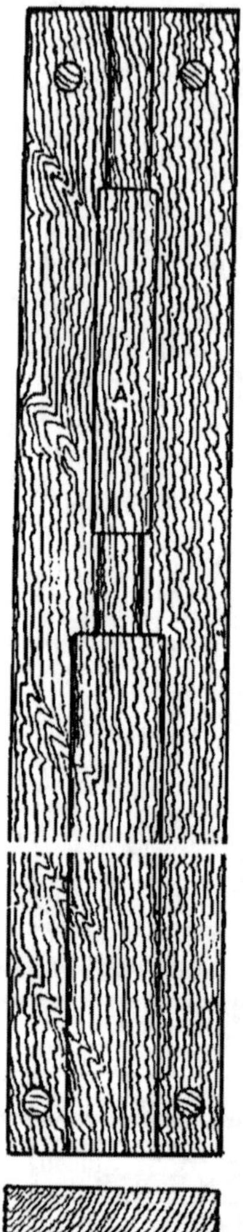

Fig. 25 .

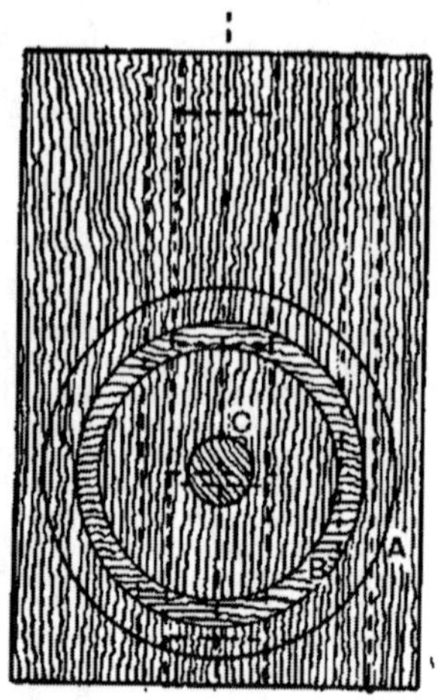

Fig. 260.

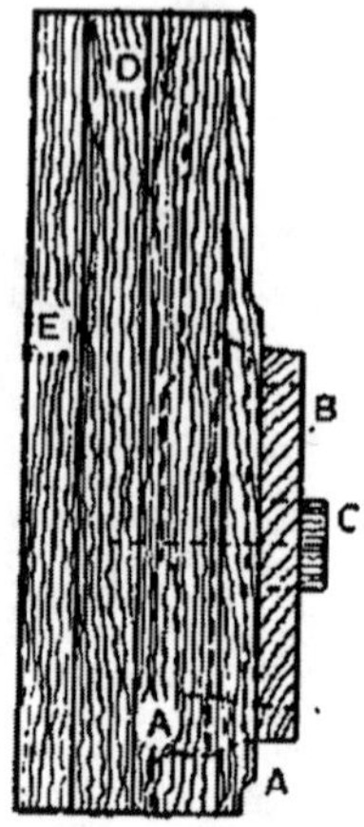

Fig. 261.

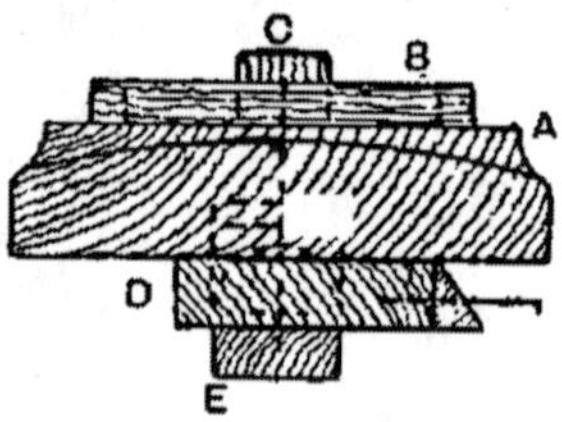

Fig. 262.

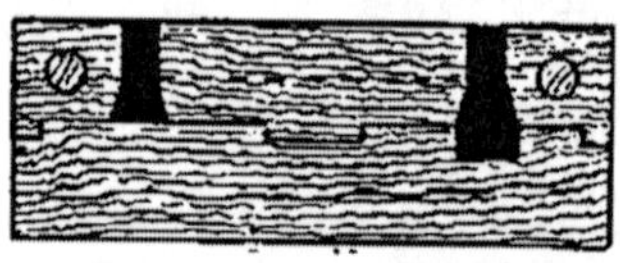

Fig. 264.

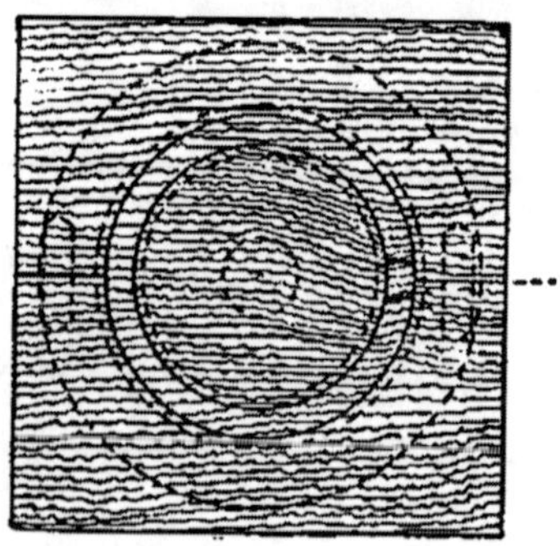

Fig. 263.

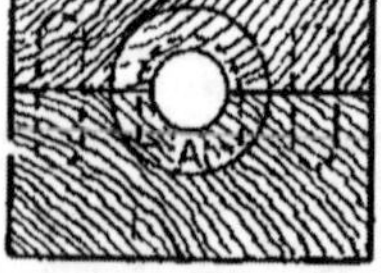

Fig. 259.

Fig. 258 and 259.—Core-box for Sliding Pinion Spindle. Figs. 260 to 262.—Surfacing Slide Pattern. Figs. 263 and 264.—Ring Core-box for Surfacing Slide.

means of the pieces A nailed on the board, or by means of dowels, the method being merely a matter of choice.

In Figs. 251 to 255 B and C show prints which core out the hole shown dotted in Fig. 251, for the spindle which makes the connection between the back shaft gear and the rack and pinion sliding movement at the front. The enlargement of the hole next the print B is for the reception of the sleeve pinion, which renders the sliding movement automatic. It is not necessary to make the prints B, C of the drop or pocket form; round prints will answer as well. In this case B will be nailed on, and the moulder will joint down to its centre; C will be nailed on its boss, but both together will be held with loose brads as shown, to be drawn backwards into the mould. The print B is twice the length of C. The moulder will thrust the core endwise into the impression of C, leaving then at the other end a bearing surface in B equal to half the length of B.

A core-box must be made for this in halves, dowelled together. It is shown in plan by Fig. 258, and in end view by Fig. 259, one half havi-- been removed to expose the hole. In the part A the core cuts through the saddle, corresponding with the portion K left clear of facings in Fig. 252. The prints D (Figs. 251, 253, 254, and 255) are for tee-grooved cores by which work is bolted to the saddle. A core-box must also be made for these, framed similarly to that in Figs. 256 and 257, but without a bottom board.

The bracket E for the back shaft (Figs. 251, 252, 254, and 255) is assumed to be cast on, as is the usual practice in small lathes. It is situated rather awkwardly for casting, being deep and having perpendicular web faces, with bosses, and being close to the edge of the saddle which slides along the rear edge of the bed. A clean and accurate way to mould it would be by putting a block print K (Fig. 255) against one face, and coring out that, with the bosses included by the print, leaving the other face to deliver itself in the top—the saddle moulding upside down. There is, however, the strip shown dotted at C, and this should be cast in order to lessen planing. But to do that would involve leaving the bracket E loosely dowelled, otherwise the edge *c* could not be moulded. But it is undesirable to leave such brackets loose, because they are liable to be rammed out of truth, and thus throw the boss for the back shaft out. On the whole the best plan to adopt is that shown.

The bracket is fastened on, and the edge C is cast square, leaving the V to be formed wholly by planing, a lesser

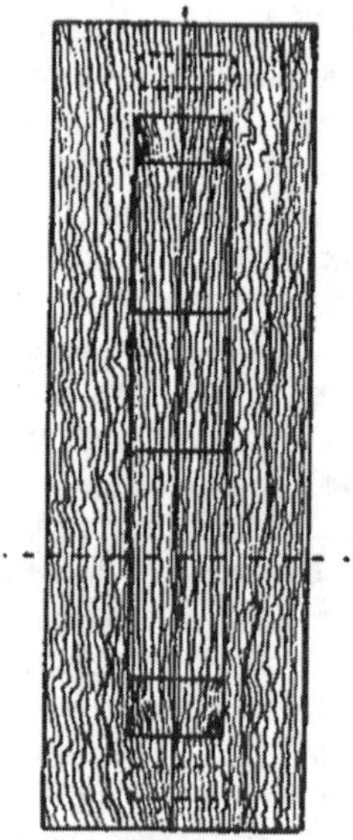

Fig. 265.

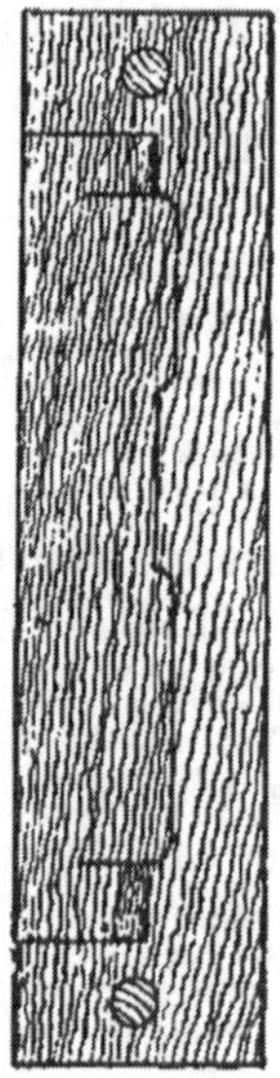

Fig. 266.

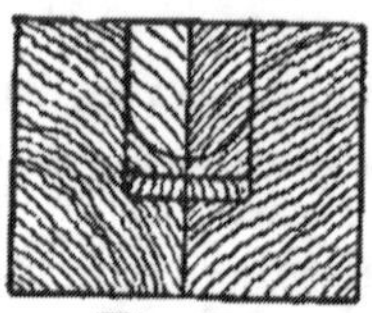

Fig. 267.

Fig. 265.—Core-box to Form Recess for Screw. Fig. 266.—Half Box Opened in Joint Face. Fig. 267.—Transverse Section of Core-box.

evil than having the bracket cast untrue. But a print might be nailed along the edge as at D, and the strip cored. The bosses on the vertical faces of the bracket are both put on loosely, as also is the one F through which the surfacing screw spindle passes, and the boss faces on E likewise should be loose (Fig. 254). The moulder then joints up to the centre *c*, and half the bracket delivers downwards and half in the top. No holes are cored in it, since that would be troublesome and unnecessary, because such holes should be lined out and drilled through the solid.

The remaindor of the pattern is self-explanatory. Against the edge G (Figs. 252 and 255) the setting-up strip

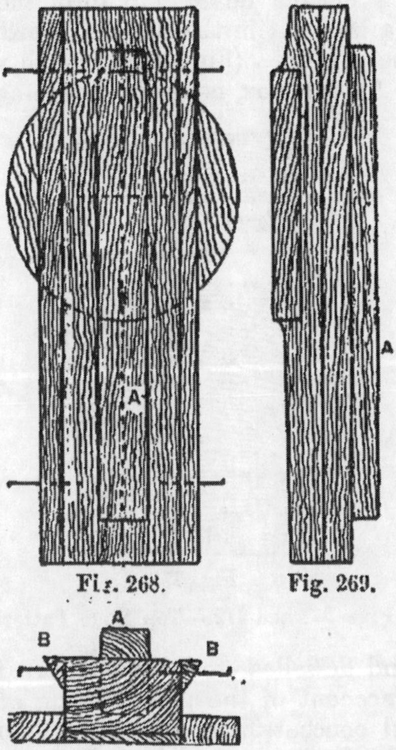

Fig. 268. Fig. 269. Fig. 270.

Figs. 268 to 270.—Swivel Slide Pattern.

goes. The faces H (Figs. 253 and 256) receive the apron casting. Such details will vary in different lathes, and need cause no difficulty. These blocks or facings are all fastened on, but taper is given to the inner edges.

The pattern of the surfacing slide is shown in Figs. 260 to 262, with dotted lines which indicate cored portions. Fig. 260 is a plan, Fig. 261 a side elevation, and Fig. 262

an end elevation; A is the face on which the top slide swivels, and B is a ring print to receive the core round which the clamping bolts move for setting the slide to any angle; C is a pin cast with the slide to act as a centre pivot. The mode of construction is indicated by the shading.

A core-box (Figs. 263 and 264) will be made for the print B. A central disc and an outer jointed ring being attached to a bottom board will form the annular veed groove, and a hole cut in the bottom board will form that portion of the core at A (Fig. 261) through which the bolts are thrust. As the box is made, the ring portion must

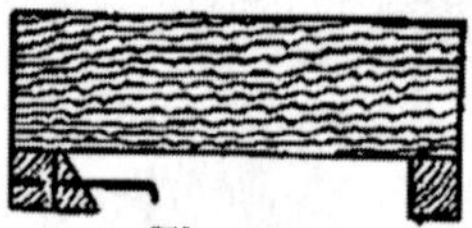

Fig. 272.

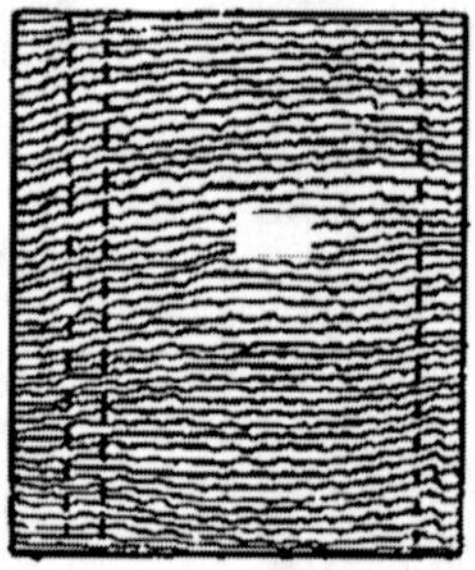

Fig. 271.

Figs. 271 and 272.—Top Slide Pattern.

be divided and dowelled, to be withdrawn in halves horizontally, on account of the undercutting of the vees. It is maintained concentrically by the annulus or shoulder (see Fig. 264). In a small slide it is better not to core this annulus but to bore it out of the solid.

The portion D of the pattern has one square edge, against which the adjustment strip fits, and a bevelled edge which must be put on loosely, either with nails or with dovetails (Fig. 262). The recess for the surfacing screw is cored, E being the print. The core-box is divided and dowelled (Figs. 265 to 267). Fig. 265 shows it in plan, Fig. 266 one half opened in the joint face, and Fig. 267 is a transverse section. The halves are dowelled together,

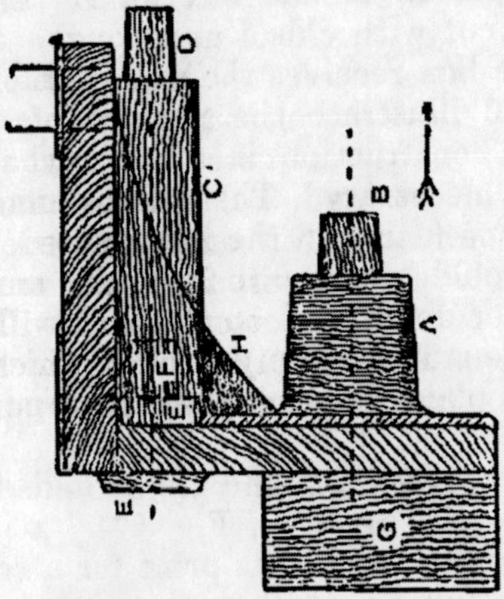

Fig. 274.

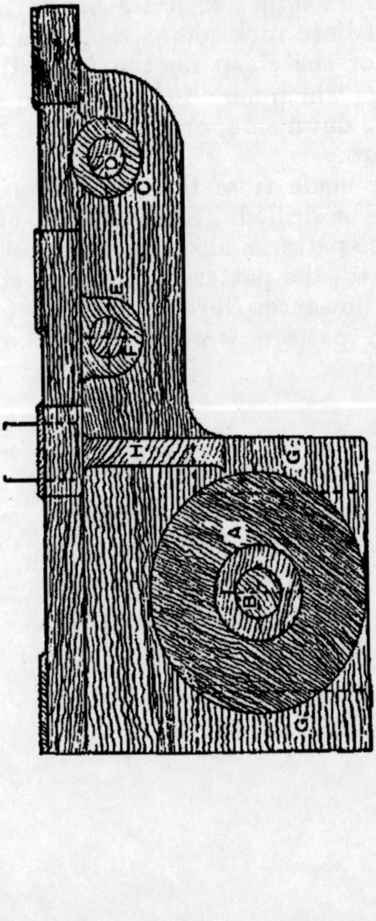

Fig. 273.

Figs. 273 and 274.—Apron Pattern.

and the shape imparted to the interior for clearing the surfacing screw is cut with chisel and gouge. The facing in the centre of the box receives the nut for the screw.

Figs. 268 to 270 illustrate the pattern of the top or swivel slide. The construction is so clearly shown that few comments are necessary. There is one core only, a plain rectangular one fitting in the impression of the print A, and the print moulds downwards. There are two loose pieces B, B tacked or dovetailed on the body. The timber grain shows how the stuff is arranged. The top slide (Figs. 271 and 272) is also plain. There is one loose strip and no coring.

The apron pattern (Figs. 273 and 274) moulds face downwards, as shown by the arrow in Fig. 274. A is the boss for the clasp-nut spindle, and B its print for a round core; C is the boss for the spindle which operates the rack pinion by hand, and D is its print; E, E are bosses for the rack pinion and intermediate rack pinion, and F is their print; G, G are guides for the clasp nut; H is a stiffening rib. The planing facings which match those on the saddle must be left loose on the down side, or else the face must be left plain in the pattern.

In the castings made from the patterns various holes not shown have to be drilled. Some amount of machining not indicated in the patterns also will be necessary. Some nuts will be required, the patterns for them being just like their castings. Allowances for tooling are to be made where required in pattern work and core-boxes to the extent of about $\frac{1}{8}$ in.

CHAPTER XIII.

MISCELLANEOUS PATTERNS AND CORE-BOXES.

In making patterns for the screw-down valve shown in section and plan by Figs. 275 and 276, the wood for the trunk of the body pattern (Fig. 277) is in two pieces; fit them together and then glue a piece of cartridge paper between. All the patterns must be made in two pieces, the joint being at the centre line. When dry the pattern can be turned in the lathe, a brass or iron plate being screwed at each end across the joint, with a countersunk hole in the centre so that it will run true.

The nose of the valve is prepared in two halves, trued to shape with the spokeshave. Test it with, say, four templates made of cardboard or thin zinc cut to suit the half finishing to the centre line; these templates can, of course, be used on both sides, a mixture of tripoli and oil termed rud being put on the edge of the template, which, when applied, leaves a mark at the irregular parts. This process must be repeated till the parts become quite true. Then the nose can be fixed to the trunk with three dowels, great care being exercised in getting it on true. A chisel driven into the joint will split the paper, leaving the pattern in two halves as desired.

The core-box must be very strong to withstand the hammering of the coremaker. Mahogany is very good wood to use, an extra piece being glued and screwed across the grain at the back of each half. The two pieces are fitted together and kept in position with dowels of brass and bushes to suit.

Make the box to the outside lines and begin setting out, laying on the flat side of half the pattern and carefully lining it round. Then remove it and complete the setting out as shown in Fig. 278. Take great care in getting the position of the seating A. Minimise the metal where the article does not require turning, such as inside the body and below the seating, as indicated by the recessed portions; of course, allow extra metal for turning and screwing where necessary.

When the core-box is put together, describe a circle at the top and bottom end of a diameter equal to the points C S (Fig. 277). Also cut a template to the core at the

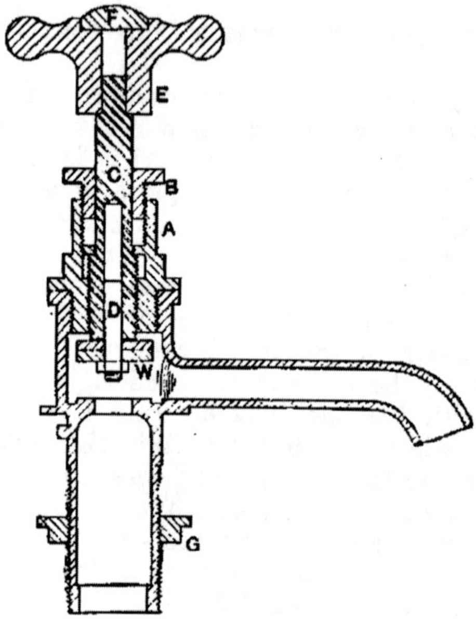

Fig. 275.

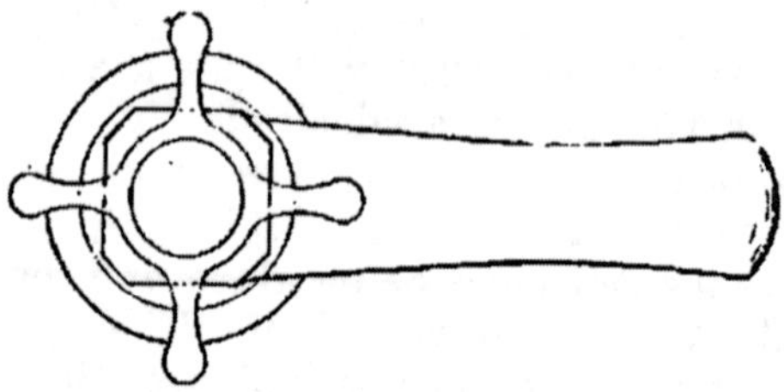

Fig. 276.

Figs. 275 and 276.—Vertical Section and Plan of Screw-down Valve.

mouth of the valve, mark it on the core-box and cut it out, using very sharp, thin gouges for this purpose. Finish carefully to the lines at the ends and put on a thin band of the rud to show the parts finished. Test the remainder of the semicircular parts with a square. The nose part of the core-box is tested by several templates, and, after being sandpapered very smooth, can be varnished with a mixture of shellac varnish and gas black.

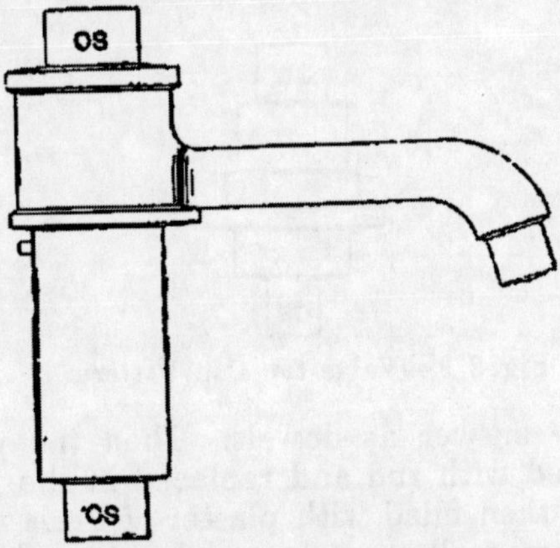

Fig. 277.—Body Pattern for Screw-down Valve.

To make a better box in iron or brass, turn a core to the size and shape required and fix the nose on the trunk. This is also made in two halves, and well varnished or

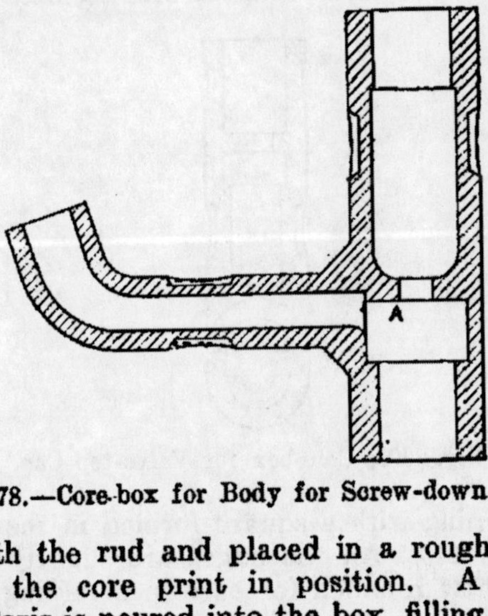

Fig. 278.—Core-box for Body for Screw-down Valve.

painted with the rud and placed in a roughly-made box that holds the core print in position. A quantity of plaster-of-Paris is poured into the box, filling it somewhat above the centre line of the print, and is allowed to dry. The plaster is carefully cut down to the centre line, and the wood core print removed, the sides trimmed, and the slots are cut as shown in Fig. 278; these afterwards form

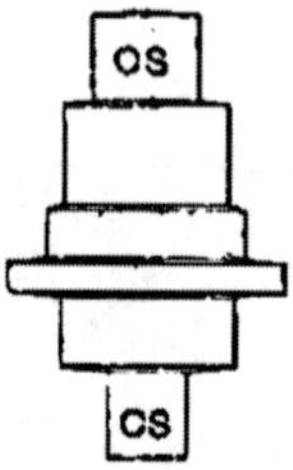

Fig. 279.—Valve-top Cap Pattern.

projections to answer as dowels. Then the whole wood print is painted with rud and replaced in the rough wood box, which is then filled with plaster-of-Paris and allowed to set. Cut away all superfluous plaster and take apart, leaving a plaster pattern for the metal core-box. This, when thoroughly dry, may be varnished, then cast, the shrinkage being sufficient to al...v of the casting being cleaned up.

The pattern of the top cap or stuffing box A (Fig. 275)

Fig. 280.—Core-box for Valve-top Cap.

is a plain turning with a square formed in the middle, as shown in Fig. 279. All the edges are slightly taper, and the ends slightly rounded for ease in moulding, C S being the points. The core-box is illustrated by Fig. 280. Where the square comes the metal is slightly reduced to lighten the casting and to assist the brass finisher. The top part of the cap receives packing cotton.

The top part of the stuffing nut B (Fig. 275) is made hexagon shape, the bottom being round for screwing.

Fig. 281.—Nut Pattern.

Fig. 282.—Half Core-box for Nut.

The nut is immersed wholly in the bottom box of the moulder, and a small core is placed as shown by C S in Fig. 281, the half core-box being shown by Fig. 282.

The spindle C (Fig. 275) has a square formed on the top to receive the knob; the hole in the bottom end is drilled to receive the jumper D. The knob E (Fig. 275) is moulded downwards. The pattern is turned in the lathe, and afterwards cut out to form the four spokes. Fig. 283 shows the core at stays at A. The top receives the pottery plate F (Fig. 275), while the bottom core is squared to fit the spindle. Fig. 284 is a section through the core-box. The jumper is a plain washer with a projection on each side, one entering the drilled spindle, and the other receiving

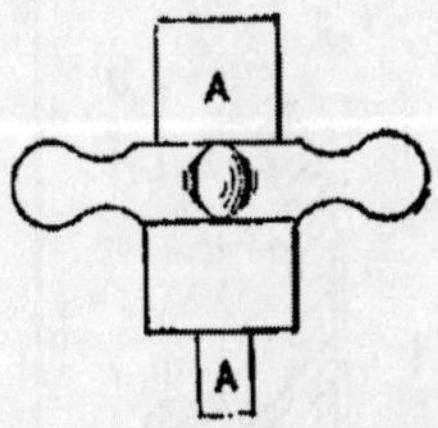

Fig 283.—Knob Pattern.

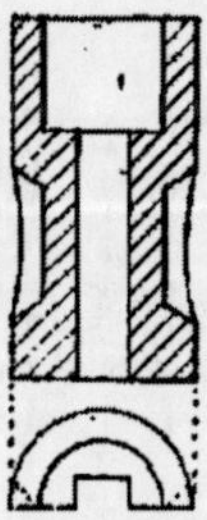

Fig. 284.—Core-box for Knob.

a nut which secures the seating washer W. The fly or running nut G (Fig. 275) is simply a circular screwed washer with a hexagon head. The shrinkage is about $\frac{1}{8}$ in. in the foot, and the amount for turning and screwing is about $\frac{3}{16}$ in.

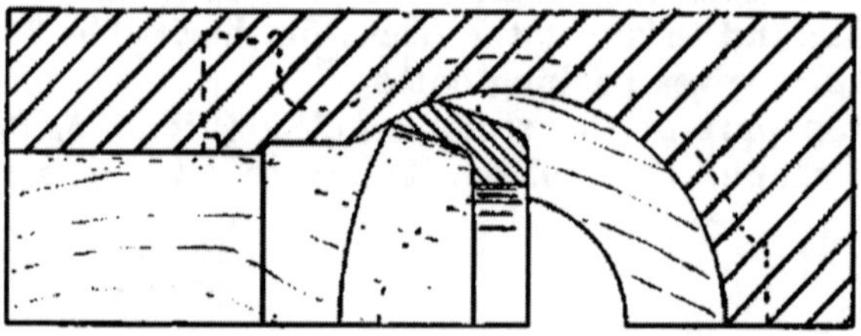

Fig. 286.

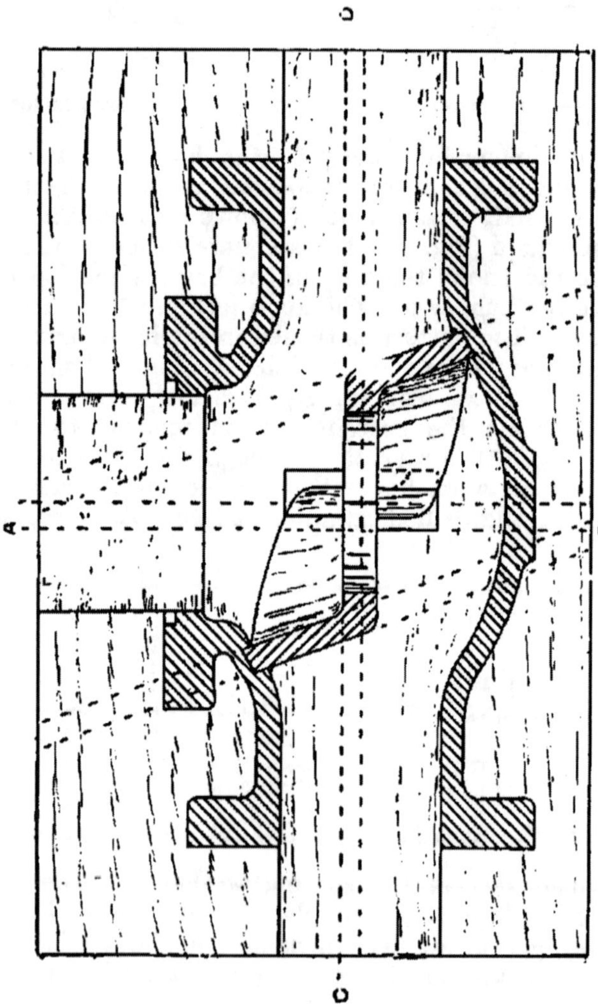

Fig. 285.

Fig. 285.—Globe Valve Core-box. Fig. 286.—Section of Globe Valve Core-box.

Fig. 285 is a face view of one half of the core-box for a globe valve of the design shown marked, Fig. 286 being a section on A B, and Fig. 287 a section on C D. Two blocks, being jointed and dowelled, are squared at the ends and on

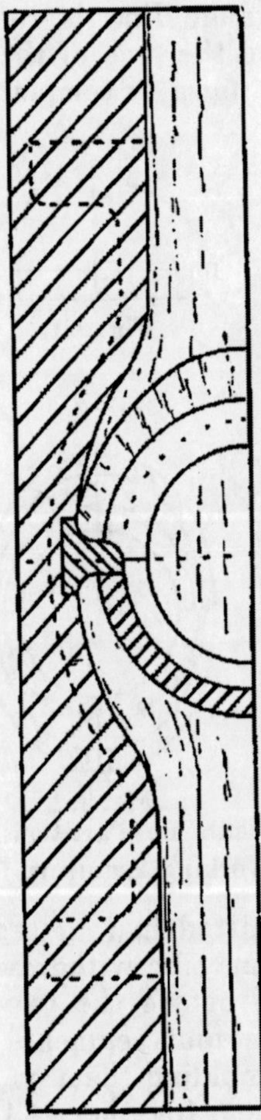

Fig. 287.—Section of Globe Valve Core-box.

Fig. 288.—Shouldered Template for Globe Valve Core-box.

the edges where the branch comes. Centre lines on the face being gauged and squared, circles are described on the ends and edge to the print diameters. The shape is scribed round one-half of the pattern when laid on the box, and the thickness of the metal is marked within the lines.

The semicircular hollow for the prints is worked straight through, and a shouldered template (Fig. 288) is then used to obtain the shape of the swelled part. The hollow for the branch is worked from the edge, the counter-bore of the flange being neglected. A gauge line is run round where the metal is set back beyond the face of the branch flange, and the set-back is worked down to template. The

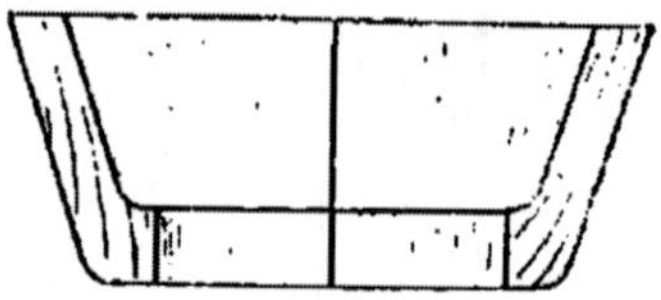

Fig. 289.

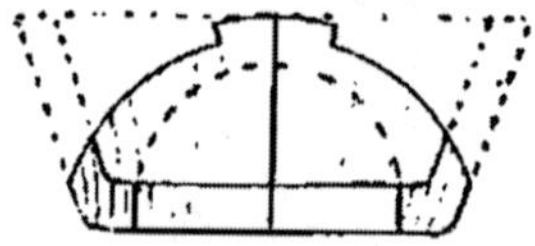

Fig. 291.

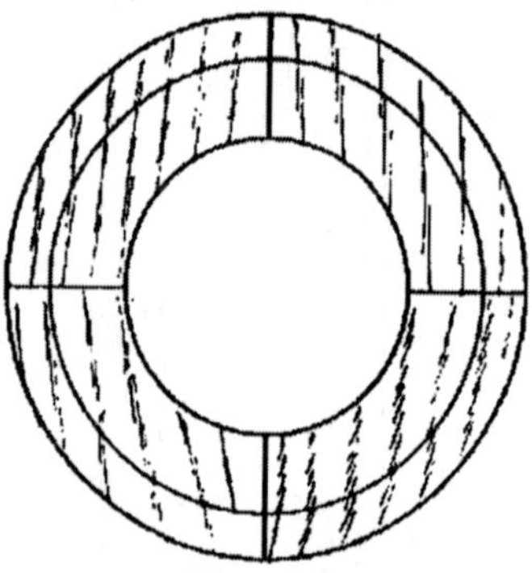

Fig. 290.

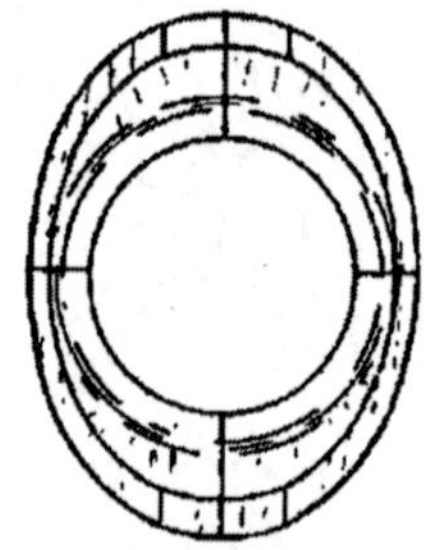

Fig. 292.

Figs. 289 and 290.—Turned Segments for Partitions.

Figs. 291 and 292.—Method of Working Segments.

partition and valve seat must be fitted in four segments, and kept loose so that each piece may be withdrawn by a circular motion from the half-core before the two halves are fastened together. Turn these four segments to the shape shown by Figs. 289 and 290, holding them on a face-plate with a paper joint. To tie them together at the top, glue on four shallow segments to break joint, as the end joints must not be glued, and are, moreover, made to coincide with transverse lines passing through the centre of the face-plate. Then fit them into the body of the box, the binding segments being cut away.

A better way is to fix two semicircular templates (Figs. 291 and 292) and to sweep around these a shouldered template cut to the reverse of Fig. 288. A shoulder, extending (say) $\frac{3}{16}$ in. into the wood and $\frac{1}{2}$ in. below the joint, determines the positions of the segments. The other extremity of each segment is cut as in Fig. 293, and ends are carried by a small block (Figs. 294 and 295) let into the centre of the box before being worked to shape. This block makes up the partition where it departs from the conical form. Most of the lines upon it may then be marked by a long-toothed gauge. Scribe the inclined dotted lines on Fig. 285 when the section is marked out

Fig. 293.

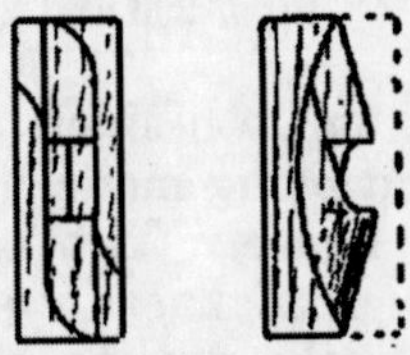

Fig. 294. Fig. 295.

Fig. 293.—End of Segment. Figs. 294 and 295.—Block for Ends of Segments.

to assist in getting the segments to position. The end of the segment must agree with a straightedge placed along the line. A set-square laid in the semicircle formed by the two segments will test the correctness. A long-toothed gauge, worked against the branch edge of the box, will test the position of the valve seat.

One half of the box being worked, the other is scribed from it and the slant lines transferred. As each half of the box is rammed separately, the ends and the branch edge are tapered and closed by pieces being screwed up to them. The transverse backing, which all such boxes should possess, is not shown, and is best fixed before the box is worked.

The pattern for a bull-nose plane will be described as a final example. A lengthways section through a brass casting intended for the body of a bull-nose plane is shown by Fig. 296, an end view being given by Fig. 297. The dimension B should be about $\frac{1}{16}$ in. greater than the width of the wide part of the cutting iron, in order to allow for filing to size. The dimension A is about $\frac{5}{16}$ in. less than B. Fig. 298 represents the pattern, the part exterior to the contour of the casting being a core-print. The pattern is made as follows:—A block of wood is planed to a parallel thickness equal to A, and the whole of the shape shown in Fig. 298 is

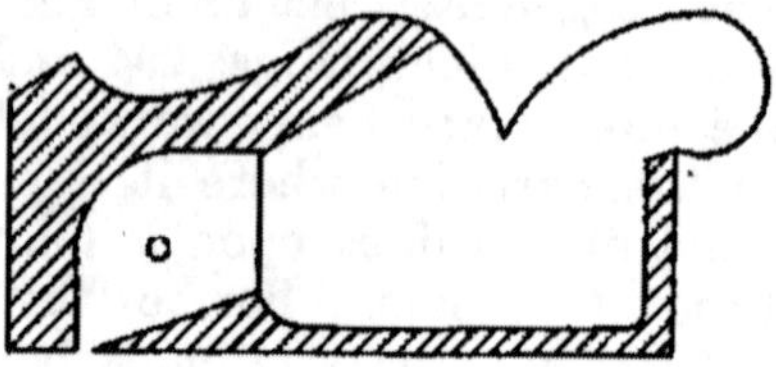

Fig. 296.

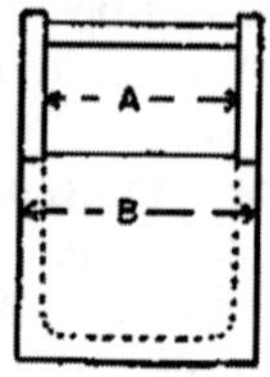

Fig. 297.

Figs. 296 and 297.—Body of Bull-nose Plane.

set out on both sides, a slight allowance for draught from the sand being made. The wood is then cut to the outline of the figure. Two thin pieces are then cut out, both having a thickness equal to half the difference between A and B, the outline of these pieces being similar to that

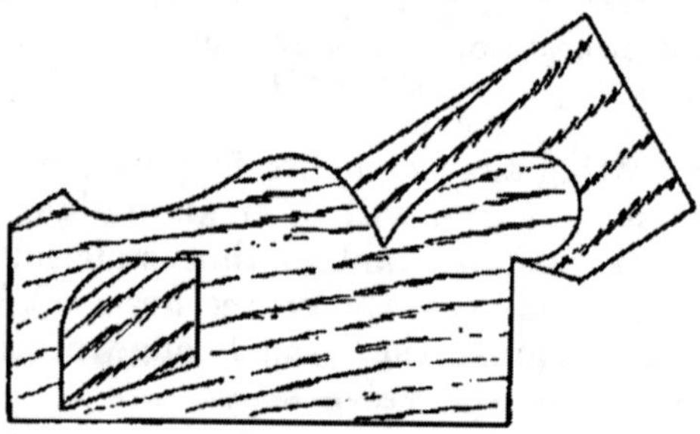

Fig. 298.

Fig. 298.—Pattern for Bull-nose Plane.

of Fig. 296. The space for the shaving escapement C (Fig. 296) is also cut away. Fig. 296 shows the face of the plane when finished, and Fig. 298 shows the face as it is to be cast. The difference between these views is due to allowances for facing the casting, and if not attended to, an unduly wide mouth will be the result. For castings to be made in iron, it is advisable to glue a little fillet about $\frac{3}{32}$ in. thick and $\frac{3}{8}$ in. wide over the part of the casting which is eventually to become the mouth. This is done in order to prevent the metal being chilled, which would occur if it were very thin. It is also necessary in an iron casting to ensure that the mould is so arranged for casting that the face of the plane occupies its lowest part, or when faced up blow-holes may be found there. The core-box (Figs. 299 and 300) is made of two pieces of wood dowelled together. After the blank pieces are dowelled they are

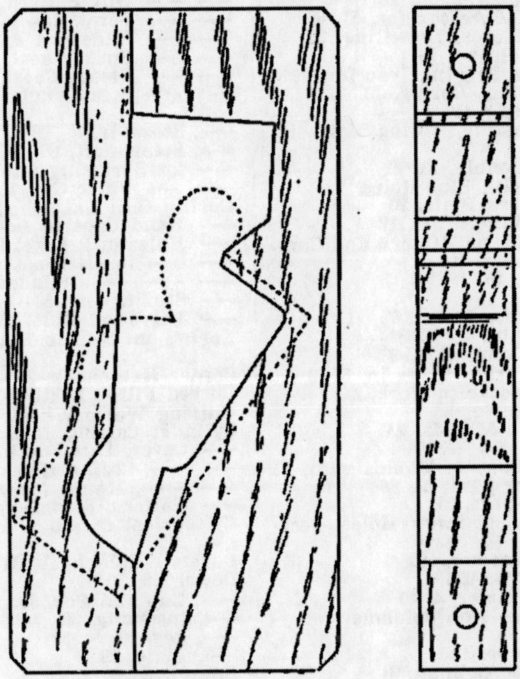

Fig. 299. Fig. 300.

Figs. 299 and 300.—Core-box for Bull-nose Plane.

planed up to a thickness equal to A. The main part of the pattern is then laid on the face of the blank core-box in the position shown in Fig. 299, and the shape scribed on the core-box. This is done, of course, before the thin pieces have been glued on it. One of the thin pieces is then laid on the core-box to fit on with the lines already scribed, and its shape transferred to the core-box. That part of the core-box which has to be cut away will then become evident.

INDEX.